Shelby Foote

THE CIVIL WAR

WAR

A NARRATIVE

Shelby Foote

THE CIVIL WAR

A NARRATIVE

6

★ ★ ★

CHARLESTON HARBOR
TO VICKSBURG

40th Anniversary Edition

BY SHELBY FOOTE
AND THE EDITORS OF TIME-LIFE BOOKS,
ALEXANDRIA, VIRGINIA

All these were honoured in their generations,
and were the glory of their times.

There be of them,
that have left a name behind them,
that their praises might be reported.

And some there be, which have no memorial;
who are perished, as though they had never been;
and are become as though they had never been born;
and their children after them.

But these were merciful men,
whose righteousness hath not been forgotten.

With their seed shall continually remain
a good inheritance,
and their children are within the covenant.

Their seed standeth fast,
and their children for their sakes.

Their seed shall remain for ever,
and their glory shall not be blotted out.

Their bodies are buried in peace;
but their name liveth for evermore.

— ECCLESIASTICUS XLIV

Contents

★ ★ ★

★

Prologue

In early January of 1863, when Jefferson Davis returned to Richmond from a twenty-five-day trip out West to boost the morale of hard-used Confederate troops and civilians alike, he had good reason to consider his mission a success. In the military actions of the war that took place around the time of his sojourn, the South's fighting men had acquitted themselves well, derailing at Walnut Hills General Sherman's efforts to reach Vicksburg, driving General Burnside from Fredericksburg, detaching Galveston from Union control, and destroying Federal supply depots and communications lines in Kentucky, Mississippi, and Tennessee in a series of swift cavalry raids. And while Rosecrans may have declared Stones River a Northern victory, in truth Bragg's troops had fought the Federals to an Antietam-style stalemate.

If Davis's trip helped flagging energies in the field, however, certainly nothing he might say or do could stay the economic ill wind that swept the South upon his return. France — although still, like Britain, unwilling to recognize the Confederacy politically — deigned to float a bond issue to a country whose trade was being choked by a naval blockade and whose transportation system and communication lines were being savaged by war. The French bonds only made the South's financial woes worse. The plunging value of Confederate currency and widespread inflation had undermined the very morale Davis had sought to shore up. By Easter, full-fledged civilian riots had broken out across Dixie. As angry crowds burned and looted stores or raided supply depots in the South, commerce boomed in the North. There industry expanded and business thrived in the face of a growing, war-fed demand for goods and services.

Even on the battlefield, the South's fortunes may not have been all Davis imagined. Burnside's attempt to retake Fredericksburg was foiled as much by bad weather as by Robert E. Lee. For all the glory garnered by cavalrymen Morgan, Van Dorn, and Forrest, the damage their lightning raids had inflicted was soon repaired. Though Vicksburg's proud, high-mounted guns still denied the Yankees free use of the Mississippi, Union Admiral Farragut had nevertheless steamed upstream past Port Hudson to cut the South off from another stretch of the mighty river. Even General Grant's hapless attempts to by-pass or encircle the city would prove more dangerous than their failure indicated. For the dogged officer learned from his mistakes, and while his seven ill-fated forays may not have given him Vicksburg, they did teach him enough about the plush delta region and the kind of operations that might succeed there for him to come up with a better plan to take the city.

In any case, news from the front that spring often gave the South much to cheer about. Yet while Grant was making new plans for Vicksburg, along the coast of South Carolina another Yankee commander was thinking, much more reluctantly, of capturing another obdurate southern town. Admiral Du Pont hoped that by taking Charleston he could strengthen the Union blockade. But General Pierre G. T. Beauregard, beloved by the people of the port city as the man who seized Fort Sumter in the first place, had built up local defenses dramatically and easily repulsed the halting Union attack.

Confederates would also emerge triumphant in the battle brewing anew around Fredericksburg, as Lee — yet again — defied long odds with superior generalship. There — yet again — Abraham Lincoln would place high hopes in a new commander of the Army of the Potomac, but Joseph ("Fighting Joe") Hooker, who replaced the discredited Ambrose Burnside, would turn out to be no match for Lee either. Such hopes would not be entirely misplaced since, in the early maneuverings around Fredericksburg, the Union cavalry would for the first time prove equal to that of the Confederates. Nevertheless, when later the guns fell silent at Chancellorsville, victory clearly fell to the South, although Lee lost one of his greatest assets — Stonewall Jackson, mortally wounded by his own men.

Meanwhile, out West, Grant developed his close-out plan: march troops overland south along the west bank of the Mississippi, sail the navy downstream past the Vicksburg bluffs, rendezvous below the city beyond the reach of its guns, ferry the army across to the east bank and drive inland to take Jackson, the state capital; then backtrack and storm Vicksburg. It was a plan that befuddled fellow officers and foes alike, since none could imagine operating without a secure supply line. The Northern-born commander of Vicksburg, John Pemberton, was dismayed not only by Grant, but also by Grierson's daring Union cavalry raid into Mississippi, by General Banks's working his way up from New Orleans toward Port Hudson, and — most of all — by Joe Johnston's refusal to come to the city's aid. But Pemberton remained determined to hold Vicksburg even as the long-dreaded siege got underway.

★   ★   ★

★

Shelby Foote

A Confederate soldier stands
beside a palmetto tree near a
"Quaker" battery, made of logs
and painted to resemble a
cannon, at Charleston Harbor.

ONE

Naval Repulse at Charleston

1863 ★ ★ ★ ★ ★ ★

Pierre Gustave Toutant Beauregard **was as flamboyant by nature as by name,** and over the course of the past two years this quality, coupled all too often with a readiness to lay down the sword and take up the pen in defense of his reputation with the public, had got him into considerable trouble with his superiors, who sometimes found it difficult to abide his Creole touchiness off the field of battle for the sake of his undoubted abilities on it. Called "Old Bory" by his men, though he was not yet forty-five, the Hero of Sumter had twice been relieved of important commands, first in the East, where he had routed McDowell's invasion attempt at Manassas, then in the West, where he had saved his badly outnumbered army by giving Halleck the slip at Corinth, and now he was back on the scene of his first glory in Charleston harbor. Here, as elsewhere, he saw his position as the hub of the wheel of war. Defying Union sea power, Mobile on the Gulf and Wilmington, Savannah, and Charleston on the Atlantic remained in Confederate hands, and of these four it was clear at least to Beauregard that the one the Federals coveted most was the last, variously referred to in their journals as "the hotbed of treachery," "the cradle of secession," and "the nursery of disunion." Industrious as always, the general was determined that this proud South Carolina city should not suffer the fate of his native New Orleans, no matter what force

★

*Confederate General
Pierre Gustave Toutant
Beauregard used his
engineering skills to
make the defenses at
Charleston harbor
impregnable against
Union attack.*

the Yankees brought against it. Conducting frequent tours of inspection and keeping up as usual a voluminous correspondence — a steady stream of requisitions for more guns and men, more warships and munitions, nearly all of which were returned to him regretfully unfilled — he only relaxed from his duties when he slept, and even then he kept a pencil and a note pad under his pillow, ready to jot down any notion that came to him in the night. "Carolinians and Georgians!" he exhorted by proclamation. "The hour is at hand to prove your devotion to your country's cause. Let all able-bodied men, from the seaboard to the mountains, rush to arms. Be not exacting in the choice of weapons; pikes and scythes will do for exterminating your enemies, spades and shovels for protecting your friends. To arms, fellow citizens! Come share with us our dangers, our brilliant success, or our glorious death."

Two approaches to Charleston were available to the Federals. They could make an amphibious landing on one of the islands or up one of the inlets to the south, then swing northeastward up the mainland to move upon the city from the rear; or they could enter through the harbor itself, braving the massed batteries for the sake of a quick decision, however bloody. Twice already they had tried the former method, but both times — first at Secessionville, three months before Beauregard's return from the West in mid-September, and again at Pocotaligo, one month after he reassumed command — they had been stopped and flung back on their naval support before they could gather momentum. This time he thought it probable that they would attempt the front-door

★

approach, using their new flotilla of vaunted ironclads to spearhead the attack. If so, they were going to find they had taken on a good deal more than they expected; for the harbor defenses had been greatly improved during the nearly two years that had elapsed since the war first opened here. Fort Moultrie, Castle Pinckney, and Fort Sumter, respectively on Sullivan's Island, off the mouth of the Cooper River, and opposite the entrance to the bay, had not only been strengthened, each in its own right, but now they were supported by other fortifications constructed at intervals along the beaches and connected by a continuous line of signal stations, making it possible for a central headquarters, itself transferrable, to direct and consolidate their fire. First Beauregard, then Pemberton, and now Beauregard again — both accomplished engineers and artillerists, advised moreover by staffs of specialists as expert as themselves — had applied all their skill and knowledge to make the place as nearly impregnable as military science and Confederate resources would allow. A total of seventy-seven guns of various calibers now frowned from their various embrasures, in addition to which the harbor channels were thickly sown with torpedoes and other obstructions, such as floating webs of hemp designed to entangle rudders and snarl propellers. Not content with this, the sad-eyed little Creole had not hesitated to dip into his limited supply of powder in order to improve the marksmanship of his cannoneers with frequent target practice. Like his idol Napoleon he believed in a lucky star, but he was leaving as little as possible to chance; for which reason he had set marker buoys at known ranges in the bay, with the corresponding elevations chalked on the breeches of the guns. As a last-ditch measure of desperation, to be employed if all else failed, he encouraged the organization of a unit known as the Tigers, made up of volunteers whose assignment was to hurl explosives down the smokestacks of such enemy ships as managed to break through the ring of fire and approach the fortress walls or the city docks. The ironclads might indeed be invincible; some said so, some said not; but one thing was fairly certain. The argument was likely to be settled on the day their owners tested them in Charleston harbor.

This was not to say that Beauregard had abandoned all notion of assuming the offensive, however limited his means. He had at his disposal two homemade rams, the *Palmetto State* and the *Chicora*, built with funds supplied by the South Carolina legislature and the Ladies' Gunboat Fair. The former mounted an 80-pounder rifle aft and an 8-inch shell gun on each broadside, while the latter had two 9-inch smoothbores and four rifled 32-pounders. Both were balky and slow, with cranky, inadequate engines and armor improvised from boiler plate and railroad iron, but as January drew to a close the general was determined to put them to the test by challenging the blockade squadron off the Charleston bar. Orders were handed Flag Officer Duncan Ingraham on the 30th, instructing him to make the attempt at dawn of the following day.

Beauregard meanwhile had in mind a more limited offensive of his own, to be launched against the 9-gun screw steamer *Isaac Smith*, which had been coming up the Stono River almost nightly to shell the Confederate camps on James and John's islands. That night he lay in wait for her with batteries of field artillery, allowed her to pass unchallenged, then took her under fire as she came back down. The opening volley tore off her stack, stopped her engines, riddled her lifeboats, and killed eight of her crew. Her captain quickly surrendered himself and his ship and the 94 survivors, including 17 wounded. Repaired and rechristened, the *Smith* became the *Stono* and served under that name as part of Charleston's miniature defense squadron, the rest of which was already on its way across the bay, under cover of darkness, in accordance with Ingraham's orders to try his hand at lifting the Union blockade.

Palmetto State and *Chicora*, followed by three steam tenders brought along to tow them back into the harbor in case their engines failed, were over the bar and among the wooden-walled blockaders by first light. Mounting a total of one hundred guns, the Federal squadron included the 1200-ton sloop-of-war *Housatonic*, two gunboats, and seven converted merchantmen. A lookout aboard one of these last, the 9-gun steamer *Mercedita*, was the first to spot the misty outline of an approaching vessel. "She has black smoke!" he shouted. "Watch, man the guns! Spring the rattle! Call all hands to quarters!" This brought the captain out on deck, clad only in a pea jacket. When he too spotted the stranger, nearer now, he cupped his hands about his mouth and called out: "Steamer, ahoy! You will be into us! What steamer is that?" It was the *Palmetto State*, but for a time she did not deign to answer. Then: "Halloo!" her skipper finally replied, and with that the ram put her snout into the quarter of the *Mercedita* and fired her guns. Flames went up from the crippled steamer. "Surrender," the rebel captain yelled up, "or I'll sink you!" The only answer was a cloud of oily smoke shot through with steam. "Do you surrender?" he repeated. This brought the reply, "I can make no resistance; my boiler is destroyed!" "Then do you surrender?" "Yes!" So the *Palmetto State* backed off, withdrawing her snout, and turned to go to the help of the *Chicora*, which meanwhile had been serving the 10-gun sidewheel steamer *Keystone State* in much the same fashion. Riddled and aflame, the Federal hauled down her flag to signify surrender, then ran it up again and limped out to sea as the two rams moved off in the opposite direction. At the far end of the line, the *Housatonic* and the gunboats held their station, thinking the racket had been provoked by a blockade runner venturing out. By full daylight the two improvised ironclads were back in Charleston harbor, their crews accepting the cheers of a crowd collected on the docks.

Beauregard was elated by the double coup. Quick to claim that the blockade had been lifted, at least for a time, he took the French and Spanish consuls out to witness the truth of his words that "the outer harbor remained in

*Federals abandon the Mercedita after the 9-gun
steamer was struck by the ironclad Palmetto State in
Charleston harbor on January 31, 1863.*

the full possession of the two Confederate rams. Not a Federal sail was visible, even with spyglasses." Next day the blockaders were back again, presumably too vigilant now to permit him to risk another such attempt, but he did not admit that this detracted in the slightest from the brilliance of the exploit. He bided his time, still improving his defenses for the all-out attack which he believed was about to be launched. "Already six monitors . . . are in the waters of my department, concentrating about Port Royal, and transports with troops are still arriving from the North," he reported in mid-March. "I believe the drama will not much longer be delayed; the curtain will soon rise." Three more weeks went past before his prediction was fulfilled. Then on Monday, April 6, the day after Easter — it was also the first anniversary of Shiloh and within a week of the second anniversary of the opening of the war in this same harbor — not six but nine brand-new Union ironclads, some single- and some double-turreted, crossed the Charleston bar and dropped anchor in the channel, bringing their great 15-inch guns to bear on the forts and batteries Beauregard had prepared for their reception. The curtain had indeed risen.

★ ★ ★ **R**ear Admiral Samuel Du Pont had the flag. It was he who, back in early November of 1861, had conceived and executed the elliptical attack on Port Royal, thereby giving the North its first substantial victory of the war, and it was hoped by his superiors — his desk-bound superiors in Washington, that is, for he had no superiors afloat — that he would repeat the triumph here in Charleston harbor. Son of a wealthy New York importer and nephew of an even wealthier Delaware powder maker, the admiral was approaching sixty, a hale, well-set-up aristocrat with a dignified but genial manner and a growth of luxuriant whiskers describing a bushy U about his chops and under his clean-shaven mouth and chin, all of which combined to give at least one journalist the impression that he was "one of the stateliest, handsomest, and most polished gentlemen I have ever seen." Gideon Welles admired him, too; up to a point. "He is a skillful and accomplished officer," the Secretary confided in his diary. "Has a fine address, [but] is a courtier with perhaps too much finesse and management." This edge of mistrust was returned by the man who was its object. It seemed to Du Pont, whose enthusiasm had been tempered by close association, that the Navy Department was suffering from an affliction which might have been diagnosed as "ironclads on the brain."

This had not always been the case, particularly in the days when John Ericsson was trying to persuade the brass to give him authority for construction of the *Monitor*. Grudgingly, despite grave objections, they had finally let him go ahead with a contract which stipulated that he would not be reimbursed in case of failure. But after Hampton Roads and the draw engagement that put an end to the overnight depredations of the *Merrimac*, the Department not only reversed itself, but went all-out in the opposite direction. Ericsson received an order for half a dozen sister ships of the one already delivered, and other builders were engaged for the construction of twenty-one more, of various shapes and sizes. Assistant Secretary Fox was especially enthusiastic, informing Du Pont that after he had used the new-fangled warships to reduce Charleston he was to move on to Savannah, then send them down to the Gulf to give Mobile the same treatment. Ironclads were trumps, according to Fox. He told Ericsson he had not "a shadow of a doubt as to our success, and this confidence arises from a study of your marvelous vessels." The Swede was less positive. "The most I dare hope is that the contest will end without loss of that prestige which your ironclads have conferred upon the nation abroad," he replied, adding the reminder: "A single shot may sink a ship, while a hundred rounds cannot silence a fort." Unwilling to have his confidence undermined or his ebullience lessened, Fox assured a congressional committee that the monitors (such was the generic name, adopted in honor of the first of what was intended to be a long line of invincible vessels) could steam into southern harbors, flatten the defenses, and emerge unscathed. His only note of caution was injected into a dispatch addressed to Du Pont. "I beg of you," he pleaded, "not to let the Army spoil it." He wanted the show to be all Navy, with the landsmen merely standing by to be ferried in to pick up the pieces when the smoke cleared. In late March, having gained nothing from nudging Porter with the promise of a ribboned star and permanent promotion, he informed Du Pont that it was up to him to make up for the reverses lately suffered in the West: "Farragut has had a setback at Port Hudson and lost the noble old *Mississippi*. It finally devolves upon you by great good fortune to avert the series of disasters that have fallen upon our Navy. That you will do it most gloriously I have no misgivings whatever."

In point of fact, Du Pont by this time had misgivings enough for them both. What was more, these doubts were shared by a majority of his ironclad skippers — and with cause. Near the mouth of the Ogeechee River, just beyond the Georgia line, the Confederates had constructed as part of the Savannah defenses a 9-gun earthwork called Fort McAllister, which Du Pont decided to use as a sort of test range to determine how well the monitors would

Rear Admiral Samuel Du Pont (second from left), who gained a Federal victory at Port Royal in November 1861, meets with his staff aboard the Wabash.

do, offensively and defensively, under fire. He gave the reduction assignment to the *Montauk*, which meant that he was giving the best he had; for her captain was Commander John L. Worden, who had skippered the *Monitor* in her fight with the *Merrimac*. Worden made his first attack on January 27 and, after expending all his ammunition in a four-hour bombardment, withdrew undamaged despite repeated hits scored by the guns of the fort, which was not silenced. Returning February 1 he tried again, with like results. Neither the ship nor the fort had done much damage to the other, aside from the concussive strain on the eardrums of the *Montauk*'s crew from the forty-six hits taken on her iron decks and turret. A third attack, February 27, was more fruitful, although not in the way intended. Finding the rebel cruiser *Nashville* aground beyond Fort McAllister, Worden took her under long-range fire with his 11- and 15-inch guns, set her ablaze, and had the satisfaction of watching her destruction when her magazine exploded. Struck only five times by the guns of the fort, the iron-

If these vaunted engines of destruction could not humble a modest 9-gun sand fort, what could they hope to accomplish against multi-gunned bastions like Sumter and Moultrie?

clad pulled back without replying, well satisfied with her morning's work, only to run upon a torpedo which blew such a hole in her bottom that she had to be beached in the mud at the mouth of the river. While she was undergoing repairs that soon restored her to full efficiency, three more monitors came down from Port Royal on March 3 and tried their hand with an eight-hour bombardment of the fort: with similar results. Neither silenced or seriously damaged the other, and the ironclads withdrew to try no more.

Fruitless though the experiment had been in positive results — aside, that is, from the fortunate interception of the *Nashville* — a lesson had been learned, on the negative side, as to the capabilities of the monitors. "Whatever degree of impenetrability they might have," Du Pont reported, "there was no corresponding degree of destructiveness as against forts." He felt much as one sailor had felt on a test run. "Give me an oyster-scow!" the man had cried. "Anything — only let it be of wood, and something that will float over instead of under the water." Most of the captains were of a similar mind, and when they looked beyond the present to the impending future, their doubts increased. If these vaunted engines of destruction could not humble a modest 9-gun sand fort, what could they hope to accomplish against multi-gunned bastions like

★

Sumter and Moultrie? They asked the question and shook their heads. "I do not feel as sure as I could wish," one skipper admitted, while another was more positive in expressing his reservations. "I begin to rue the day I got into the iron clad business," he wrote home.

Still, orders were orders, and as April came in Du Pont completed his final preparations for the attack. In addition to his flagship the *New Ironsides*, a high-bulwarked 3500-ton frigate whose ponderous armor and twenty heavy guns mounted in broadside made her the most powerful battleship in the world, he had eight low-riding monitors, mounting one or two guns each in revolving turrets: which meant that, in all, he would be opposing 77 guns ashore with 33 afloat. These odds were rather evened by the fact that the naval guns, in addition to being mounted on moving targets, which made them far more difficult to hit, were heavier in caliber and threw about an equal weight of metal. Other odds were irreducible, however, one being that in order to reach the city from the sea his ships would have to steam for seven winding miles in a shoal-lined channel, much of which had been fiendishly obstructed and practically all of which was exposed to the plunging fire of forts whose gun crews had been anticipating for months this golden opportunity to disprove the claim that monitors were indestructible. On April 2, despite increasing doubts and reservations, Du Pont left Port Royal and reached Edisto Island, twenty-odd miles below the entrance to Charleston harbor, before nightfall. There the ships were cleared for action, the exposed armor of their decks and turrets covered over with slippery untanned hides and their bulwarks slopped with grease to lessen the "bite" of enemy projectiles. (That at least was the hoped-for effect, when the vessels should come under fire. The more immediate result, however, was that they stank fearfully under the influence of the Carolina sun.) On the 5th — Easter Sunday — they cleared North Edisto and crossed the Charleston bar next morning. Du Pont had intended to attack at once, but finding the weather hazy, which as he said "prevent[ed] our seeing the ranges," he decided to drop anchors and wait for tomorrow, in hopes that it would afford him better visibility. (It would also afford the same for the gunners in the forts; but Du Pont was not thinking along these lines, or else he would have made a night attack.) Finally, against his better judgment — and after much prodding from above, including jeers that he had "the slows" and taunts that identified him as a sea-going McClellan, overcautious and too mindful of comparative statistics — he was going in.

*T*omorrow — April 7 — brought the weather he thought he wanted, and soon after noon the iron column started forward, the nine ships moving in single file, slowly and with a certain ponderous majesty not lost on the beholders in the forts. Originally the admiral had intended to lead the way in the flagship, but on second

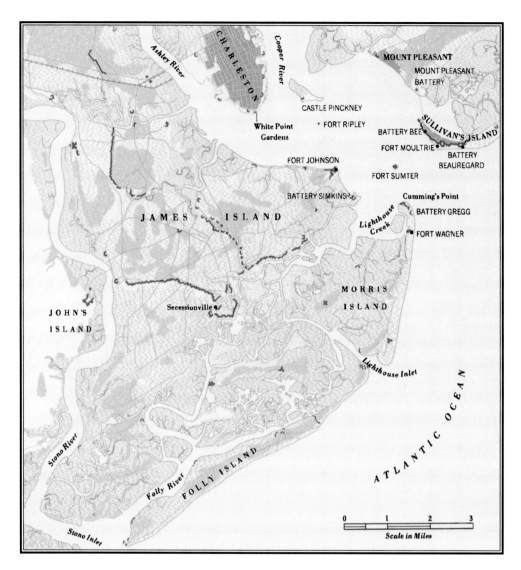

*The Confederate defenses at Charleston
harbor included batteries on
Morris, James, and Sullivan's islands.*

thought he decided to take the center position from which "signals could be
better made to both ends of the line," so that the resultant order of battle was
*Weehawken, Passaic, Montauk, Patapsco; New Ironsides; Catskill, Nantucket,
Nahant, Keokuk.* There was an exasperating delay of about an hour when the
lead monitor's heavy anchor chain became entangled with the bootjack raft designed to protect her bow from torpedoes; then the column resumed its forward

motion, passing Morris Island in an ominous silence as the rebel cannoneers on Cummings Point held their fire. As the ships approached the inner works, however, the Confederate and Palmetto flags were hoisted over Sumter and Moultrie, while bands on the parapets struck up patriotic airs and the guns began to roar in salute. Captain John Rodgers of the *Weehawken*, spotting the rope obstructions dead ahead, commanded the helmsman to swing hard to starboard in order to avoid becoming entangled in the web and immobilized under the muzzles of guns whose projectiles were already hammering the monitor like an anvil. This was well short of the point at which Du Pont had intended to open fire, however, and the result was that the whole line was thrown into confusion by the abrupt necessity, confronting each ship in rapid sequence, of avoiding a collision with the ship ahead. Moreover, as the *Weehawken* turned she encountered a torpedo which exploded directly under her. "It lifted the vessel a little," Rodgers later reported, "but I am unable to perceive that it has done us any damage."

Aboard the flagship, with her deeper draft, the confusion was at its worst. When she lost headway she had to drop her anchor to keep from going aground, and as she hung there, trying to get her nose into the tide, she received two disconcerting butts from two of the monitors astern as they swept past in response to her signal to move up and join the action. Hoisting anchor at last, the *Ironsides* chugged forward a short distance, only to have to drop it again in order to avoid piling up on a shoal. This brought her, unbeknownst, directly over a huge submerged torpedo which the Confederates had fashioned by packing an old boiler with explosives and connecting it to an observation post ashore, to be used to detonate the charge at the proper time. Now the proper time was very much at hand; the rebel electrician later said that if he himself had been allowed to spot the Yankee flagship he could not have placed her more precisely where he wanted her. However, his elation quickly faded, turning first to dismay and then to disgust, when the detonating mechanism failed time after time to send a spark to the underwater engine of destruction. Meanwhile, happily unaware that he and his ship were in mortal danger of being hoisted skyward in sudden flame and smoke, Du Pont signaled the monitors to "disregard motions of commander in chief" and continue to press the attack without his help. The *Ironsides*, as one of her surgeons complained, was as completely out of the fight as if she had been moored to a dock in the Philadelphia Navy Yard, but this did not prevent her taking long-range punishment from the rebel guns. Presenting if not the closest, then at any rate the largest and least mobile target in the harbor, she was struck no less than ninety-five times in the course of the engagement. Despite the din, according to one of her officers, "the sense of security the iron walls gave to those within was wonderful, a feeling akin to that which one experiences in a heavy storm when the wind and hail beat harmlessly against the windows of a well-protected house."

No such feeling was experienced by the crews of the monitors, the officer added; "for in their turrets the nuts that secured the laminated plates flew wildly, to the injury and discomfiture of the men at the guns." Up closer, they were harder hit. "The shots literally rained around them," a correspondent wrote, "splashing the water up thirty feet in the air, and striking and booming from their decks and turrets." The flagship was a mile from Sumter, the nearest monitors about half that far, but the captain of the twin-turreted *Nahant* quickly found what it would cost to close the range. "Mr Clarke, you haven't hit anything yet," he protested to the ensign in charge of the 15-inch gun, which was throwing its 420-pound shells at seven-minute intervals. When the young man replied, "We aint near enough, Captain," the skipper went into a rage. "Not near enough? God damn it," he cried, "I'll put you near enough! Starboard your helm, Quartermaster!" As the ship came about, a rebel projectile slammed against the sight-slit, killing the helmsman and mangling the pilot. "Retire! Retire!" the captain shouted. Others caught it as hard or harder, with similar results: smokestacks perforated, turrets jammed, decks ripped up, guns knocked out of action. The only effect on the enemy a journalist could see, examining the brick northeast face of Sumter through his glasses, was that of "increasing pock marks and discolorations on the walls, as if there had been a sudden breaking out of cutaneous disease." But there was no corresponding slackening of fire from within the fort, whose cannoneers were jubilant over the many hits they scored. Frenzied at being kept from a share in the fun of pummeling the ironclads, Confederates locked in the Moultrie guardhouse screamed above the roar of the bombardment: "For God's sake, let us come out and go to the guns!"

After peering through the drifting smoke for about two hours, Du Pont was told that it was nearly 5 o'clock. "Make signal to the ships to drop out of fire," he said quietly. "It is too late to fight this battle tonight. We will renew it early in the morning." Below decks, when the gun captains received word of this decision, they sent up an urgent request that they be allowed to fire at least one broadside before retiring. It was granted, and as the *Ironsides* turned to steam down the channel an eight-gun salvo was hurled at Moultrie, the only shots she fired in the course of the engagement. This brought the total to an even 150 rounds expended by the flotilla, and of these 55 were scored as hits. The Confederates, on the other hand, had fired 2209, of which no less than 441 had found their mark, despite the fact that the targets had not only been comparatively small, and moving, but had also been mostly submerged. That this was remarkably effective shooting Du Pont himself began to appreciate when the retiring monitors came within hailing distance of the flagship and he got a close-up look at their condition. The first to approach was the *Keokuk*, limping badly. Last in and first out, she had ventured nearest to Sumter's 44 guns, and she had the scars of 90 point-blank hits to prove it. She was "riddled like a

In a painting by Xanthus Smith, a U.S. naval officer with the Federal fleet at Charleston, a tugboat steams to aid the Keokuk off Morris Island.

colander," one witness remarked, "the most severely mauled ship one ever saw." That night, in fact, she keeled over and sank at her anchorage off Morris Island. Others also had been roughly handled; *Weehawken* had taken 53 hits, *Nantucket* 51, *Patapsco* 47, *Nahant* 36, *Passaic* 35, *Catskill* 20, and *Montauk* 14. In general, the damage suffered was in inverse ratio to the individual distance between them and the rebel guns, and none had been closer than 600 yards.

The admiral's intention to "renew [the battle] early in the morning" was modified by the sight of his crippled monitors. Five of the eight were too badly damaged to be able to engage if ordered, and of these five, one would sink before the scheduled time for action. Equally conclusive were the reports and recommendations of the several captains when they came aboard the flagship that evening. "With your present means," John Rodgers advised, "I could not, if I were asked, recommend a renewal of the attack." The redoubtable Worden was no less emphatic. "After testing the weight of the enemy's fire, and observing the obstructions," he reported, "I am led to believe that Charleston cannot be taken by the naval force now present, and that had the attack been continued [today] it could not have failed to result in disaster." This gave Du Pont pause, and pausing he reflected on the risks. Here was no New Orleans, where the problem had been to run the fleet through a brief, furious gauntlet of fire in order to gain a safe haven above the forts and place a defenseless city under the muzzles of its guns; this was Charleston, whose harbor, in the words of a staff officer, "was a *cul-de-sac*, a circle of fire not to be passed." The deeper you penetrated the circle, the more you were exposed to destruction from its rim. Moreover, as the admiral saw the outcome, even if he pressed the attack "in the end we shall retire, leaving some of our ironclads in the hands of the enemy, to be refitted and turned against our blockade with deplorable effect." This last was unthinkable — though he thought about it in his cabin all night long. By daybreak he had made up his mind. "I have decided not to renew the attack," he told his chief of staff. "We have met with a sad repulse; I shall not turn it into a great disaster."

"I am by no means confident that we are acting wisely in expending so much strength and effort on Charleston, a place of no strategic importance."

— Gideon Welles

Next afternoon he recrossed the bar. "I attempted to take the bull by the horns, but he was too much for us," he admitted to the army commander whose troops had been standing by to pick up the pieces. By the end of the week the flotilla again was riding at anchor inside Port Royal, swarmed over by armorers hammering the vessels back into shape. The admiral knew the reaction in Washington would be severe, coming as it did on the heels of such great expectations, but he also knew that he had the support of his monitor captains, who stood, as one of them said, "like a wall of iron" around his reputation, agreeing with his chief of staff's opinion that "Admiral Du Pont never showed greater courage or patriotism than when he saved his ships and men, and sacrificed himself to the clamor and disappointment evoked by his defeat." In point of fact, however, part of the expressed disappointment, if not the outright clamor, occurred within the fleet itself. A chief engineer was clapped in arrest for complaining in his ship's mess that the attack had not been pressed to the victory point, and at least one junior officer remarked wryly that "the grim sort of soul like Farragut was lacking." Welles and Fox, though hot enough at the outcome and in no doubt at all as to where the blame lay, were considerably hampered in their criticisms by the political necessity for delay in bringing the matter out into the open with the publication of the adverse battle reports. After all, it was they — especially Fox — who had announced that the monitors were irresistible, and contracts already had been signed for the delivery of eighteen more of the expensive naval monsters. Two weeks after the repulse, Welles was attempting to shrug it off by telling his diary: "I am by no means confident that we are acting wisely in expending so much strength and effort on Charleston, a place of no strategic importance."

The grapes had soured for him; but not for Beauregard. The Louisiana general's only regrets were that the boiler-torpedo had not gone off beneath the *Ironsides* and that the Yankees had slunk away without attempting a renewal of the assault, which he felt certain would have been even more decisively repulsed. In a congratulatory address to his troops, his enthusiasm knew no bounds. He spoke of "the stranded, riddled wreck" of the *Keokuk*, whose big guns now were part of the harbor defenses, and of the ignominious flight of "her baffled coadjutors," whose defeat had reinspired world-wide confidence in the ultimate and glorious triumph of the Confederate cause. In his official report to Richmond, though — for he had recently confided to a friend that, from now on, he was adopting a more restrained style in his dispatches, in order to counteract a rumor that he was prone to exaggerate his accomplishments — the little Creole, with his bloodhound eyes, his swarthy face, and his hair brushed forward in lovelocks at the temples, contented himself for the most part with factual observations. "It may be accepted, as shown," he wrote, "that these vaunted monitor batteries, though formidable engines of war, after all are not invulnerable or invincible, and may be destroyed or defeated by heavy ordnance, properly placed and skillfully handled." However, in the glow and warmth of congratulations being pressed upon him, including one that he had made Sumter "a household word, like Salamis and Thermopylae," he could not resist the temptation to add a closing flourish to the report: "My expectations were fully realized, and the country, as well as the State of South Carolina, may well be proud of the men who first met and vanquished the iron-mailed, terribly armed armada, so confidently prepared and sent forth by the enemy to certain and easy victory."

★   ★   ★

Shelby Foote

The 1st Rhode Island and 6th
Ohio clash with the 4th Virginia at
Kelly's Ford on March 17, 1863.

T W O

Lee, Hooker; Mosby; Kelly's Ford

1863 ★ ★ ★ ★ ★

Though he grew snappish at the first report that the fleet had been repulsed — "Hold your position inside the bar near Charleston," he instructed Du Pont in a message sent posthaste down the coast; "or, if you shall have left it, return to it, and hold it till further orders" — Lincoln was in a better frame of mind for the reception of bad news than he had been for months. The reason for this was that he had just returned from a five-day Easter vacation combined with a highly satisfactory inspection of the Army of the Potomac, whose tents were pitched along the Rappahannock in the vicinity of Falmouth. The visit was a heartening experience, not only because it showed him that the condition of the troops was excellent, but also because it abolished his main previous doubt as to the fitness of the man he had appointed as their commander. After saying, "Now there is Joe Hooker. He can fight. I think that is pretty well established," Lincoln had added: "But whether he can 'keep tavern' for a large army is not so sure." If the trip down the bay had done nothing else, it had reassured the President on that score. Fighting Joe had taken hold with a vengeance, and the results were plain to see on the faces and in the attitude of the men. Fredericksburg and the Mud March, though the letters of the former were embroidered on the rippling blue of their regimental colors, were no longer even a part of their vocabulary.

★

Hooker could indeed keep tavern. Within a week of his assumption of command he jolted the commissary department by ordering the issue of rations expanded to include fresh vegetables and soft bread; he supervised a thorough cleanup of the unsanitary camps, shrinking the overlong sick lists in the process, and he instituted a liberal system of furloughs which, combined with a tightening of security regulations, did much to reduce desertion. "Ah! the furloughs and vegetables he gave!" one infantryman still marveled years later. "How he did understand the road to the soldier's heart!" In the midst of all this welcome reform, army paymasters came down from Washington with bulging satchels and surprised the troops with six months' back pay. It was no wonder another veteran recalled that "cheerfulness, good order, and military discipline at once took the place of grumbling, depression, and want of confidence." Idleness, that breeder of discontent, was abolished by a revival of the old-time grand reviews, with regiment after regiment swinging past the reviewing stand so that when the men executed the command "eyes right" they saw their chieftain's clean-shaven face light up with pleasure at seeing their appearance improved by their diurnal spit-and-polish preparations. Unit pride, being thus encouraged, increased even more when Hooker, expanding the use of the so-called Kearny patch — a device improvised by the late Phil Kearny, about this time last year, to identify the men of his division in the course of their march up the York-James peninsula — ordered the adoption of corps insignia of various shapes, cut from red, white, or blue cloth, thus indicating the first, second, or third division, and stitched to the crown of the caps of the troops, so that he and they could tell at a glance what corps and division a man was gracing or disgracing, on duty or off. Moreover, after the gruff and dish-faced Pope and the flustered and fantastically whiskered Burnside, Hooker himself, by the force of his personality and the handsomeness of his presence, infused some of the old McClellan magnetism into the reviving army's ranks. "Apollo-like," a Wisconsin major called the forty-eight-year-old Massachusetts-born commander, and a visiting editor wrote of him as "a man of unusually handsome face and elegant proportions, with a complexion as delicate and silken as a woman's." Another remarked, along this same line, that the general looked "as rosy as the most healthy woman alive."

Some claimed that this glow, this rosiness, had its origin in the bottle (the men themselves apparently took pride in the assertion;

"Joe Hooker is our leader —

He takes his whiskey strong!"

they sang as they set off on practice marches) while other dissenters from the prevalent chorus of praise, although admitting that the general was "handsome and picturesque in the extreme," directed attention to what one of them called

★

This forage cap is adorned with a corps badge made from Union General Phil Kearny's red blanket.

his "fatally weak chin." Still others believed they detected inner flaws, below the rosy surface. "He could play the best game of poker I ever saw," a former West Coast intimate recollected, "until it came to the point when he should go a thousand better, and then he would flunk." But the harshest judgment of all came from a cavalry officer, Charles F. Adams, Jr. According to this son of the ambassador to England, the new commander was "a noisy, low-toned intriguer" under whose influence army headquarters became "a place to which no self-respecting man liked to go, and no decent woman could go. It was a combination of barroom and brothel." Young Adams' own "tone" was exceptionally high, which made him something less than tolerant of the weakness of others — particularly the weaknesses of the flesh, from which he himself apparently was exempt — but in support of at least a part of the accusation was the fact that, from this time on, the general's surname entered the language as one of the many lower-case slang words for prostitute. As for the rest, however, a friend who was with him almost daily insisted that Hooker had gone on the wagon the day he took command. Headquarters might have some of the aspects of a barroom, as Adams said, but according to this observer the general himself did not imbibe.

The fact was, it did indeed appear that he as well as the army had experienced a basic change of character. Much of his former bluster was gone; he had even acquired a dislike for his *nom-de-guerre*, though perhaps this was largely because the story was beginning to get around that he had come by it as the result of an error made in a New York composing room during the Peninsula campaign, when a last-minute dispatch arrived from the front with additional news involving his division. "Fighting — Joe Hooker," the follow-up was tagged, indicating that it was to be added to what had gone before, but the typesetter dropped the dash and it was printed as a separate story, under the resultant heading. The nickname stuck despite the general's objections. "Don't call me Fighting Joe," he said. "[It] makes the public think that I am a hot-headed, furious young fellow, accustomed to making furious and needless dashes at the enemy." Nor was this the only change in Hooker. All his military life, at West Point, in Mexico, and in the peacetime army — from which he had resigned in 1853, after sixteen years of service, in order to take up California farming and civil engineering, only to fail at both so utterly that when news came that the war had begun his friends had to pass the hat to get up money for his fare back East — he had been quick to resent the authority and criticize the conduct of his superiors. Just recently, he had sneered at the President and the Cabinet as a flock of bunglers and had asserted that what the country needed was a dictator, making it more or less clear that the man he had in mind for the job was himself. Now, though, all that had gone by the board. He had not even resented Lincoln's "beware of rashness. Beware of rashness" letter, calling him to account for his derogations while appointing him to command the army. Soon afterwards, in the privacy of his tent, Hooker read the letter to a journalist, only taking exception to the charge that he had "thwarted" Burnside. "The President is mistaken. I never thwarted Burnside in any way, shape, or manner," he broke off reading to say — though even now he could not resist adding: "Burnside was pre-eminently a man of deportment. He fought the battle of Fredericksburg on his deportment; he was defeated on his deportment; and he took his deportment with him out of the Army of the Potomac, thank God." He returned to the letter, and when he had finished reading it he folded it and put it back into his breast pocket, as if to emphasize the claim that he had taken it to heart. "That is just such a letter as a father might write to his son," he mused aloud, and the reporter thought he saw tears beginning to mist the general's pale blue-gray eyes. "It is a beautiful letter," Hooker went on, "and although I think he was harder on me than I deserved, I will say that I love the man who wrote it." Again he paused. Then he said, "After I have got to Richmond I shall give that letter to you to have published."

This last, variously phrased as "When I get to Richmond" or "After we have taken Richmond," cropped up more frequently in his talk as the spirit and strength of his army grew, and it was one of the few things that struck Lincoln unfavorably when he arrived for his Easter visit. "If you get to Richmond, General — " he remarked at their first conference, only to have Hooker break in with "Excuse me, Mr President, but there is no 'if' in this case. I am going straight to Richmond if I live." Lincoln let it pass, though afterwards he said privately to a friend: "That is the most depressing thing about Hooker. It seems to me that he is over-confident." Presently, however, as the inspection tour progressed, he began to see for himself that the general's ready assurance was solidly based on facts and figures. Even after the detachment of Burnside's old corps — which took with it, down the coast to Newport News, whatever resentment its

★

members might be feeling as a result of the supersession of their former chief — Hooker still had seven others, plus a newly consolidated corps of cavalry, including in all no less than twenty divisions of infantry and three of horsemen, here on the Rappahannock, with a present-for-duty total of 133,450 effectives, supported by seventy batteries of artillery with a total of 412 guns. Across the way, the Confederates had less than half as many men and a good deal less than half as many guns, and Hooker not only knew the approximate odds, he was also preparing to take advantage of them. On the eve of Lincoln's arrival he had put his corps commanders on the alert by ordering all surplus baggage sent to the rear, and he had warned

"Don't call me Fighting Joe. It makes the public think that I am a hot-headed, furious young fellow."

— Joseph Hooker

the War Department to have siege equipment ready for shipment to him in front of the rebel capital. In addition to 10,000 shovels, 5000 picks, 5000 axes, and 30,000 sandbags, he wanted authentic maps of the Richmond defenses, to be used in laying out saps and parallels, and he requested that a flotilla of supply boats be kept standing by at all times, ready to deliver 1,500,000 rations up the Pamunkey River as soon as the army got that far. He did not say "if," he said "as soon as," and when this was repeated at Falmouth on Easter Sunday Lincoln shook his head in some perplexity. He admired determination and self-reliance, especially in a military man, but he also knew there was such a thing as whistling in the dark. He had known men — John Pope, for one — who assumed those qualities to hide their doubts, not only from their associates but also from themselves. In fact, the louder a man insisted that there was no room for doubt in his make-up, the more likely he was to belong to the whistler category, and Lincoln feared that Hooker's brashness might be assumed for some such purpose. "It is about the worst thing I have seen since I have been down here," he remarked.

Most of what he saw he found encouraging, however. He agreed with Hooker's estimation of the army as "the finest on the planet," and he particularly enjoyed the temporary relief the visit afforded him from the day-to-day pressure of White House paperwork and the importunities of favor-seekers. Not that he was entirely delivered from the latter. Now that the career officers had

★

him where they could get at him, out of channels and yet with no great strain on their ingrained sense of propriety, they did not neglect the opportunity. Even so stiff a professional as Meade, whose testiness had caused his troops to refer to him as "a God-damned old goggle-eyed snapping turtle," could not resist the chance to curry favor, difficult though he found it to unbend. "In view of the vacant brigadiership in the regular army," he wrote his wife, "I have ventured to tell the President one or two stories, and I think I have made decided progress in his affections." But this was all comparatively mild and even enjoyable — even the stories — in contrast to what the Chief Executive had left behind, and presently would be returning to, in Washington. What was more, his wife and younger son, who accompanied him on the outing, appeared to enjoy it every bit as much as he did. Mary Lincoln responded happily to the all-too-rare opportunity of being with her husband, in and out of office hours, and playing the role of First Lady in a style she considered fitting. Riding one day through a camp of Negro refugees, who crowded about the presidential carriage and lifted their children overhead for a look at the Great Emancipator, she asked her husband how many of "those piccaninnies" he supposed were named Abraham Lincoln. "Let's see," he calculated. "This is April, 1863. I should say that of all

General Joseph Hooker and President
Abraham Lincoln review the cavalry at
Falmouth Heights, Virginia, in April 1863.

★

those babies under two years of age perhaps two thirds have been named for me." Mrs Lincoln, who enjoyed the notion — it was fairly customary in her native Bluegrass for slaves to name their offspring for the master — smiled. But ten-year-old Tad had an entirely different notion of what was fun. He wanted to see some real, live rebels. And Lincoln obliged him. Proceeding one blustery morning to Stafford Heights, they looked across the Rappahannock and down into the ruined streets of Fredericksburg, where the army had staged its two-day carnival before crossing the "champaign tract" to be brought up short in front of the sunken road at the foot of Marye's Heights, and to Tad's delight they saw floating from the eaves of one of the town's few unwrecked houses the Stars and Bars. Nearby, moreover, alongside a tall scorched chimney like a monument erected to commemorate a home, stood two sentinels: genuine, armed gray-backs, though one of them — perversely, as if to lessen Tad's pleasure — wore a light-blue U.S. Army overcoat. Their voices faint with distance, they began yelling across the river at the Yankee spectators, something about Fort Sumter and the ironclads being "licked," which brought an officer out of one of the Fredericksburg bomb-proofs to investigate the shouting. He took out his binoculars, beginning to sweep the opposite heights, and when he spotted the presidential group he paused, adjusted the focus, and peered intently. Whether or not he recognized the tall form, made still taller by the familiar stovepipe hat, they never knew; but at any rate he seemed to. He lowered the glasses and struck an attitude of dignity, then removed his wide-brimmed hat, made a low, formal bow, and retired.

★ ★ ★ *F*or the Confederates across the way — less than 60,000 in all, including the punctilious officer and the two sentinels, one of whom had been lucky enough to scavenge a Yankee overcoat to put between him and the chill of Virginia's early spring — there had been no corresponding improvement, but rather a decline, in the quantity as well as the quality of the supplies provided by their government. The basic daily ration at this time consisted of a quarter-pound of bacon, often rancid, and eighteen ounces of cornmeal, including a high proportion of pulverized cob, supplemented about every third day by the issue of ten pounds of rice to each one hundred men, along with an occasional few peas and a scant handful of dried fruit when it was available, which was seldom. "This may give existence to the troops while idle," Lee complained to the War Department, "but [it] will certainly cause them to break down when called upon for exertion." Scurvy had begun to appear, and though he attempted to combat this by sending out details to gather sassafras buds, wild onions, and such antiscorbutics — together with other, more substantial windfalls, unofficial and in fact illegal; "Ah, General," he chided Hood, "when you Texans come about, the chickens have to roost mighty

★

high" — Lee felt, as he said, "painfully anxious lest the spirit and efficiency of the men should become impaired, and they be rendered unable to sustain their former reputation or perform the service necessary for our safety."

Yet their morale was as high as ever, if not higher: not only because they managed to forget, or at least ignore, their hunger pangs by staging regimental theatricals and minstrel shows, attending the mammoth prayer meetings which were a part of the great religious revival that swept like wildfire through the army at this time, and organizing brigade-size snowball battles which served much the same purpose on this side of the river as Hooker's grand reviews were serving on the other; but also because they could look back on a practically uninterrupted series of victories which they had grounds for believing would be continued, whatever the odds. In the ten months Lee had been in command of the Army of Northern Virginia, including the past three spent in winter quarters, they had fought no less than thirteen battles, large and small, and in all but one of these — South Mountain, where they had been outnumbered ten to one — they had maintained the integrity of their position from start to finish, and in all but one other — Sharpsburg, where the odds were never better than one to three and mostly worse — they had dominated the field when the smoke cleared. Although they had generally assumed the more costly tactical role of the attacker, they had inflicted more than 70,000 casualties, at a cost of less than 50,000 of their own, and had captured about 75,000 small arms while losing fewer than one tenth as many. In guns, the advantage was greatest of all in this respect; losing 8, they had taken 155. ("I declare," a North Carolina private said as his Federal captors were taking him rearward through their lines. "You-uns has got about as many of them 'U.S.' guns as we have.") The over-all result was confidence, in Lee and in themselves, and a pride that burned fiercely despite privation and grim want. One Confederate, writing home, expressed amazement at the contrast between the army's bedraggled appearance in camp and its efficiency in combat. He marveled at the spirit of his companions, "so ragged, slovenly, sleeveless, without a superfluous ounce of flesh upon their bones, with wild matted hair, in mendicants' rags — and to think when the battle-flag goes to the front how they can and do fight!" Nor was praise of Lee's scarecrow heroes limited to those who stood in his army's ranks. An exchanged Union officer, returning to his own lines this spring after a term spent beyond them as a captive, put his first-hand observations on the record in a letter home. "Their artillery horses are poor, starved frames of beasts, tied to their carriages and caissons with odds and ends of rope and strips of raw hide; their supply and ammunition trains look like a congregation of all the crippled California emigrant trains that ever escaped off the desert out of the clutches of the rampaging Comanche Indians. The men are ill-dressed, ill-equipped, and ill-provided, a set of ragamuffins that a man is ashamed to be seen among, even when he is a prisoner and

★

*During the winter of 1863, Confederate
soldiers near Fredericksburg engaged
in a huge snowball fight.*

can't help it. And yet they have beaten us fairly, beaten us all to pieces, beaten us so easily that we are objects of contempt even to their commonest private soldiers, with no shirts to hang out the holes of their pantaloons, and cartridge-boxes tied around their waists with strands of rope."

Lee himself could silence grousing with a jest. "You ought not to mind that," he reassured a young officer who complained about the toughness of some biscuits; "they will stick by you the longer." He referred in much the same tone of levity to the threats made by his new opponent, who had no sooner taken charge of the blue army than he began showing signs of living up to his nickname, Fighting Joe. "General Hooker is obliged to do something," the gray commander wrote home in early February. "I do not know what it will be. He is playing the Chinese game, trying what frightening will do. He runs out his guns, starts wagons and troops up and down the river, and creates an excitement generally. Our men look on in wonder, give a cheer, and all again subsides *in statu quo ante bellum.*" When nothing came of all this show of force before the month was out, Lee expressed a wry impatience. "I owe Mr F. J. Hooker no thanks for keeping me here," he told his wife. "He ought to have made up his mind long ago what to do." At the same time, though, he was warning subordinates that the bluecoats would "make every effort to crush us between now and June, and it will require all our strength to resist them." His confidence, while as firm as that of the men he led, did not cause him to ignore the present odds or the fact that if they continued to lengthen they would stretch beyond endurance. Within a month of the destructive but fruitless repulse of the Federal host that ventured across the river in mid-December, he made his warning explicit in a dispatch to the Secretary of War. "More than once have most promising opportunities been lost for want of men to take advantage of them, and victory itself has been made to put on the appearance of defeat because our diminished and exhausted troops have been unable to renew a successful struggle against fresh numbers of the enemy. The lives of our soldiers are too precious to be sacrificed in the attainment of successes that inflict no loss upon the enemy beyond the actual loss in battle." And he added, with a new note of bitterness which had come with the sack of Fredericksburg and the issuance of the Emancipation Proclamation: "In view of the vast increase of the forces of the enemy, of the savage and brutal policy he has proclaimed, which leaves us no alternative but success or degradation worse than death, if we would save the honor of our families from pollution [and] our social system from destruction, let every effort be made, every means be employed, to fill and maintain the ranks of our armies, until God in his mercy shall bless us with the establishment of our independence."

Instead of an increase, what followed hard on the heels of this appeal was a drastic reduction of his fighting strength, beginning January 14 with the detachment of D. H. Hill to contest the further invasion of the crusty Tarheel general's home state, presaged by the Federals' mid-December advance on Goldsboro. Lee himself went to Richmond two days later to confer with Davis on this and other problems, but had to hurry back to the Rappahannock on the 18th — the eve of his fifty-sixth birthday — when the high-level council of war was disrupted by news that Burnside's army was astir in its camps around Falmouth. As it turned out, all that came of this was the Mud March and Joe Hooker's elevation; Lee detached Robert Ransom's demi-division, which had played a leading role in Longstreet's defense of the sunken road the month before, and sent it south to North Carolina, as he had agreed to do at the interrupted strategy conference. Shortly afterwards, however, word came that Burnside's old corps had boarded transports at Aquia Landing and steamed down Chesapeake Bay to Hampton Roads. It seemed likely that these men were being returned to the scene of their year-old triumph below Norfolk, with instructions to extend their conquest eastward to the Weldon Railroad, Lee's vital supply connection with the factories and grainfields of Georgia and the Carolinas, or to Petersburg, whose fall would give them access to the back door of the capital itself. This two-pronged menace could not be ignored, whatever risk might be involved in attempting to contest it by a further weakening of the Rappahannock line. On February 15 the dismemberment of Longstreet's corps was resumed. Pickett's division was hastened south to Richmond; Hood's followed two days later, accompanied by Old Peter himself, who was charged with the defense of the region beyond the James. These two divisions combined with the troops already there would give him 44,000 men in all, whereas the Federals had 55,000 on hand, exclusive of the corps that presumably was about to join them from Hampton Roads. It was at best a chancy business for the Confederates, north and south of their threatened capital; for even if these blue reinforcements arrived, as was expected momentarily, the command on the south side of the James would be no worse outnumbered than the one on the south side of the Rappahannock, now that more than a fourth of the latter's strength had been subtracted in favor of the former. All Lee could do in this extremity was urge Longstreet to be ready to hurry northward, if possible — that is, if he could find a way to disengage without inviting the destruction of his command or the capture of Richmond — as soon as he got word that Hooker had left off playing the Chinese game and was on the move in earnest. "As our numbers will not admit of our meeting [the enemy] on equality everywhere," the gray commander wrote his detached lieutenant in mid-March, "we must endeavor, by judicious dispositions, to be enabled to make our troops available in any quarter where they may be needed [and] after the emergency passes in one place to transfer them to any other point that may be threatened."

With fewer First Corps troops on hand than had departed, he was down to 58,800 effectives and 170 guns, to be used in opposing a good deal better than twice as many of both. He was almost precisely aware of his opponent's numerical preponderance, not only because of information he received from spies beyond the northern lines, but also because he read the northern papers, one of which was quite specific on the point. Quoting Hooker's medical director, this journal showed 10,777 men on the current sick list, and then went on to state that the sick-well ratio was 67.64 per 1000. By computation Lee arrived at a figure close to 160,000. (Awesome though this total was, it was even a bit low. In late March the Federal commander, lumping teamsters, cooks, and other extra-duty personnel with all the rest, reported an "aggregate present" of 163,005. (Against such odds, and with the knowledge that Hooker would choose the time and place of attack, Lee's only hope for salvation was superior generalship — his own and that of his chief subordinates — coupled with the valor of his soldiers and the increased efficiency of his army. To help achieve this last, he reorganized the artillery into battalions of four four-gun batteries each, four of which battalions were attached to each of the two corps, with two more in general reserve. His hope was that this arrangement, besides strengthening the close-up support of the infantry on the defensive, would provide the "long arm" with a flexibility that would permit a more rapid massing of fire from several quarters of the field at once, either for counterbattery work or for softening an enemy position as a prelude to attack. Whether such measures would produce the desired effect remained to be seen in combat, but another innovation required no testing, its effectiveness being apparent even to a casual eye. This was a legacy left by Longstreet on his departure beyond the James: left, indeed, not only to the Army of Northern Virginia, but also to military science, since in time it would be recognized as perhaps the Confederacy's main contribution to the art of war, which was never the same thereafter.

From such crude beginnings, fathered by the necessity for defending a fixed position against a greatly superior foe, grew the highly intricate field fortifications of the future.

In mid-January, while Lee was away on his brief trip to Richmond, Old Peter had been left in command on the Rappahannock by virtue of his seniority. His corps, still intact at the time, occupied the northern half of the position, from Hamilton's Crossing to Banks Ford, five miles above Fredericksburg, while Jackson's occupied the rest, from Massaponax Creek down to Port Royal, twenty miles below the town. Lee had no sooner left than Longstreet invited Stonewall to inspect the First Corps defenses, and what the grim Virginian saw when he arrived was in the nature of a revelation. Located so as to dominate the roads and open ground, the fieldworks had been designed for use by a skeleton force which could hold them against a surprise attack until supports came up from the reserve. There was nothing new about that; Lee had conceived and used intrenchments for the same purpose on the Peninsula, nearly a year ago. The innovation here involved was the traversed trench. Formerly such works had been little more than long, open ditches, with the spoil thrown forward to serve as a parapet, which gave excellent protection from low-trajectory fire from dead ahead but were vulnerable to flank attack and the lateral effect of bursting shells. To offset these two disadvantages — particularly the latter, intensified by the long-range rifled cannon of the Federals, firing from positions well beyond the reach of most Confederate batteries — Longstreet's engineers had broken the long ditches into quite short, squad-sized rifle trenches, staggered in depth, disposed for mutual support, and connected by traverses which could be utilized against flank attacks and afforded solid protection from all but direct artillery hits. Jackson took a careful look, then returned to his own lines, where the dirt began at once to fly anew. From such crude beginnings, fathered by the necessity for defending a fixed position against a greatly superior foe, grew the highly intricate field fortifications of the future. Presently the whole Rappahannock line, from Banks Ford to Port Royal, was thus protected throughout its undulant, winding, 25-mile length, and when Old Peter left next month with more than half of his men, so well had he and they designed and dug, Lee did not find it necessary to reinforce the two-division remnant by shifting troops from Jackson. "The world has never seen such a fortified position," a young Second Corps artillerist declared some weeks later. "The famous lines at Torres Vedras could not compare with them. . . . They follow the contour of the ground and hug the bases of the hills as they wind to and from the river, thus giving natural flanking arrangements, and from the tops of the hills frown the redoubts for sunken batteries and barbette batteries *ad libitum*, far exceeding the number of our guns; while occasionally, where the trenches take straight across the fields, a redoubt stands out defiantly in the open plain to receive our howitzers." Hooker might, as Lee said, "make every effort to crush [the defenders] between now and June," but he was going to find it a much harder job, from here on out, if he tried anything like the approach his predecessor had adopted in December.

On the face of it, that seemed unlikely; Hooker did not resemble Burnside in manner any more than he did in looks. Clearly, if he continued to develop along the lines he had followed so far, Lee was going to have a far thornier problem on his hands, even aside from the lengthened numerical odds, than any he had overcome in frustrating the two all-out offensives that had succeeded his repulse of McClellan, within sight and sound of Richmond, nine months back. The new chieftain's reorganization of his mounted force was a case in point; "Hooker *made* the Federal cavalry," an admiring trooper later declared. Formerly parceled out, regiment by regiment, to infantry commanders whose handling of them had been at best inept, whether in or out of combat, the three divisions — 11,500 strong, with about 13,000 horses — were grouped into a single corps under Brigadier General George Stoneman, a forty-year-old West Pointer, all of whose previous service had been with the mounted arm, before and during the present war, except for a brief term as an infantry corps commander, in which capacity he had won a brevet for gallantry at Fredericksburg. His current rank was one grade below that of the other seven heads of corps; Hooker was withholding promotion until Stoneman proved that he could weld his inherited conglomeration of horsemen into an effective striking force. That was his basic task, and he seemed well on the way toward pushing it to fulfillment, helped considerably by the fact that, after nearly two years in the saddle, the early blue-jacket volunteers — formerly sneered at by their fox-hunt-trained opponents as "white-faced clerks and counter jumpers" who scarcely knew the on side from the off — were becoming seasoned troopers, no longer mounted on crowbait nags fobbed off on the government by unprincipled contractors, but on strong-limbed, sound-winded, well-fed animals who, like their riders, had learned the evolutions of the line and had mastered the art of survival in all weathers.

This improvement came moreover at a time of crisis for the gray cavalry on the opposite bank of the Rappahannock. Not only was there a critical shortage of horses in the Army of Northern Virginia; there was also the likelihood that those on hand, survivors for the most part of a year of hard campaigning, would die for lack of forage. This second danger increased the threat implicit in the first. So clean had the region been swept of fodder that such few remounts as could be found outside the immediate theater of war could not be brought northward. For example, four hundred artillery horses procured that winter in Georgia had to be kept in North Carolina because they could not be foraged with the army, all but a dozen of whose batteries had already been withdrawn from the lines in order to save the animals from starvation. A man could subsist, at least barely, on a couple of pounds of food a day, whereas a horse required about ten times that amount, and this was a great deal more than the rickety single-track railroad from Richmond could bring forward, even if that much grain had been available there. The result was that the cavalry's activity was severely limited. Brigadier General Wade Hampton's brigade, for instance — the first of Stuart's three, which contained in all about 5000 men — had staged three highly successful small-scale raids, deep in the Federal rear at Dumfries and Occoquan, immediately before and after the Battle of Fredericksburg, returning with some 300 captives and their mounts, mostly unwary vedettes picked up in the course of the gray column's advance by starlight, together with a sizeable train of mule-drawn wagons loaded with captured stores, including 300 pairs of badly needed boots — a real windfall. But the end result of these three coups was that Hampton's underfed horses were so utterly broken down by their exertions that the whole brigade had to be sent south to recover, thus weakening Lee still further at a time when he expected Hooker to make up his mind to come booming over the river any day.

Stuart chafed under the restriction thus imposed. His one exploit this winter was an 1800-trooper raid on Fairfax Court House, fifteen miles from the Federal capital, beginning the day after Christmas and ending New Year's Day; but all it earned him — in contrast to the enormously successful forays by Forrest and Morgan, launched simultaneously in the West — was 200 mounted prisoners, 20 wagons, and the contents of a dozen sutler stalls; which scarcely made up for the wear and tear of the long ride. Though as usual he made the most of the adventure in his report, it was followed by two months spent in winter quarters, where he was obliged to give less attention to the fast-developing enemy cavalry than to the problem of finding forage for his hungry horses. In such surroundings, though he sought diversion for himself and his men in regimental balls and serenades, the plumed hat, red-lined cape, and golden spurs lost a measure of their glitter, at least in certain eyes. "Stuart carries around with him a banjo player and a special correspondent," one high-ranking fellow officer remarked. "This claptrap is noticed and lauded as a peculiarity of genius, when in fact it is nothing else but the act of a buffoon to attract attention." Down to two brigades after Hampton's departure — one under W. H. F. Lee, called "Rooney," and the other under Fitzhugh Lee, respectively the commanding general's son and nephew — Jeb was obliged to take his pleasure at second hand, from the occasional exploits of subordinates and even ex-subordinates. Among the latter was Captain John S. Mosby, a former cavalry scout who had been given permission in January to recruit a body of partisans for operations in the Loudoun Valley, part of a region to be known in time as "Mosby's Confederacy," so successful were he and his Rangers in bedeviling and defeating the

*Confederate guerrilla John S. Mosby,
standing second from left, poses with the officers
of the 43rd Battalion of Partisan Rangers.*

★

bluecoats sent there to capture or destroy him. Twenty-eight years old and weighing barely 125 pounds, the slim, gray-eyed Virginian first attracted wide attention by his capture, at Fairfax on a night in early March, of Brigadier General E. H. Stoughton, a Vermont-born West Pointer, together with two other officers, 30 men, and 58 horses. Mosby, who at present had fewer men than that in his whole command, entered the general's headquarters, stole upstairs in the darkness, and found the general himself asleep in bed. Turning down the covers, he lifted the tail of the sleeper's nightshirt and gave him a spank on the behind.

"General," he said, "did you ever hear of Mosby?"

"Yes," Stoughton replied, flustered and half awake; "have you caught him?"

"He has caught you," Mosby said, by way of self-introduction, and got his captive up and dressed and took him back through the lines, along with virtually all of his headquarters guard, for delivery to Fitzhugh Lee the following morning at Culpeper.

Fitz Lee, a year younger than the clean-shaven Mosby, though he disguised the fact behind an enormous shovel beard that outdid even Longstreet's in length and thickness, could appreciate a joke as well as the next man, and in this case he could appreciate it perhaps a good deal better, since he and the captive Vermonter had been schoolmates at the Point. Besides, he was in an excellent frame of mind just now, having returned the week before from a similar though less spectacular exploit involving still another fellow cadet of his and Stoughton's: New York-born Brigadier General W. W. Averell, who commanded the second of Stoneman's three divisions. Young Lee was sent by his uncle to investigate a rumor that Hooker was about to repeat McClellan's strategy by transferring his army to the Peninsula. Crossing the Rappahannock well upstream at Kelly's Ford on February 24, Lee's 400-man detachment pushed on to the Warrenton Post Road, then down it, penetrating the blue cavalry screen to the vicinity of Hartwood Church, eight miles short of Falmouth. Here the graybacks encountered their first serious opposition in the form of the 3d Pennsylvania Cavalry, Averell's old regiment before his promotion to divisional command. Lee promptly charged and routed the Keystone troopers, capturing 150 of them at a cost to himself of 14 killed and wounded. Then, having secured the information he had come for — Hooker, whose headquarters were a scant half-dozen miles away by now, obviously was planning no such move as had been rumored — Lee successfully withdrew without further incident, leaving behind him a note for his former schoolmate, whose entire division had been turned out, along with two others of infantry, in a vain attempt to intercept the raiders and avenge the defeat of one of its best regiments. The note was brief and characteristic. "I wish you would put up your sword, leave my state, and go home," Fitz told his old friend, adding in reference to the speed with which the bluecoats had retreated when attacked: "You ride a good horse, I ride a better. Yours can beat mine running." The close was in the nature of a challenge. "If you won't go home, return my visit and bring me a sack of coffee."

Averell returned the visit within three weeks, and he took care to bring along a sack of coffee in his saddlebags. What was more, he repaid the call in force, splashing through the shallows of Kelly's Ford on the morning of March 17 with 3000 troopers. Lee had fewer than 1000 at the time, but his pickets put up such a scrap at the crossing that Averell, though he was pleased to have captured about two dozen of them in the skirmish, persuaded himself that it would be wise to leave a third of his force there to protect his rear, thereby of his own accord reducing the odds to only a little better than two to one. Also, being aware of his old schoolmate's impulsive nature, he halted about mid-morning, less than a mile beyond the river, dismounted his men, and took up a strong defensive position behind a stone wall crossing a pasture on the farm of a family named Brooks. Sure enough, at noon Lee came riding hard from Culpeper and attacked without delay, his lead regiment charging dragoon-style, four abreast. The result, as the defenders poured a hot fire from behind their ready-made breastworks, was a quick and bloody repulse. Averell cautiously followed it up, but was struck again, one mile north, with like results. While the blue riders held their ground, the Confederates crossed Carter's Run and re-assembled; whereupon the two commands settled down to long-range firing across the creek, relieving the monotony from time to time with limited charges and countercharges which did nothing to alter the tactical stalemate. This continued until about 5.30, when Averell, having learned from captured rebels that Stuart and his crack artillerist Pelham were on the field, decided that the time had come for him to recross the Rappahannock. "My horses were very much exhausted. We had been successful so far. I deemed it proper to withdraw." So he stated later in his report. However, before terminating the requested "visit" he took care to observe the amenities by leaving the sack of coffee Lee had asked for, together with a note: "Dear Fitz. Here's your coffee. Here's your visit. How do you like it? Averell."

The truth was, Fitz did not much like it. Though he could, and did, claim victory on grounds that he had remained in control of the field after the enemy withdrew, this was not very satisfactory when he considered that the Federals could make the same claim with regard to every similar Confederate penetration, including his own recent raid on Hartwood Church and Stuart's dazzling "rides" the year before. Then too, there was the matter of casualties. Suffering 133, Lee had inflicted only 78, or not much over half as many. If this was a victory, it was certainly a strange one. But there was more that was alarming about this St Patrick's Day action: much more, at least from the southern point of view. For the first time on a fair field of fight — the two-to-one odds

Brigadier General W.W. Averell, seated,
commanded a Union cavalry division
under George Stoneman.

were not unusual; moreover, they had been the source of considerable underdog glory in the past — Confederate cavalry had fallen back repeatedly under pressure from Federal cavalry. Nothing could have demonstrated better the vast improvement of this arm of the Union war machine, especially when it was admitted that only Averell's lack of the true aggressive instinct, which twice had left the rebel horsemen unmolested while they reformed their broken ranks, had kept the blue troopers from converting both repulses into routs. Unquestionably, this proof that the Federal cavalry had come of age, so to speak, meant future trouble for the men who previously had ridden around and through and over their awkward opponents almost at will. . . . Nor was that all either. This light-hearted exchange of calling cards, accompanied in one case by the gift of a pound of coffee, had its more immediate somber consequences, too. After all, a man who died on this small field was every bit as dead as a man who died in the thunderous pageantry of Fredericksburg, and his survivors were apt to be quite as inconsolable in their sorrow. They might possibly be even more inconsolable,

★

since their grief did not take into account the battle or skirmish itself, but rather the identity of the man who fell. What made Kelly's Ford particular in this respect was that it produced one casualty for whom the whole South mourned.

One of Averell's reasons for withdrawing had been the report that Stuart was on the field. It was true, so far as it went; Jeb was there, but he had brought no reinforcements with him, as Averell supposed; he had come to Culpeper on court-martial business, and thus happened to be on hand when the news arrived that bluecoats were over the river. Similarly, the day before, John Pelham had left cavalry headquarters to see a girl in Orange, so that he too turned up in time to join Fitz Lee on the ride toward Kelly's Ford; "tall, slender, beautifully proportioned," a friend called the twenty-three-year-old Alabamian, and "as grand a flirt as ever lived." With his own guns back near Fredericksburg — including the brass Napoleon with which he had held up the advance of a whole Federal division for the better part of an hour — he was here supposedly as a spectator, but anyone who knew him also knew that he would never be content with anything less than a ringside seat, and would scarcely be satisfied even with that, once the action had been joined. And so it was. When the first charge was launched against the stone wall, the young major smiled, drew the sword which he happened to be wearing because he had gone courting the night before, and waved it gaily as he rode hard to overtake the van. "Forward! Forward!" he cried. Just then, abrupt as a clap of blue-sky thunder, a shell burst with a flash and a roar directly overhead. Pelham fell. He lay on his back, full length and motionless, his blue eyes open and the smile still on his handsome face, which was unmarked. Turning him over, however, his companions found a small, deep gash at the base of his skull, just above the hair line, where a fragment of the shell had struck and entered. When Stuart, who had ridden to another quarter of the field, heard that his young chief of artillery was dead he bowed his head on his horse's neck and wept. "Our loss is irreparable," he said.

Others thought so, too: three girls in nearby towns, for instance, who put on mourning. Word spread quickly throughout the South, and men and women in far-off places, who had known him only by reputation, received with a sense of personal bereavement the news that "the gallant Pelham" had fallen. Robert Lee, who had attached the adjective to the young gunner's name in his report on their last great battle, made an unusual suggestion to the President. "I mourn the loss of Major Pelham," he wrote. "I had hoped that a long career of usefulness and honor was still before him. He has been stricken down in the midst of both, and before he could receive the promotion he had richly won. I hope there will be no impropriety in presenting his name to the Senate, that his comrades may see that his services have been appreciated, and may be incited to emulate them." Davis promptly forwarded the letter, with the result that Pelham was promoted even as he lay in state in the Virginia capitol. For once, the Senate had acted quickly, and the dead artillerist, who just under two years ago had left West Point on the eve of graduation in order to go with his native state, went home to Alabama as Lieutenant Colonel Pelham.

At this time of grief, coupled with uncertainty as to the enemy's intentions, Lee fell ill for the first time in the war. A throat infection had settled in his chest, giving him pains that interfered with his sleep and made him testy during his waking hours. By the end of March his condition was such that his medical director insisted that he leave his tent and take up quarters in a house at Yerby's, on the railroad five miles south of Fredericksburg. He did so, much against his wishes, and complained in a home letter that the doctors were "tapping me all over like an old steam boiler before condemning it." After the manner of most men unfamiliar with sickness, he was irritable and inclined to be impatient with those around him at such times (which in turn provoked his staff into giving him the irreverent nickname "the Tycoon") but he never really lost the iron self-control that was the basis of the character he presented to the world. Once, for example, when he was short with his adjutant over some administrative detail, that officer drew himself up with dignity and silently defied his chief; whereupon Lee at once got hold of himself and said calmly, "Major Taylor, when I lose my temper don't let it make you angry." Nor did his illness detract in any way from the qualities which, at the time of his appointment to command, had led an acquaintance to declare: "His name might be Audacity. He will take more desperate chances, and take them quicker, than any other general in this country, North and South." Confirmation of these words had come in the smoke and flame of the Seven Days, in the fifty-mile march around Pope with half of an outnumbered army, and in the bloody defense of the Sharpsburg ridge with his back to a deep river. Yet nothing gave them more emphasis than his reaction now to the early-April news that Burnside's old corps, after lingering all this time at Newport News, was proceeding west to join its old commander, who had been assigned to head the Department of the Ohio. This signified trouble for Johnston and Bragg in Tennessee, since it probably meant that these troops would reinforce Rosecrans. At Charleston, moreover, Beauregard even now was under what might well be an irresistible attack by an ironclad fleet, with thousands of bluecoats waiting aboard transports for the signal to steam into the blasted harbor and occupy the city. Lee's reaction to this combination of pressures, sick though he was, and faced with odds which he knew were worse than two to one here on the Rappahannock, was to suggest that, if this bolstering of the Union effort down the coast and in the West indicated a lessening of the Union effort in the East, the Army of Northern Virginia should swing over to the offensive. "Should Hooker's army assume the defensive," he wrote the Secretary of War on April 9, "the readiest method of relieving the pressure on General Johnston and General Beauregard would be for this army to cross into Maryland." The wretched condition of the roads, plus the cramping shortage of provisions and transportation, made such a move impossible at present, he added; "But this is what I would recommend, if practicable."

Such audacity, though ingrained and very much a part of the nature of the man, was also based on the combat-tested valor of the soldiers he commanded. He knew there was nothing he could ask of them that they would not try to give him, and he believed that with such a spirit they could not fail; or if they failed, it would not be their fault. "There never were such men in an army before," he said this spring. "They will go anywhere and do anything if properly led." And if his admiration for them was practically boundless, so too was his concern. "His theory, expressed upon many occasions," a staff officer later wrote, "was that the private soldiers — men who fought without the stimulus of rank, emolument, or individual renown — were the most meritorious class of the army, and that they deserved and should receive the utmost respect and consideration." Not one of them ever appealed to him without being given a sympathetic hearing, sometimes in the very heat of battle, and he turned down a plan for the formation of a battalion of honor because he did not believe there would be room in its ranks for all who deserved a place there. Quite literally, nothing was too good for them in the way of reward, according to Lee, and this applied without reservation. To him, they all were heroes. One day he saw a man in uniform standing near the open flap of his tent. "Come in, Captain, and take a seat," he said. When the man replied, "I'm no captain, General; I'm nothing but a private," Lee told him: "Come in, sir. Come in and take a seat. You ought to be a captain."

★ ★ ★ *L*incoln **apparently felt much the same way about the enlisted men in blue.** One correspondent observed that at the final Grand Review, staged on the last full day of his Falmouth visit, "the President merely touched his hat in return salute to the officers, but uncovered to the men in the ranks." Seated upon a short, thick-set horse with a docked tail, the tall civilian in the stovepipe hat and rusty tailcoat presented quite a contrast to the army commander, who wore a dress uniform and rode his usual milk-white charger. A Maine soldier noticed Hooker's "evident satisfaction" as the long blue files swung past in neat array, and spoke of "the conscious power shown on his handsome but rather too rosy face," whereas another from Wisconsin remarked that "Mr Lincoln sat his cob perfectly straight, and dressed as he was in dark clothes, it appeared as if he was an exclamation point astride of the small letter *m*." He seemed oddly preoccupied with matters far removed from the present martial business of watching the troops pass in review. This was shown to be the case when he turned without preamble to Major General Darius N. Couch, the senior corps commander, and asked:

★

"What do you suppose will become of all these men when the war is over?" Couch was somewhat taken aback; his mind had not been working along those lines; but he said later, "It struck me as very pleasant that somebody had an idea that the war would sometime end."

Four days of intimate acquaintance with the Army of the Potomac had indicated to Lincoln, despite the blusterous symptoms of overconfidence on the part of the man beside him on the big white horse — despite, too, the rumored repulse of the ironclads at Charleston, the loss of the Union foothold on Texas, the upsurge of guerillas in Missouri, the apparent stalemate in Middle Tennessee, and Grant's long sequence of failures in front of Vicksburg — that the end of the war might indeed be within reach, once Hooker decided the time had come for a jump-off. Morale had never been higher, the Chief Executive found by talking with the troops in their renovated camps and hospitals. Moreover, the reorganizational shake-up seemed to have brought the best men to the top. Sumner and Franklin were gone for good, along with the clumsy Grand Division arrangement which had accomplished little more than the addition of another link to the overlong chain of command, and of the seven major generals now at the head of the seven infantry corps, less than half — Couch, Reynolds, and Henry W. Slocum — had served in the same capacity during the recent Fredericksburg fiasco, while the remaining four were graduates of the

Near Falmouth, Virginia, the 110th Pennsylvania forms for inspection during its stay at winter headquarters.

★

hard-knocks school of experience and therefore could be presumed to have achieved their current eminence on merit. Daniel E. Sickles, the only nonregular of the lot, had taken over from Stoneman after that officer's transfer to the cavalry; Meade had succeeded Dan Butterfield, who had moved up to the post of army chief of staff; John Sedgwick had inherited the command of W. F. Smith, now in charge of Burnside's old corps on its way out to Ohio; Oliver O. Howard, who had lost an arm last year on the Peninsula, had replaced Sigel when that general, already miffed because Hooker had been promoted over his head, resigned in protest because his corps, being next to the smallest of the seven, was incommensurate with his rank. Lincoln had known most of these men before, but in the course of the past four days he had come to know them better, with the result that he felt confident, more confident at any rate than he had felt before, as to the probable outcome of a clash between the armies now facing each other across the Rappahannock. In fact his principal admonition, in a memorandum which he prepared in the course of his visit — perhaps on this same April 9 of the final Grand Review, while Lee was recommending to his government that the Army of Northern Virginia swing over to the offensive in order to break up the menacing Federal combinations — was that "our prime object is the enemy's army in front of us, and is not . . . Richmond at all, unless it be incidental to the main object." Having observed from Stafford Heights the strength of the rebel fortifications, he did not think it would be wise to "take the disadvantage of attacking [Lee] in his intrenchments; but we should continually harass and menace him, so that he shall have no leisure or safety in sending away detachments. If he weakens himself, then pitch into him."

One further admonition he had, and he delivered himself of it the following morning as he sat with Hooker and Couch before departing for Aquia Landing, where the steamer was waiting to take him and his party back to Washington. "I want to impress upon you two gentlemen," he said, "in your next fight, put in all your men." He pronounced the last five words with emphasis, perhaps recalling that in the December fight a good half of the army had stood idle on the left while the conflict wore toward its bloody twilight finish on the right, and then he was off to join his wife and son for the boat ride up the Potomac. Although the trip unquestionably had done him good, providing him with a rare chance to relax, it was after all no more than an interlude in the round of administrative cares, a brief recess from the importunities of men who sought to avail themselves of the power of his office. When a friend remarked that he was looking rested and in better health as a result of his visit to the army, Lincoln replied that it had been "a great relief to get away from Washington and the politicians. But nothing touches the tired spot," he added.

★　★　★

★

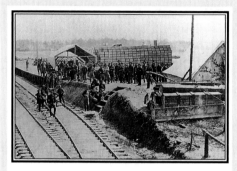

*Wooden crates of hardtack
and other supplies lie stock-
piled along a railroad siding
at Stoneman's Switch
near Fredericksburg.*

THREE

Suffolk: Longstreet Southside

1863 ★ ★ ★ ★ ★ **L**ongstreet, on his own at last — at least in a manner of speaking — was finding no such opportunities for glory beyond the James as his fellow corps commander Jackson had found the year before, on detached service out in the Shenandoah Valley. There Stonewall had not only added a brisk chapter to military history and several exemplary paragraphs to future tactics manuals, but had also earned for himself, according to admirers, the one thing his senior rival, according to detractors, wanted more than anything on or off the earth: a seat among the immortals in Valhalla. However, this southside venture, being a different kind of thing, seemed quite unlikely to be productive of any such reward. Designed less for the gathering of laurels than for the gathering of the hams and bacon which for generations had made and would continue to make the Smithfield region famous, it was aimed at satisfying the hunger of the stomach, rather than the hunger of the soul. What was more, throughout his ten weeks of "independent" command, Old Peter was obliged to serve three masters — Davis, Seddon, and Lee — who saddled him with three separate, simultaneous, and sometimes incompatible assignments: 1) the protection of the national capital, threatened by combinations of forces superior to his own, 2) the gathering of supplies in an area that had been under Federal domination for nearly a year, and 3) the disposition of his

★

troops so as to be able to hurry them back to the Rappahannock on short notice. To these, there presently was added a fourth, the investment of Suffolk, which had more men within its fortifications than he could bring against them. The wonder, under such conditions as obtained, was not that he failed in part, but that he succeeded to any degree at all in fulfilling these divergent expectations.

In Richmond itself there had been no talk of failure at the outset, only a feeling of vast relief as the battle-hardened divisions of Hood and Pickett arrived to block the approach of blue forces reported to be gathering ominously, east and southeast of the city, beyond the rim of intrenchments mainly occupied by part-time defenders recruited in the emergency

> *"We are much more likely to succeed by operating ourselves than by lying still to await the enemy's time for thorough preparations before he moves upon us."*
>
> — James Longstreet

from the host of clerks and other government workers who had escaped conscription up to now. One of these, an industrious diarist, influenced perhaps by a far-fetched sense of rivalry — or perhaps by the fact that in the past six months, since Lee's army had set out northward after Pope, he had forgot what a combat soldier looked like — thought the First Corps veterans "pale and haggard" when he saw them on February 18, slogging through snow deposited calf-deep in the streets by a heavy storm the night before. Four days later, however, Seddon wrote Lee that their "appearance, spirit, and cheerfulness afforded great satisfaction," not only to the authorities but also to the fretful populace. "General Longstreet is here," the Secretary added, "and under his able guidance of such troops no one doubts as to the entire security of the capital." On February 25 he appointed the burly Georgian commander of the Department of Virginia and North Carolina, which was created by combining the three departments of Richmond, Southern Virginia, and North Carolina, respectively under Major Generals Arnold Elzey, Samuel G. French, and D. H. Hill, together with the independent Cape Fear River District under Brigadier General W. H. C. Whiting, who was charged with protecting Wilmington from attack by land or water. Longstreet's total number of men present for duty, including those in the two divisions he brought with him, plus Ransom's demi-division forwarded earlier, was 44,193 of all arms, mostly scattered about the two states in ill-equipped and poorly administered garrisons of defense. Already outnumbered by the Federals on hand — whose current strength of 50,995 effectives he considerably overestimated — he was alarmed by reports, received on the day he assumed command, that transports were arriving daily in Hampton Roads, crowded to the gunwales with reinforcements for the intended all-out drive on Richmond. So far, they had unloaded an estimated "40,000 or 50,000" troops at Newport News, he wired Lee, and there were rumors that Joe Hooker himself had been seen at Fort Monroe, presaging the early arrival of the balance of the Army of the Potomac.

In such alarming circumstances, and schooled as he had been in strategy under Lee, Old Peter reasoned that the time had come for him to attack, if only by way of creating a diversion. As he put it, "We are much more likely to succeed by operating ourselves than by lying still to await the enemy's time for thorough preparations before he moves upon us." However, it was in the attempted application of this commendable principle that his troubles really began; for it was then that he came face to face with the fact that the exercise of independent command, especially in the armies of the Confederacy, involved a good deal more than a knowledge of tactics and logistics. Like him, his three ranking subordinates were West Pointers in their early or middle forties, and like him, too, they had their share of temperamental peculiarities — as he discovered when he issued instructions for a joint attack on New Bern. Held by the Federals for nearly a year now, the town had been the base for their mid-December advance against the Wilmington & Weldon Railroad, sixty miles away at Goldsboro, and it was Longstreet's belief that an attack on both banks of the Neuse River, farther down, would pinch off the blue garrison and expose it to capture or destruction. His plan was for Hill to move against the place with his whole command, reinforced by one of Whiting's two brigades, which would give him about 14,000 men in all. Hill was altogether willing, having recently excoriated the Yankee invaders by calling upon his infantry to "cut down to 6 feet by 2 the dimensions of the farms which these plunderers propose to appropriate." But Whiting was not, even though the brigade asked for was Ransom's, detached from the First Corps and forwarded to him only the month before. In response to Longstreet's call for "half your force and as many more as can be spared from the Wilmington garrison," along with one of his three long-range Whitworth guns, Whiting — a brilliant thirty-nine-year-old Mississippian who, three years after Old Peter had finished near the bottom of the West Point class of '42, had not only graduated at the top of his class, but had done so with the highest marks any cadet had ever made — promptly wrote: "I perceive you are not acquainted with this vicinity. . . . So far from considering myself able to spare troops from here, I have applied for and earnestly urged that another brigade be sent here immediately. The works here are by no means completed and I need the services of every man I can raise."

The result was that Hill moved against New Bern without the help of Whiting's men or the loan of the precious long-range gun, and though he converted what was to have been an attack into a demonstration — it was March 14, the anniversary of the fall of the town to the Federals as a follow-up of their capture of Roanoke Island — even that was repulsed decisively when the defenders towed gunboats up the river from Pamlico Sound and opened a scorching fire against the Confederates on both banks, inflicting 30-odd casualties at a cost of only 6. Back in Goldsboro two days later, Hill was furious. "The spirit manifested by Whiting has spoiled everything," he protested in his report. As he saw it, the proper correction for this was for the government to keep its word that he would be given command of all the troops in the state, including those at Wilmington, in which case he would be able to bend the fractious Whiting to his will. "I have received nothing but contemptuous treatment from Richmond from the very beginning of the war," he complained hotly, "but I hope they will not carry matters so far as to perpetuate a swindle." Longstreet, receiving his caustic friend's report, sought to protect him from the wrath of their superiors. "I presume that this was not intended as an official communication," he replied, "and have not forwarded it. I hope that you will send up another account of your trip." Hill neither insisted that the document stand nor offered to withdraw it, but he declined to submit a new or expurgated account of what Old Peter referred to as his "trip."

For all his obstreperous ways of protesting the injustice he saw everywhere around him, Hill was only one among the many when it came to presenting his chief with problems. Arnold Elzey, in charge of the Richmond defenses north of the James, had only recently returned to duty after a long and painful convalescence from the face wound he had suffered at Gaines Mill. A Marylander, he originally had had the last name Jones, but had dropped it in favor of his mother's more distinctive maiden name. Erratic and moody, perhaps because of his disfigurement and the internal damage to his mouth which made his words scarcely intelligible, he was said to be drinking heavily — a particular yet not uncommon type among the casualties of war, injured as much in pride as in body. At any rate, neither he nor his command could be counted on for anything more than the desperate last-ditch resistance that was his and their assignment. Moreover, Longstreet had no high opinion of the abilities of Sam French, who was charged with the defense of Petersburg, that vital nexus of rail supply lines connecting Virginia and the deeper South. A New Jersey–born adoptive Mississippian and a veteran of the Mexican War, French had attained high rank without distinction in the field of the present conflict, and Old Peter had the usual combat officer's prejudice in this and other such cases he encountered when he crossed the

James. Because of Lee's policy of quietly getting rid of men he found unsatisfactory, not by cashiering them but by transferring them to far or adjoining theaters where he considered their shortcomings would cost their country less, Longstreet might have thought he was back with the old Army of the Potomac, as it had been called before the advent of Lee and its transfiguration into the Army of Northern Virginia, so familiar were the faces of many of the officers he found serving under him when he took over his new department. All too many of those faces reflected failure, and all too many others identified men who were inexperienced in combat.

Not that there appeared to be any considerable need for such experience just now. Foraging operations were in full swing, with commissary details scouring the countryside and sending back long trains of wagons heavily loaded with hams and bacon, side meat, salted fish, and flour and cornmeal, all of which were plenteous in the region. Increasingly, as the Federals failed to press their rumored drive on Richmond, the removal of such badly needed stores was becoming the prime concern of the department commander and his troops.

On March 17 their work was interrupted by a dispatch from Lee. Bluecoats were over the Rappahannock at Kelly's Ford; Longstreet was to hurry

*Confederate soldiers augment their rations
with donations from sympathetic civilians.*

north with Hood and Pickett to help drive them back. Before he could obey, however, the order was countermanded. The threat had been no more than a cavalry raid; the enemy troopers had retired. Old Peter returned to his foraging duties with new zeal. Now that the nearer counties had been picked clean, he wanted to move eastward into those beyond the Blackwater and Chowan Rivers, out of reach for the past year because of the Union occupation. He figured that if the Yankees could be driven back within their works and held there for a reasonable length of time, his commissary agents — unhampered by the enemy and aided by the citizens of those regions, who had remained intensely loyal to the Confederacy through long months when they might have thought themselves forsaken — would be able to effect a quick removal of the stores. However, this was at best a risky business for him to undertake. He would not only have to keep his two most effective divisions ready to disengage on short notice, in order to be able to speed them north on call from Lee; he would also have to detail a considerable portion of his force for commissary duties behind the lines if he was to accomplish the main purpose underlying his reason for advancing in the first place. In short, with these two disadvantages added to the fact that he was outnumbered before he even began, he would be reversing the required two-to-one numerical ratio between the two parties engaged in siege operations. But he decided to give the thing a try in any event, for the sake of all those thousands of slabs of bacon and barrels of herring awaiting removal from areas previously inaccessible to the soldiers who were fighting here and elsewhere for their eventual deliverance from the blue forces now in occupation.

He made his plans accordingly. Hood and Pickett would join French for a movement against Suffolk, which would serve the double purpose of bringing the fertile Blackwater–Chowan watersheds within the grasp of his commissary agents and of blocking the path of a Federal drive on Petersburg from the lower reaches of the James. Nor was that all. Hill — reinforced at last by Ransom's brigade, pried loose from Whiting over that general's violent protest that he was being stripped of two thirds of his infantry on the eve of an all-out assault on Wilmington by the ironclad fleet Du Pont was assembling at Port Royal — would move simultaneously against Washington, North Carolina, the Tar River gateway to a region which was lush with agricultural produce and gave access to the fisheries of upper Pamlico Sound. This lower movement under Hill, while equally rich in foraging possibilities, was more in the nature of a diversion, favoring the main effort against Suffolk, which would be under Longstreet's personal direction. It was Old Peter's hope that the Unionists, being threatened in two places at once, would not only be prevented from strengthening either at the expense of the other, but would also be thrown off balance by the expectation of additional strikes, all down the long perimeter of their coastal holdings. Though he made it clear at the outset, to his superiors as

★

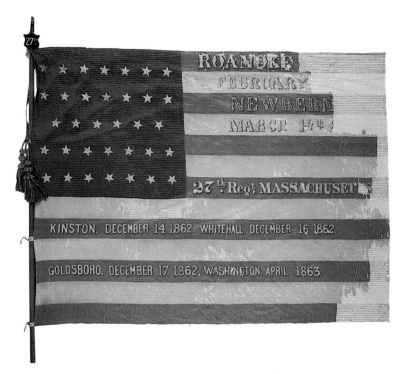

ROANOKE
FEBRUARY
NEWBERN
MARCH 14th
27th Regt MASSACHUSET

KINSTON, DECEMBER 14 1862, WHITEHALL, DECEMBER 16, 1862

GOLDSBORO, DECEMBER 17 1862, WASHINGTON APRIL 1863,

The flag of the 27th Massachusetts Volunteers was adorned with the names and dates of battles in which they fought, including Washington, North Carolina.

well as to his subordinates, that both advances were intended to be no more than demonstrations, staged primarily to drive the bluecoats within their works so that his foraging details would be free to scour the area unmolested, he did not overlook the possibility of taking advantage of any opening the enemy might afford. Food for Lee's soldiers was his main concern, but he intended to draw blood, too — despite the numerical odds — whenever and wherever the tactical risk appeared slight enough to justify grasping the nettle. "The principal object of the expedition was to draw out supplies for our army," he reminded the War Department after the movement against Suffolk was under way. "I shall confine myself to this unless I find a fair opportunity for something more."

Hill took off first, however, advancing so rapidly from Goldsboro that on March 30 he had Washington invested before the Federal department commander, Major General John G. Foster, had a chance to reinforce its 1200-man garrison. With ten times that many troops on hand, the Confederates would have little trouble keeping the defenders penned up, but Hill did not believe their capture would be worth the casualties he would suffer in an assault. Consequently, while his foragers were busily rounding up hogs and cattle, he continued to hover about the place, making threatening gestures from time to time in the face of highly accurate fire from gunboats anchored off the town. His chief worry was that Foster — one of Burnside's three aggressive brigadiers in last year's smashing attack on Roanoke Island — would order an advance against his rear by the

★

*R*esidents of New Bern, North Carolina, gather
at the stationer's store to follow the progress of the
war through the town's newspapers and magazines.

Union force at New Bern, only thirty miles away. As the siege progressed through the first week in April he vibrated with alternate emotions of jubilation and despair, much to the confusion of Longstreet, who scarcely knew what to make of his lieutenant's fluctuant dispatches. "Up to the 2d instant," he replied from Petersburg on April 7, apparently in something of a daze, "you gave me no reason to hope that you could accomplish anything. . . . Then came your letter of the 2d, which was full of encouragement and hope. . . . After your letter of the 2d came one of the 4th, which I believe was more desponding than your previous letters. . . . Your letter of the 5th revives much hope again." Old Peter was understandably confused, but in point of fact Hill was doing much better than he knew or would admit. Not only were large quantities of supplies moving swiftly back to Goldsboro for forwarding to Richmond and the Rappahannock line, but Foster was reacting exactly as the Confederates had hoped he would do to their pretense of great strength and earnestness. Drawing in his horns in expectation of being struck next at almost any point in his department, he left Hill's commissary agents a clear field for exploitation. "I am confident," he warned Halleck on Easter Sunday, "that heavy operations will be necessary in this state, and that the most desperate efforts are and will continue to be made to drive us from the towns now occupied."

At any rate Longstreet's main concern was centered presently on matters closer at hand than Hill's pendulum swings from gloom to elation down on the banks of the Tar. On April 9 — the day Lee recommended an advance into Maryland as the best Confederate strategy for contesting the over-all Union menace, East and West, and also the day Hooker staged the last of the Grand Reviews in honor of Lincoln's Falmouth visit — First Corps troops moved out of their camps near Petersburg and took up the march southeastward in the direction of the lower Blackwater crossings less than twenty miles from Suffolk, which the Federals had been fortifying ever since they occupied it formally in September. Two divisions were quartered there now, under Major General John J. Peck and Brigadier General George W. Getty, with a combined total of 21,108 effectives. Hood, Pickett, and French had 20,192 between them; but Peck, estimating the rebel strength at "40,000 to 60,000 men," reacted much as Foster had done, ten days ago, to Hill's advance on Washington. Calling in all his detachments from the surrounding countryside, he skirmished briefly along the Blackwater to gain time for a concentration, then fell back on Suffolk, where he buttoned himself up tightly. While his troops were at work improving the intrenchments, he notified his superiors at Fort Monroe and Washington that he was prepared to fight to the last man, despite the enemy's "great preponderance of artillery as well as other branches." Longstreet moved up deliberately. On April 11 he invested the town, taking the bluecoats under fire from the opposite bank of the Nansemond River while extending his right southward all the way to Dismal Swamp. Behind this long, concave front, which he held with a minimum number of men in order to provide details for his all-important foraging operations, commissary officers were soon busy purchasing everything in sight that a man could eat or wear. Long trains of wagons, piled high with goods and forage, soon were grinding westward amid a din of cracking whips, ungreased axles, and teamster curses. After unloading at newly established dumps along the Petersburg & Norfolk Railroad, they returned eastward, rattling empty across the muddy landscape, for new loads. Day and night, to Longstreet's considerable satisfaction — as well as to that of the hungry men on the Rappahannock, whose rations improved correspondingly — the shuttle work continued. Supplies appeared inexhaustible in this region scarcely touched by war till now.

★

Meanwhile, by way of keeping up the bluff, the troops on line were demonstrating noisily, as if in preparation for an assault on the blue intrenchments across the way. Although the duty was mostly dull, there were occasional incidents that provided all the excitement a man could want, and more. For instance, there was the affair at Fort Huger, an old Confederate redoubt constructed originally as part of the Suffolk defenses but abandoned by the Federals when they took over. As it turned out, they showed wisdom by this action. On April 16, French moved five guns and three companies of infantry into the fort on the far left of his line, intending to deny enemy gunboats the use of the adjoining Nansemond River. Three nights later, however, six companies of Connecticut infantry crossed the river, a quarter of a mile upstream, and swooped down in a surprise attack that captured the works, along with all five of the guns and 130 officers and men. Joined before dawn by the other four companies of their regiment, they held the place all the following day and returned to their own lines after dark, taking along the captured men and guns. Longstreet had scarcely had time to absorb the news of this setback when he heard from Hill that the Washington siege had been abandoned on the same day Fort Huger was occupied by French. Two weeks had sufficed for the removal of most of the stores from the region; so that when, at the end of that span, the Federals succeeded in running in two ships to replenish the supplies of the garrison, Hill decided the time had come for him to withdraw. Back at Goldsboro before the week was out, he praised his troops for their "vigilance on duty and good behavior everywhere." His scorn he reserved for homeguarders, especially those of lofty rank, whose avoidance of combat duty he blamed for his lack of the strength required to drive the detested Yankees not only "into their rat holes at New Bern and Washington," but into Pamlico Sound as well. "And such noble regiments they have," he sneered at these stay-at-home Tarheel warriors. "Three field officers, four staff officers, ten captains, thirty lieutenants, and one private with a misery in his bowels. . . . When our independence is won, the most trifling soldier in the ranks will be more respected, as he is now more respectable, than an army of these skulking exempts."

Longstreet accepted vexation far more philosophically. Even the overrunning of Fort Huger, though it showed, as he said, "a general lack of vigilance and prompt attention to duties," did not arouse his ire. "Many of the officers were of limited experience," he concluded his report of the affair, "and I have no doubt acted as they thought best. I do not know that any of them deserve censure. This lesson, it is hoped, will be of service to us all." Others reacted differently as the Suffolk siege wore on. Hood, for example, had small use for this buttoned-up style of warfare. "Here we are in front of the enemy again," he wrote Lee toward the end of April. "The Yankees have a very strong position, and of course they increase the strength of their position daily. I presume we

★

shall leave here so soon as we gather all the bacon in the country." Boyishly the Kentucky-born Texan added: "When we leave here it is my desire to return to you. If any troops come to the Rappahannock please don't forget me." Thirty-one and a bachelor, Hood was bored. But that could scarcely be said of his fellow division commander Pickett. This thirty-eight-year-old widower, a handsome if rather doll-faced man with long chestnut curls which he anointed regularly with perfume, was in the full flush of a sunset love affair with a south-side girl not half his age. LaSalle Corbell was her name; he styled her "the charming Sally" — his dead wife had been called Sally, too — and wrote her ardent letters signed "Your Soldier" despite the fact that he saw her almost nightly, riding up to her home at Chuckatuck by twilight and back to his lines before the first red glow of dawn. When Longstreet at last began to frown on this inattentiveness to duty, not to mention the abuse of horseflesh, Pickett tried to persuade the corps adjutant, Major G. Moxley Sorrel, to give him permission

> *"I presume we shall leave here so soon as we gather all the bacon in the country."*
>
> — John Bell Hood

to take off without Old Peter's knowledge. Sorrel, who did not approve of what he called "such carpet-knight doings in the field," declined to accept the responsibility for what might happen in Pickett's absence, and referred him back to Longstreet. "But he is tired of it and will refuse," the ringleted Virginian protested. "And I must go; I must see her. I swear, Sorrel, I'll be back before anything can happen in the morning." Sorrel still said no; but recalling the scene years later he added that "Pickett went all the same. Nothing could hold him back from that pursuit."

Increasingly, as spring wore on and the end of the campaign drew near — he himself had set a May 3 closing date by notifying Richmond on April 19 that two more weeks would suffice for draining the region of its stores — Longstreet grew dissatisfied: not so much with what he had done, which was after all considerable, as with the thought of what he had not done. While it was true that he had carried out, practically to the letter, his difficult triple assignment — that is, he had kept the Yankees out of Petersburg, he had secured enormous quantities of previously inaccessible supplies, and he had kept his First Corps troops on the alert for a swift return to Lee — it was also painfully true that he had accomplished nothing that would compare in tactical brilliance with even the smallest battlefield victory scored by Jackson out in the Valley a year ago. As a result, the taking of Suffolk, along with its thousands of bluecoats and tons of matériel, began to appeal to him more and more as a fitting end to these two months of detached service. Moreover, as the notion grew more attractive in his mind's eye, it also began to appear more feasible to his military judgment, despite the fact that the Federals inside the place were stronger now, by some 9000 reinforcements brought in from Hampton Roads, than they had been at the outset. There were several ways of assessing this last, however, and one was that the grandeur of the triumph would be in direct ratio to the plumpness of the prize. Accordingly, Old Peter wrote to Lee, telling him what he had in mind and asking if he could not be sent the rest of his corps in order to assure the success of his assault on the blue intrenchments. Foreseeing objections — as well he might — he suggested that Lee, if need be, could fall back to the line of the Annas, though it was his own conviction that one corps would be able to stand fast on the Rappahannock in the event of an attack. Lee replied on April 27 that Hooker was far too strong, and just now far too active, for him to consider a further weakening of his army. In fact, he countered by asking his lieutenant if he could spare him any of the troops in North Carolina. But he

Mules haul a wagon across a brook in Virginia
just before James Longstreet's Confederate troops
withdrew westward in early May 1863.

★

certainly did not veto the proposal for ending the southside siege with an assault. "As regards your aggressive movement upon Suffolk," he wrote, "you must act according to your good judgment. If a damaging blow could be struck there or elsewhere of course it would be advantageous." He added some doubts as to whether the game would be worth the candle in this case, but Longstreet could see in the letter a relaxation of the urgency for keeping his First Corps divisions practically uncommitted in order to have them ready to hurry north on short notice. Consequently, while his foraging crews kept busy, hauling out the last of the precious wagonloads of hogs and corn and herring, he turned his thoughts to tactical details of the assault that would cap the climax by adding the one element — glory — so far lacking in a campaign already productive of much else.

Three days later, however — April 30 — his plans were shattered by a wire from Adjutant General Cooper in Richmond, quoting a dispatch just received from Lee. Hooker was over the Rappahannock in great strength, above as well as below Fredericksburg, Lee had announced, "and it looks as if he was in earnest." Cooper's instructions to Longstreet were brief and to the point: "Move without delay your command to this place to effect a junction with General Lee."

Longstreet inquired by telegraph whether this meant that he was to abandon his wagons, still scattered about on foraging operations, and risk a quick withdrawal of his men, which would bring out the Federals hot on his heels. By no means, Cooper replied on May Day. What had been intended was for him "to secure all possible dispatch without incurring loss of trains or unnecessary hazard of troops." Having thus avoided going off half-cocked, Old Peter turned to the always difficult task of designing a disengagement. After the wagons had been called in and sent rearward, orders were issued on May 2 for all the troops to withdraw from the intrenchments the following evening and retire westward under cover of darkness, burning bridges and felling trees in their wake to discourage pursuit. This came off on schedule, and after some sharp skirmishing by rear-guard elements, the whole command was across the Blackwater by sundown of the 4th. Leaving French to defend that line, Hood and Pickett moved to Petersburg next day. Dawn of the 6th found them on the march for the James, leg-weary but eager, and Longstreet himself was in Richmond before noon, making preparations to speed both divisions northward by rail for a share in the great battle reportedly still raging along the near bank of the Rappahannock. All this ended the following day, however, when he received a wire from Lee: "The emergency that made your presence so desirable has passed for the present, so far as I can see, and I desire that you will not distress your troops by a forced movement to join me, or sacrifice for that purpose any public interest that your sudden departure might make it necessary to abandon."

★ ★ ★

★

Shelby Foote

Federals use a telescope and field glasses to check the Confederate positions near Fredericksburg during an informal truce prior to the Battle of Chancellorsville.

F O U R

Hooker, Stoneman; The Crossing

1863 ★ ★ ★ ★ ★ "Go forward, and give us victories," Lincoln had written, and that was what Hooker had in mind when he crossed the Rappahannock. Nor was that all. "I not only expected victory," he would recall when the smoke had cleared, "I expected to get the whole [rebel] army." That this had indeed been his intention was confirmed by his chief of staff, who also declared in retrospect that the real purpose of the campaign had been "to destroy the army of General Lee where it then was." Earlier, on the eve of committing what he called "the finest body of soldiers the sun ever shone on," Fighting Joe had expressed his resolution in terms that were even more expansive. "My plans are perfect," he announced, "and when I start to carry them out, may God have mercy on Bobby Lee; for I shall have none."

Just what those plans were he was not saying, even to those whose task it would be to translate them into action. In point of fact, however, they were influenced considerably by the man who had preceded him in command. In addition to having demonstrated the folly of launching headlong attacks against prepared intrenchments — intrenchments which, incidentally, had been enormously strengthened and extended since December — Burnside had explored, at least on paper, several other approaches to the problem of how to prise the rebels loose from their works and come to grips with them in the open, where the

★

advantage of numbers would be likely to decide the issue in favor of the Union. Now he had departed, taking "his deportment with him out of the Army of the Potomac, thank God," but Hooker could remember how the lush-whiskered general had stressed the need for secrecy and then proceeded to talk with all and sundry about his plans, with the result that his opponent's only surprise had been at his foolhardiness. So the new commander, who, by ordinary, was anything but a close-mouthed man, profited in reverse from his predecessor's example. He kept his plans to himself.

Not that he did not have any; he did, indeed, and he did not care who knew it, so long as the particulars remained hidden. These too had been inherited, however, for the most part. Originally, like Burnside on the eve of his bloody mid-December commitment, Hooker had planned to cross the Rappahannock well below Fredericksburg; but this had two serious disadvantages. It would uncover the direct route to Washington, which he knew would distress

---

Hooker could remember how the lush-whiskered general had stressed the need for secrecy and then proceeded to talk with all and sundry about his plans . . .

Lincoln, and it would have to be announced to the Confederates in advance by the laying of pontoons. Upstream, on the other hand, the river narrowed and was comparatively shallow. There were fords in that direction — Banks Ford, five miles above the town, and United States Ford, seven miles farther west — behind which he could mass and conceal his troops in order to send them splashing across in a rush that would smother the south-bank gray outpost detachments, thus forcing Lee to face about and meet his assailants without the advantage of those formidable intrenchments. This had been Burnside's intention in the campaign that ground to a soggy halt in January, but Hooker, by waiting for the advent of fair weather, had greatly reduced the likelihood of the movement's coming to any such premature and ignominious end. Besides, there would be tactical embellishments, designed to increase the Federal chances for an all-out victory.

Principal among these was a plan for taking advantage of the recently demonstrated improvement of the blue cavalry. With Stoneman outnumbering Stuart better than three to one — just over 11,500 sabers opposed to just under 3500 — it was Hooker's belief that if his troopers crossed the river in strength they would be able to have things pretty much their own way in the Confederate rear. Damage to Lee's communications and supply lines, coupled with strikes at such vital points as Gordonsville and Hanover Junction, might throw him into sudden retreat; in which case the Federal infantry, coming down on the run from the upstream crossings, would catch him in flight, strung out on the roads leading southward, and destroy him. No one so far in this war had been able to throw Lee into such a panic, it was true, but the reason for this might be that no one had dared to touch him where he was tender. At any rate Hooker thought it worth a try, and he had his adjutant general draw up careful instructions for Stoneman. His entire corps, less one brigade but accompanied by all 22 of its guns, was to cross Rappahannock Bridge, thirty miles above Fredericksburg, not later than 7 a.m. on April 13, "for the purpose of turning the enemy's position on his left, throwing the cavalry between him and Richmond, isolating him from his supplies, checking his retreat, and inflicting on him every possible injury which will tend to his discomfiture and defeat." Lest there be any doubt that the cavalry chief was to be vigorous in his treatment of the fleeing Lee, the adjutant then broke into what might one day have become the model for a pregame Rockne pep talk: "If you cannot cut off from his column large slices, the general desires that you will not fail to take small ones. Let your watchword be fight, fight, fight, bearing in mind that time is as valuable to the general as rebel carcasses."

Stoneman and his 10,000 chosen troopers, along with their 22 guns and a train of 275 wagons containing enough additional food and forage to sustain them for nine days beyond the lines, were poised for a crossing at the specified hour. One brigade had already forded the river a few miles above Rappahannock Bridge, with instructions to come sweeping down and clear out the rebel horsemen watching from across the way. But as the three divisions stood to their mounts, awaiting the order that would send them about their task of cutting slices large and small from Lee's retreating column, rain began to patter and then to drum, ominously reminiscent of the downpour that had queered the Mud March. Now as then, roads became quagmires and the river began to swell, flooding the fords and tugging at the shaky pilings of the bridge. Stoneman decided to wait it out. Recalling the brigade that had crossed, he wired headquarters that his rolling stock was stalled. Hooker replied that he was to shuck his guns and wagons and proceed without them. Stoneman said he would, and set dawn of the 15th as his new jump-off time. Then the wire went dead. Hooker, having promised to keep the President posted on the progress of the movement, struck an optimistic note in a dispatch sent to Washington on that date: "I am rejoiced that Stoneman had two good days to go up the river, and was able to cross it before it had become too much swollen. If he can reach his position [deep in the enemy rear] the storm and mud will not damage our prospects." Lincoln was not so sure. It was his belief, he replied within the hour, that "General S. is not moving rapidly enough to make the expedition come to anything. He has now been out three days, two of which were unusually fair weather, and all three without hindrance from the enemy, and yet he is not 25 miles from where he started. To reach his point he still has 60 to go, another river (the Rapidan) to cross, and will be hindered by the enemy. By arithmetic, how many days will it take him to do it? . . . I greatly fear it is another failure already."

His fears were confirmed the following day when a courier reached Falmouth with a letter from upstream. "I cannot say what has been the state of affairs away from this vicinity," Stoneman wrote, "but here, at the hour of my last dispatch, the condition of things may be judged of when I tell you that almost every rivulet was swimming, and the roads next to impassable for horses or pack-mules. . . . The railroad bridge has been partly carried away by the freshet. The river is out of its banks, and was still on the rise a few hours ago. . . . My dispatch [setting a new date for the crossing] was based upon the expectation that we were to be favored with a continuation of fair weather. It certainly was not predicated upon the expectation of being overtaken by one of the most violent rainstorms I have ever been caught in." There was much else by way of explanation and excuse, including the news that three men and several horses had been drowned that morning while attempting to cross what had been a nearly dry stream bed the day before. But the gist of the long letter came about midway: "The elements seem to have conspired to prevent the accomplishment of a brilliant cavalry operation."

Hooker was disappointed. He told Stoneman to stay where he was, keep up his reserve supply of rations, and be ready to take off southward "as soon as the roads and rivers will permit." However, the rain showed no sign of a real letup. For nearly two weeks it kept falling, with only a few fair days mixed in to mock the army's immobility, and all this time Hooker was champing at the bit, anxious to put his troops in motion for the kill. As the days went by, his bitterness increased. He began to doubt that Stoneman and the cavalry were up to carrying out the mission he had assigned them; he began, in fact, to see room for improvement in the plans he had called perfect. Since he had the Confederates outnumbered better than two to one — as he knew by reports from the excellent intelligence service he had established as part of his staff — he had a rare chance to attack them, front and back, with separate columns each of which would be superior to the gray mass clamped between them. Instead of 10,000 cavalry, he would put 60,000 infantry and artillery in Lee's immediate rear, blocking his retreat while the other 60,000 pounded his front and the troopers far in his rear slashed at his lines of supply and communication. Isolated and surrounded, prised out of his intrenchments and grievously outnumbered, Lee would be pulverized; Hooker would "get the whole army." It was a pleasant thing to contemplate, not only because of its classic tactical simplicity, but also because it would involve what might be called poetic justice, a turning of the tables on the old fox who so often had divided his own army, but without the advantage of numbers, in hopes of destroying the very soldiers who now were about to destroy him.

What was more, as Hooker pored over his maps to plan the logistical details of the proposed envelopment, he found that the terrain seemed made to order for just such a maneuver. Banks Ford was stoutly defended from across the way, the rebels having honeycombed the dominant south-bank heights with trenches that formed the left-flank anchor of their line, and U.S. Ford was guarded nearly as heavily by an intrenched outpost detachment; besides which, the recent rains had swollen them both well past wading depth, so that his previous design to seize them in a sudden, splashing rush was now impractical. On the other hand Kelly's Ford, fifteen miles above the junction of the Rappannock

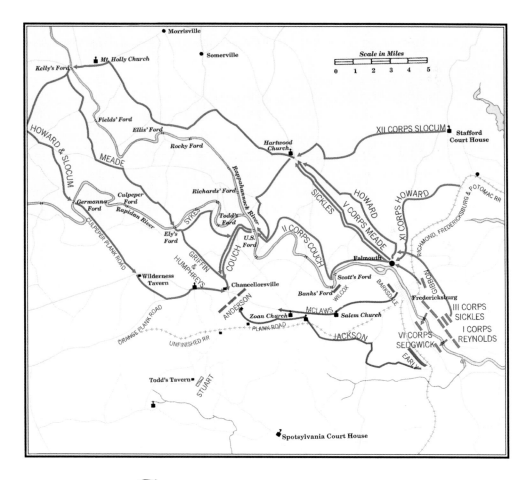

*The Army of the Potomac crossed the Rappa-
hannock and Rapidan rivers in a flanking
movement around Robert E. Lee's left.*

and the Rapidan, which occurred just over a mile above U.S. Ford, was lightly held, unfortified, and comparatively shallow. Although crossing there would call for a long approach march and would involve another river crossing when the column reached the Rapidan, the advantages greatly outweighed the drawbacks. For one thing, Kelly's Ford was far enough out beyond the enemy flank to give hope that, with luck, the march and perhaps both crossings could be accomplished before the rebs knew what was afoot, and for another it would afford a covered approach, along excellent roads traversing a wooded region known locally as the Wilderness, to within striking distance of the Confederate rear. Moreover, as the column moved eastward along the south bank of the Rappahannock it would uncover both U.S. and Banks Fords, which would not only shorten considerably its lines of supply and communication, thereby making it possible for the two halves of the blue army to reinforce each other quickly if an emergency arose in either direction, but would also give the flankers, in the case of the Banks Ford defenses, control of high ground that dominated much of the present rebel line of fortifications; Lee would be obliged to come out into the open, whether he wanted to or not. All this sounded fine to Hooker. Admittedly he was about to engage in the risky business of dividing his army in the presence of the enemy, but Lee had proved on more than one occasion that the profits more than justified the risk, even though he had done so with the numerical odds against him; whereas with Hooker it would be the other way around. It was this last that gave him substantial reason to hope for the Cannae which so far, and for all his vaunted skill in battle, had eluded Lee.

Translating theory into action, Fighting Joe sent orders on April 26 for the corps of Slocum, Howard, and Meade to march for Kelly's Ford at sunrise the following morning. They were to be in position there not later than 4 p.m. of the 28th, at which time they were to head south for the Rapidan, cross that river at Ely's and Germanna Fords, and take the roads leading southeast to the Orange Turnpike, then proceed due east along it to a position covering a crossroads hamlet called Chancellorsville, eight miles west of Lee's line and less than half that far from the ragged eastern rim of the Wilderness. Couch — minus Gibbon's division, which could not be moved just yet because its Falmouth camp was in plain view of the enemy on Marye's Heights — was to march at dawn of the 29th to a position in the rear of Banks Ford and stand ready to throw pontoons for a crossing as soon as Slocum's advance flanked the rebels out of the trenches across the way. Meanwhile, with 60,000 Federal soldiers marching against the Confederate rear, the corps of Sedgwick, Reynolds, and Sickles, aggregating another 60,000, would move down to the riverbank south of Fredericksburg, near the point of Franklin's crossing in December, where they would establish a west-bank bridgehead on the 29th for the purpose of demonstrating against Lee's front, thus distracting his attention

★

from what would be going on behind him and keeping him in doubt as to where the heaviest blow would fall. Stoneman would add to the confusion by striking first at the Virginia Central Railroad, then eastward along it to the Richmond, Fredericksburg & Potomac, where he was to harass and slow down the gray army if it attempted to escape the jaws of the blue vise by falling back on its threatened capital. Still mindful of the need for secrecy, Hooker enjoined the generals with the upstream column to regard the "destination of their commands as strictly confidential." Apparently his left hand was to be kept from knowing what his right hand was about, but he lifted the veil a little by telling Sedgwick, who was in charge of the downstream column, to carry the enemy works "at all hazards" in case Lee detached "a considerable part of his force against the troops operating . . . west of Fredericksburg." Whether the main attack would be delivered against the enemy's front or his rear — that is, by Sedgwick's 60,000 or by Slocum's — remained to be seen. At the critical moment, probably on the 30th but certainly by May Day, Hooker would ride to Chancellorsville, make his estimate of the situation, and then, like an ambidextrous boxer, swing with either hand for the knockout.

The upstream march began on schedule Monday, April 27, despite a slow drizzle that threatened to undo the good which three days of fair weather had done the roads. Slogging toward Hartwood Church and Morrisville, where they would turn off south for Kelly's Ford, the veterans chanted as they trudged:

> *"The Union boys are moving on the left and on the right,*
>
> *The bugle call is sounding, our shelters we must strike;*
>
> *Joe Hooker is our leader, he takes his whiskey strong,*
>
> *So our knapsacks we will sling, and go marching along."*

Sweating under fifty to sixty pounds of weight, which included eight days' rations, a pair of blankets, a thick wool overcoat, and forty rounds of ammunition each, they interpreted the word "sling" as they saw fit, shedding knapsacks by the roadside to be gleaned by civilian scavengers — "ready finders," the army called them — who moved in their wake and profited from their prodigality. Hooker's administrative sensibilities were offended by the waste, but he was consoled by the fact that the march was otherwise orderly and rapid in spite of the showers, which fortunately left off before midday without softening the roads. In response to a wire that afternoon from a fretful Lincoln — "How does it look now?" — he managed to be at once reticent and reassuring: "I am not sufficiently advanced to give an opinion. We are busy. Will tell you all soon as I can, and have it satisfactory." Riding next day up to Morrisville, through rain that had come on again to slow the march and throw it several hours behind schedule, he was pleased all the same to note that the column had turned south for the Rappahannock, and he sent an aide ahead with a message urging Slocum to make up for lost time: "The general desires that not a moment be lost until our troops are established at or near Chancellorsville. From that moment all will be ours."

He sounded buoyant, and presently he had cause for feeling even more so. By dusk the head of the flanking column was approaching Kelly's Ford, and Hooker received word from his chief of staff at Falmouth that Couch had his two divisions in position behind Banks Ford, as ordered, and was improving the waiting time by extending the telegraph to U.S. Ford, in case that proved to be a better point for crossing. Sedgwick had been delayed by the rain, Butterfield added, but he had his three corps on the march and would begin throwing five pontoon bridges across the river below Fredericksburg on schedule in the morning. Moreover, though the weather had been too gusty to permit spyglass observation from the bobbing gondolas of Professor T. S. C. Lowe's two balloons, the ruse of leaving Gibbon's division in its exposed camp seemed to have worked as intended; Lowe reported that, from what he could see, the Confederate trenches "appeared to be occupied as usual," indicating that Lee almost certainly had no intimation that the various Federal columns were on the move for positions from which to accomplish his destruction. All this was about as encouraging as could be, but Hooker, being painfully familiar with the tricks of the old fox across the way, was leaving as little as possible to chance. He wired Lowe to send a balloon up anyhow, despite the wind and darkness, "to see where the enemy's campfires are," not forgetting to add: "Someone acquainted with the position and location of the ground and of the enemy's forces should go up."

By the time the Professor — the title was complimentary; his official designation was "Chief of Aeronauts, Army of the Potomac," and his basic uniform was a voluminous linen duster — got a balloon up into the windy night for a look at the rebel campfires, Howard's corps was over the Rappahannock, crossing dry-shod on a pontoon bridge just completed by the engineers, and had taken up a position on the south bank to guard against a surprise attack while the other two corps were crossing. Slocum came over at dawn, followed by Meade, who struck out southeastward for Ely's Ford; then Howard fell in behind Slocum, who had already headed south for Germanna Ford. Behind all three came Stoneman, a full day late and complaining bitterly that the alert order had not allowed him time to call in his 10,000 horsemen from their camps around Warrenton. He set out for Raccoon Ford, ten miles west of Germanna, for a descent on the Virginia Central in the vicinity of Louisa Court House, leaving Hooker a single 1000-man brigade of three slim regiments to accompany the infantry on the march and another 500 troopers to guard the deserted

Alfred Waud sketched the 8th Pennsyl-vania Cavalry crossing the Rapidan River at Ely's Ford on April 29.

north-bank camps and installations. The foot soldiers pushed ahead, stepping fast but warily now; for it was here in the V of the rivers that Pope, for all his bluster, had nearly come to grief in August. Neither column encountered any real difficulty, however, in the course of its daylong hike to the Rapidan. Nor did Slocum's run into much trouble after it got there. His advance guard, splashing its way through the chest-deep water, surprised a drowsy 100-man rebel detachment at Germanna, capturing a number of graybacks before they knew what was upon them. Finding timbers collected here on the south bank for the construction of a bridge, the jubilant bluecoats set to work and put them to use in short order, with the result that the rest of their corps, and all of Howard's, made a second river crossing without having to wet their socks.

Meade's troops had no such luck. Though he too encountered no opposition in the V, his march to Ely's was longer than Slocum's to Germanna, and he found no bridge materials awaiting him at its end. Coming down to the ford at sunset the advance guard plunged across the cold, swift-running Rapidan, chased off the startled pickets on the opposite bank, and set to work building fires to light the way for the rest of the corps approaching the crossing in the dusk. Regiment by regiment the three road-worn divisions entered the foam-flecked, scrotum-tightening water and emerged to toil up the steep south bank, which became increasingly slippery as the slope was churned to gumbo by the passage of nearly 16,000 soldiers, all dripping wet from the armpits down. Once across, they gathered about the fires for warmth, some in good spirits, some in bad, each arriving cluster somewhat muddier than the one before, but all about equally wet and cold. By midnight the last man was over. Low in the east, the late-risen moon, burgeoning toward the full, had the bruised-orange color of old gold, and while all around them the whippoorwills sang plaintively in the moon-drenched woods, the men lay rolled in their blankets, feet to the fire, catching snatches of sleep while awaiting the word to fall back into column. Meade had them on the go again by sunup of the last day of April, still marching southeast, but now through an eerie and seemingly God-forsaken region; the Wilderness, it was called, and they could see why. Mostly a tangle of second-growth scrub oak and pine, choked with vines and brambles that would tear the clothes from a man's back within minutes of the time he left the road, it was interrupted briefly at scattered points by occasional small clearings whose abandoned cabins and sag-roofed barns gave proof, if such was needed, that no amount of hard work could scratch a living from this jungle. To make matters worse, rebel cavalry slashed at the column from time to time, emerging suddenly from ambush, then back again, apparently for the purpose of taking prisoners who would identify their units. Meade did not like the look of things any better than the men did. He rode with the van and set a rapid pace, wanting to get them out of here, and for once they were altogether willing. Chancellorsville was less than half a dozen miles from the ford, and though it was still a good three miles short of open country where he could deploy his troops and bring his guns to bear, he remembered that Hooker had said that once the flankers were "established" in that vicinity, "all will be ours."

Arriving about an hour before noon, still without having encountered anything more than token resistance from the enemy cavalry and none at all from the famed, hard-marching rebel infantry, he found that for all its grand-sounding name the crossroads hamlet — if it could be called even that — consisted of nothing more than a large, multi-chimneyed brick-and-timber mansion, with tall slim pillars across its front supporting a double-decked veranda, and three or four outbuildings scattered about the quadrants of the turnpike intersection. There was, however, a hundred-acre clearing, which seemed expansive indeed after what he had just emerged from and would reënter when he moved on, and there were also four ladies, of various ages and in bright spring dresses, who likewise were a relief of sorts despite their show of pique at having to receive unwelcome guests. At any rate, Meade's spirits rose as he waited for Slocum and Howard, whose troops had the longer march today. Much that he previously had not understood, mainly because of Hooker's refusal to give out details of his plan — "It's all right" had been his usual and evasive reply to questions from commanders of all ranks — suddenly became much clearer to Meade, now that he was within a half-day's march of Lee's rear without its having cost him anything more than the handful of men gobbled up by the graybacks in the course of his plunge through the heart of the Wilderness. Now that he believed he saw the whole design, his dourness gave way to something approaching exaltation. By 2 o'clock, when Slocum arrived at the head of his two-corps column, Meade was fairly beside himself. "This is splendid, Slocum," he cried, displaying an exuberance that seemed all the more abandoned because it was so unlike him; "hurrah for Old Joe! We are on Lee's flank and he doesn't know it."

What he wanted now, he added with no slackening of enthusiasm, was to push on eastward without further delay, at least another couple of miles before nightfall, "and we'll get out of this Wilderness." Slocum felt much the

---

Low in the east, the late-risen moon, burgeoning toward the full, had the bruised-orange color of old gold, and . . . the men lay rolled in their blankets, feet to the fire, catching snatches of sleep while awaiting the word to fall back into column.

---

same way about it. But while they talked a courier arrived with a dispatch signed by Butterfield, relaying an order from Hooker: "The general directs that no advance be made from Chancellorsville until the columns are concentrated. He expects to be at Chancellorsville tonight."

Somewhat crestfallen, and nearly as puzzled now as he had been before he saw what he had believed was the light, Meade went about the business of getting his troops into bivouac. Slocum and Howard were doing the same when presently, at about 4.30 and true to his word, Fighting Joe himself came riding up on his big white horse, cheered lustily by the men along the roadside, and explained the logic behind the restraining order. The easterly advance along the turnpike had already flanked the rebels out of their U.S. Ford defenses, permitting Couch to sidle upstream for a crossing there instead of at Banks Ford, where the defenders were still in occupation; he was on the march for Chancellorsville even now, and Gibbon had been alerted to join him from Falmouth with his third division. This would put four whole corps in the

★

Confederate rear, as had been intended from the start, but the northern commander had it in mind to do even more by way of cinching the victory already within reach. Sedgwick's bridgehead having been established across the river below Fredericksburg with a minimal resistance from the rebels on the heights — who thus were clamped securely between two superior Union forces which now could reinforce each other, rapidly and at will, by way of U.S. Ford — Hooker had decided to summon Sickles from the left to add the weight of his corps to the blow about to be delivered against the more vulnerable enemy rear. His arrival tonight or tomorrow morning would bring the striking force up to a strength of 77,865 effectives within the five corps. With three regiments of cavalry added, along with several batteries detached from the artillery reserve, engineer troops, and headquarters personnel, the total would reach about 80,000 of all arms, who then could be flung in mass against Lee's rear to accomplish his destruction with a single May Day blow.

Meade was considerably reassured; he saw in fact, or believed he saw, a brighter light than ever. A rare attention to detail — pontoons in place on time, road space properly allotted to columns on the march, surprise achieved through ruse and secrecy — had made possible, at practically no cost at all, one of the finest maneuvers in military history. Now this same attentiveness, with regard to the massing of troops for the ultimate thrust, would also make possible one of the grandest victories. Sure enough, Couch arrived before nightfall and went into bivouac a mile north of the crossroads; Sickles sent word that he was on the way. Once more careful planning had paid off. A New York *Herald* correspondent who had accompanied the flankers shared the pervading optimism. "It is rumored that the enemy are falling back toward Richmond," he wrote, "but a fight tomorrow seems more than probable. We expect it, and we also expect to be victorious." Hooker expected it, too, because he knew the rumor to be untrue. Sedgwick, from his low-lying, close-up position south of Fredericksburg, and Professor Lowe, from the gondola of one of his big yellow balloons riding high over Stafford Heights, had both assured him that the Confederates still occupied the ridge beyond the town. Reynolds, in fact, had reported to headquarters this afternoon that he believed some of the troops in his front had just arrived from Richmond: which brought the reply, "General Hooker hopes they are from Richmond, as the greater will be our success."

His spirits were high, and so were those of his men, who cheered him to the echo, especially when a congratulatory order was read to them that evening in their camps around Chancellorsville: "It is with heartfelt satisfaction that the commanding general announces to the army that the operations of the last three days have determined that our enemy must either ingloriously fly, or come out from behind his defenses and give us battle on our own ground, where certain destruction awaits him."

★ ★ ★ **B**attle on his "own ground" — setting aside for the moment the question of whether any part of the Old Dominion could ever properly be so termed in relation to the man Lee called Mr F. J. Hooker — was exactly what Stonewall Jackson had been aching to give him for the past three months. "We must make this campaign an exceedingly active one," the Virginian declared as spring approached. "Only thus can a weaker country cope with a stronger. It must make up in activity what it lacks in strength." Fredericksburg, for all its one-sided tactical brilliance, had been a strategic disappointment to him, and he hoped to compensate for this in the great battle he knew would be fought as soon as the Federals decided the time had come for them to attempt another Rappahannock crossing. "My trust is in God," he said quietly, seated one day in his tent and musing on the future. But then, anticipating the hour when the blue host would venture within his reach, his patience broke its bounds and he rose bristling from his chair, eyes aglow. "I wish they would come!" he cried.

These past three months had been perhaps the happiest of his military life. In fact, despite his eagerness to interrupt any or all of them with bloodshed, February, March, and April, following as they did his thirty-ninth birthday in late January, had been idyllic, at least by Jacksonian standards. Aside from administrative concerns, such as the usual spate of court-martials and the preparation of battle reports, grievously neglected up to now because he had been too busy fighting to find time for writing — the total was fourteen full-scale battles in the previous eight months, with the reduction and capture of Harpers Ferry added for good measure — his principal occupation was prayer and meditation, relieved from time to time by evenings of unaccustomed social pleasure. His quarters, an office cottage on the grounds of a Moss Neck estate, were comfortable to the point of lavishness, which prompted Jeb Stuart to express mock horror at the erstwhile Presbyterian deacon's evident fall from spirituality, and Lee himself, in the course of a particularly fine meal featuring oysters, turkey, and a waiter decked out in a fresh white apron, taunted the high-ranking guests and their host with the remark that they were merely playing at being soldiers; they should come and dine with him, he said, if they wanted to see how a real soldier lived. Stonewall took the raillery and the chiding in good part, at once flustered and delighted. But the best of the idyl came at its close. The last nine days, beginning April 20, were spent with the wife he had not seen in just over a year and the five-month-old daughter he had never seen at all.

He had moved by then, back into his tent near Hamilton's Crossing, which did much to reduce the Calvinistic twinges. "It is rather a relief," he said, "to get where there will be less comfort in a room." But for the occasion of the

This portrait of Stonewall Jackson was made in the hallway of the Yerby house, above, where he and his family spent nine days in April 1863.

long-anticipated visit he accepted the hospitality of the Yerby house, in which Lee had stayed for a time under doctor's orders, and was given a large room, with no less than three beds, where he could be alone with his wife and get to know the baby. Outside duty hours, the couple took walks in the woods and along the heights overlooking the Fredericksburg plain whose December scars were beginning to be grassed over. It was the happiest of times for them both. The days went by in a rush, however, for there in full view across the way were the enemy guns and the yellow observation balloons, reminders that the idyl was likely to have a sudden end. And so it was. Dawn, Wednesday, April 29; booted

★

feet on the stairs and a knock at the bedroom door; "That looks as if Hooker were crossing," Jackson said. He drew on some clothes and went out, was gone ten minutes, and then returned to finish dressing. The visit was over, he told Anna as he buckled on his sword. He would come back if he could, but if he could not he would send an aide to see her to the train. After a last embrace, and a last long look at the baby, he was gone. Presently the staff chaplain arrived to tell her the general would not be coming back. While she was packing she began hearing the rattle of musketry from down by the river. It grew louder behind her, all the way to Guiney Station, where she boarded an almost empty train for Richmond.

Lee expressed even less surprise when an aide sent by Jackson came into his tent before sunup to give him the news. Still abed, Lee said teasingly: "Captain, what do you young men mean by waking a man out of his sleep?" Hooker had thrown his pontoons near the site of the lower December crossing, the aide replied; he was over the river in force. "Well, I thought I heard firing," Lee said, "and I was beginning to think it was time some of you young fellows were coming to tell me what it was all about. You want me to send a message to your good general, Captain? Tell him that I am sure he knows what to do. I will meet him at the front very soon."

Shortly afterwards, peering through rifts in the early morning fog, he saw for himself that the Federals had one bridge down and others under construction, all near the point now known as Franklin's Crossing, just over a mile below the town. They did not attempt an advance across the plain, but seemed content to stay within their bridgehead, at least for the present, covered by the long-range guns on Stafford Heights. Resisting the temptation to attack while the build-up was in progress, Lee decided to make his defense along the ridge, as he had done in December. Accordingly, he told Jackson to bring up the rest of his corps from below, and ordered the reserve artillery to leave its rearward camps and move forward into line. In notifying Richmond of these developments, although he knew it was unlikely that the two detached divisions would arrive in time for a share in the battle now shaping up, he requested that Longstreet be alerted for a return from Suffolk as soon as possible. Before noon, the situation was complicated by a dispatch from Stuart, informing Lee that a blue force of about 14,000 infantry and six guns had crossed at Kelly's Ford and appeared to be headed for Gordonsville. This was corrected a few hours later, however, when the cavalry commander sent word that the enemy column had turned in the direction of Ely's and Germanna Fords; so far, Jeb added, he had taken prisoners from three different Union corps, though he did not say whether he thought all three were present in full strength. In reaction, Lee sent instructions for Stuart to move eastward at once and thus avoid being cut off from headquarters. This would leave the Federal cavalry free to operate practically unmolested against his lines of supply; yet, bad as that was, it was by no means as bad as having to fight blind when he and the greatly superior Federal main body came within grappling distance of each other, here on Marye's Heights or elsewhere. Just after sundown a third courier arrived to report the bluecoats across both Rapidan fords. Though Lee still had no reliable information as to the strength of this flanking column, it was clear by now that some part of Hooker's army — a considerable part, for all he knew — was in the Confederate rear and moving closer, hour by hour. Whatever its strength, the threat it offered was too grave to be ignored. Nor did he ignore it. Two brigades of Richard Anderson's division were already at U.S. Ford; Lee instructed him to draw them in and move the others rearward to meet them in the vicinity of Chancellorsville, where the roads leading south and east from Ely's and Germanna Fords came together, "taking the strongest line you can and holding it to the best advantage." To McLaws, who commanded Longstreet's other remaining division, went orders alerting him for a possible westward march, in case it turned out that Anderson was not strong enough to stop the blue columns last reported to be moving in his direction. Anderson pulled out of the line at 9 o'clock, and after a three-hour march through driving rain informed headquarters that his division was concentrated near Chancellorsville by midnight. Knowing that his rear was protected at least to this extent, Lee turned in to rest for tomorrow.

Alfred Waud sketched this I Corps division resting on the west bank of the Rappahannock. Across the river, two more Federal divisions await orders to cross on pontoon bridges.

Morning of the 30th disclosed a total of five bridges spanning the river below Fredericksburg. Though the bluecoats had enlarged their west-bank foothold, they showed no disposition to advance. In fact, they were intrenching their perimeter — as if in expectation, not of delivering, but of receiving an attack. Jackson, for one, was eager to give it to them, whereas Lee preferred to draw them farther away from their heavy guns on Stafford Heights. Both men thus reacted as they had done to the similar situation in December; but this time Lee offered to defer to his lieutenant's judgment. "If you think you can effect anything," he said, "I will give orders for the attack." While Stonewall went about conducting a more thorough examination of the bridgehead, preparatory to moving against it, Lee received another cavalry report that the Federals were advancing eastward from Germanna Ford, along the Orange Turnpike, while a substantial train of wagons and artillery was across Ely's Ford with a heavy infantry escort, following in the wake of the column that had crossed at that point the night before. A little later — it was now past noon — Anderson sent word that he had taken up a good defensive position east of Chancellorsville, along the near fringe of the Wilderness, and was preparing to resist the blue advance. So far, all he had seen of the enemy were cavalry outriders, he added, but he thought he was going to need support when the infantry came up. Lee replied at 2.30 that Anderson was to dig in where he was, providing hasty fortifications not only for his own division but also for McLaws',

Bridges built for Reynolds Corps — sketched from Rebel rifle pits

which was on call to join him in case it was needed. "Set all your spades to work as vigorously as possible," Lee urged, and sent him some engineers to assist in drawing his line, as well as a battalion of artillery from the reserve. Then he turned back to see how Jackson was doing.

The fact was, Jackson was not doing so well, at least by his own interpretation. A careful reconnaissance had shown the enemy bridgehead to be stronger than he had supposed; he regretfully admitted that an assault would be unwise. Lee took out his binoculars for a better look at the bluecoats massed on the plain below and on the heights beyond the river. He took his time, evaluating reports while he peered. There was by now much disagreement among his officers as to whether Hooker was planning to deliver his heaviest blow from upstream or down. Presently, however, Lee returned the glasses to their case and snapped it shut with a decisive gesture. "The main attack will come from above," he said.

Having made this estimate of the situation he proceeded to act on it with an urgency required by the fact that a farther advance by the Federals approaching his rear would put them between him and Richmond, in which case he would have no choice except to retreat. He might have to do so anyhow, under the menace of Hooker's skillful combinations, but he was determined, now as always, to yield no ground he saw any chance of holding. His decision, then — announced in orders which he retired to his tent to write and issue soon after nightfall — was to turn on the rearward Union column with a preponderance of his badly outnumbered army, leaving a skeleton force to defend his present position against a possible frontal assault by the blue mass on the plain. Early's division of Jackson's corps drew the latter assignment, reinforced by a brigade from McLaws, whose other three brigades were to proceed at once to join Anderson in the intrenchments he was digging four miles east of Chancellorsville. Jackson was to follow McLaws with his remaining three divisions "at daylight tomorrow morning . . . and make arrangements to repulse the enemy." This would give Lee a total of 45,000 troops, plus Stuart when he came up, to block the path of the enemy columns moving eastward through the Wilderness, and barely 10,000, including the artillery reserve, to hold the Fredericksburg ridge, which by tomorrow would have become his rear. The risks were great, but perhaps no greater than the odds that led him to accept them. At any rate, if it came to a simultaneous fight in both directions, he would have the advantage of interior lines, even though he would have gained it by inviting annihilation.

McLaws pulled back at midnight, leaving Barksdale's Mississippians behind for a possible repetition of their mid-December exploit. Early spread his lone division all up and down the five-mile stretch of intrenchments from Marye's Heights to Hamilton's Crossing, mindful of Lee's admonition that he was to keep up a bristling pretense of strength and aggressive intentions. Jackson, told to move at daylight, was on the march by 3 a.m. Riding ahead of his troops he arrived soon after sunrise at Tabernacle Church, the left-flank anchor of Anderson's newly established line, which McLaws was busy extending northward to the vicinity of Duerson's Mill, covering Banks Ford. His instructions were to "make arrangements to repulse the enemy," and to Stonewall this meant, quite simply, to attack him. If he had no orders to proceed beyond this point, neither did he have any to remain here. Besides, there was no enemy in sight except an occasional scampering blue horseman in brief silhouette against the verdant background of the Wilderness. Before he could repulse the enemy he would have to find him, and the obvious way to find him would be to go where he was — reportedly, four miles dead ahead at Chancellorsville. So he told Anderson and McLaws to leave off digging and get their men in motion. He would go forward with them. If they ran into trouble up ahead, and it was clear by now that trouble was what they definitely were going to find in that direction, his three divisions would soon be up to lend support.

It was about 11 o'clock of a fine May Day morning by the time they got their troops into march formation and set out, preceded by clouds of skirmishers. The advance was by two main roads, the turnpike on the right and the plank road on the left; McLaws took the former, Anderson the latter, accompanied by Jackson himself. Almost as soon as they entered the green hug of the Wilderness, McLaws made contact with the enemy advancing on the turnpike. At 11.20 the first gun of the meeting engagement boomed. Then others began to roar in that direction. Jackson's instructions were for both divisions to keep pushing west until they ran into something solid. Presently he received a dispatch from Stuart, who was near at hand. "I will close in on the flank," Jeb wrote, "and will help all I can when the ball opens. . . . May God grant us victory." Stonewall replied, "I trust that God will grant us a great victory." But he added, by way of showing what he had in mind to reinforce his trust: "Keep closed on Chancellorsville."

★ ★ ★ *H*ooker too had started forward at 11 o'clock, so that the meeting engagement occurred about midway between Chancellorsville and Tabernacle Church. Sickles having come up that morning, the northern commander was set to throw a five-corps Sunday punch. This was no time for wild blows, however, and he made his preparations with the same concern for detail as before. Slocum would advance along the plank road on the right, supported by Howard; Meade would take the left, along the turnpike, supported by Couch; Sickles would remain in general reserve, on call to add the extra weight that might be needed in either direction. Nor was Fighting Joe committing the amateur's gaffe of forgetting he had another hand to box with. Orders had gone the previous evening to Sedgwick: "It is not known, of course, what effect the advance will have upon the enemy, and the general commanding directs that you observe [Lee's] movements with the utmost vigilance, and, should he expose a weak point, attack him in full force and destroy him." This was made even more specific by instructions sent to Sedgwick as the advance got under way. No matter whether the rebels weakened their Fredericksburg line or not, he was "to threaten an attack in full force at 1 o'clock and to continue in that attitude until further orders. Let the demonstration be as severe as can be," Hooker added, "but not an attack," unless of course the enemy afforded a real opening, in which case the earlier instructions would obtain and Sedgwick would go for a left-hand knockout.

Slocum and Meade stepped off smartly, much encouraged by a circular prescribing the order of march and closing: "After the movement commences,

---

As the gray mass started forward, overlapping both of his open flanks, he began a rearward movement down the pike, dribbling casualties as he went.

---

headquarters will be at Tabernacle Church." It sounded as if Hooker meant business this time. Also it made considerable tactical sense, for the turnpike and the plank road, after branching off from one another at Chancellorsville, converged near that objective. Out of the woods at last, the two lead corps would be concentrated for the final lunge, supported by Howard, Couch, and Sickles, who would follow close behind. For more than half the distance, however, these two main Wilderness arteries diverged: with the result that as the two columns moved eastward, hemmed in by the dense jungle of stunted trees and brambly underbrush, they lost contact with each other. As an additional complication, Meade had one division on the pike and two on the River Road, which curved northward to outflank the rebel intrenchments at Banks Ford; so that here, too, contact was quickly lost. Two miles from its crossroads starting point, out of touch with Slocum on the right and the rest of its own corps on the left, the division on the turnpike came under fire from enemy skirmishers as it plodded up a long slope whose crest would bring the eastern rim of the Wilderness in view. It so happened that this division, commanded by Major General George Sykes, could lay substantial claims to being the sturdiest in the Army of the Potomac, two of its three brigades being composed exclusively of U.S. Regulars, while the third was made up of battle-hardened New York volunteers who had stood fast on Henry Hill and thereby saved the fleeing remnant of Pope's army from utter destruction at Bull Run. As steady now as then, they went smoothly into attack formation and drove the rebel skirmishers back to the crest of the low ridge. There, however, they came upon the Confederate main body, long gray lines of infantry supported by clusters of guns that broke into a roar at the sight of bluecoats. Calling a halt, Sykes sent back word that he was badly in need of help. Then, as the gray mass started forward, overlapping both of his open flanks, he began a rearward movement down the pike, dribbling casualties as he went. What would be known as the Battle of Chancellorsville had opened.

Couch was already coming up with Major General Winfield S. Hancock's division, which he threw into the line at once to stabilize the situation preparatory to resuming the advance. Before this last could be accomplished, however, a courier arrived with orders from Hooker: "Withdraw both divisions to Chancellorsville." Couch was amazed. Here he was, as he later said, with "open country in front and the commanding position," yet his chief was telling him to retire. Sykes and Hancock were equally puzzled. They too wanted to push ahead in accordance with the original instructions. With their approval, Couch sent an aide to inform Hooker that the situation was under control and the troops were about ready to continue their drive along the pike. Off to the right, a mounting bank of smoke and the rumble of guns told them that Slocum was likewise engaged and seemed to be holding his own, while Meade's other two divisions apparently had encountered no resistance at all on the left. But within half an hour the aide returned with a peremptory repetition of the order: Pull back to Chancellorsville without delay. Couch considered outright disobedience. Brigadier General G. K. Warren, chief engineer of the army, urged him to adopt just such a course while he himself rode back to explain its advantages to Hooker. He spurred rearward; but as soon as he left, Couch's West Point–inculcated instinct for obedience took over. Complying with the order to retire, he withdrew the two divisions, first Sykes, then Hancock. The disengagement had been completed, except for two rear-guard regiments still in line, when a third message arrived from Hooker: "Hold on until 5 o'clock." Evidently Warren had stated his case persuasively, but Couch by now was disgusted. "Tell General Hooker he is too late," he replied testily. "The enemy are already on my right and rear. I am in full retreat."

In point of fact, his right was more seriously threatened than he knew. Slocum, followed as closely by Anderson as Couch himself was being followed by McLaws, had already fallen back down the plank road in accordance with similar instructions from headquarters. Meade too was backtracking by now, but unpursued, having encountered nothing substantial in the way of resistance on the left. As a result he was even more astounded than Couch had been at receiving the order to withdraw. Within sight of Duerson's Mill, he had been within easy reach of Banks Ford, control of which would shorten greatly the lines of supply and communication between the army's divided wings. To be told to fall back under such circumstances, with clear going to his front and his lines extending along the crest of the eastward rise, was more exasperating than anything he had encountered up to now. Once again Hooker had built up his hopes only to dash them with a peremptory order which not only called for a halt, as before, but also insisted on a retirement. Meade was furious. "If he thinks he can't hold the top of a hill, how does he expect to hold the bottom of it?" the Pennsylvanian stormed as he complied with the instructions to fall back.

That was about 2 o'clock. All three corps commanders were hard put to understand what had come over Fighting Joe in the scant three hours since they had set out from the crossroads they now were under orders to return to. At the outset, with the announcement that his headquarters would be leapfrogged four miles forward while the movement was in progress, he had seemed confident of delivering a knockout blow. Then suddenly, at the first sputter of musketry on the turnpike, he had abandoned all his aggressive intentions and ordered everything back for a defense of Chancellorsville, deep in the Wilderness. Why? They did not know, but already they were beginning to formulate theories which they and others down the years would enlarge on. For one thing, that excellent intelligence section back at Falmouth was hard at work, forwarding information disturbing enough to jangle the nerves of the steadiest man alive. According to one rebel deserter, brought in for interrogation the night before, Longstreet's whole corps had left Suffolk, presumably by rail, and had "gone to Culpeper," which would place it directly in rear of the Union flanking column and scarcely a day's march away. The prisoner added "that Lee said it was the only time he should fight equal numbers," which if true was alarming in the extreme, considering all the old fox had been able to accomplish with inferior numbers in the past. Another deserter — "from New York state originally; an intelligent man," Butterfield commented — avowed that Hood's division was already with Lee; he knew this, he said, because he had "asked the troops as they passed along." One of the two informers must be lying, at least so far as Longstreet's location was concerned. Indeed, both might be lying; it was not unusual for the Confederates to send out bogus "deserters" to confuse an opponent with misleading information. But the fact was, Lee was not reacting to his present predicament at all as he ought to be doing if he was heavily outnumbered. He was reacting, in fact, as if the numerical advantage was with him even more than either deserter claimed. And just what that reaction was Hooker had learned shortly after Meade and Slocum left him. Until that time, Professor Lowe's balloons had been fogbound high over Stafford Heights, but all of a sudden the weather faired, permitting the aeronaut to tap out a steady flow of information regarding the panorama now spread out before his

Troops of the 1st New York Artillery form for inspection beside their 12-pounder Napoleons on the eve of the Battle of Chancellorsville.

eyes. He could see various rebel columns in motion, he wired Hooker at 11 o'clock, but the largest of these was "moving on the road toward Chancellorsville." This tallied with the intelligence summation forwarded shortly thereafter by Butterfield. Completing his tabulation of the Confederate order of battle, the chief of staff declared: "Anderson, McLaws, A. P. Hill, and Hood would, therefore, be in your front."

It also explained — all too clearly — the sudden clatter of musketry and the boom of guns, first down the turnpike, then down the plank road, not long after the two columns set out eastward through the forest. In part, as well, it accounted for Hooker's reaction, which in effect was a surrendering of the initiative to Jackson, who plunged deeper into the Wilderness in pursuit. But there was a good deal more to it than this: a good deal more that was no less valid for being less specific. Perhaps Hooker at last had recalled Lincoln's

★

admonition, "Beware of rashness." Perhaps at this critical juncture he missed the artificial stimulus of whiskey, which formerly had been part of his daily ration but which he had abjured on taking command. Perhaps he mistrusted his already considerable accomplishment in putting more than 70,000 soldiers in Lee's immediate rear, with practically no losses because he had met practically no resistance. It had been altogether too easy; Lee must have wanted him where he was, or at any rate where he had been headed before he called a halt and ordered a pull-back. Or perhaps it was even simpler than that. Perhaps he was badly frightened (not physically frightened: Hooker was never that: but morally frightened) after the manner of the bullfighter Gallo, who, according to Hemingway, "was the inventor of refusing to kill the bull if the bull looked at him in a certain way." This Gallo had a long career, featuring many farewell performances, and at the first of these, having fought the animal bravely and well, when the time came for killing he faced the stands and made three eloquent speeches of dedication to three distinguished aficionados; after which he turned, sword in hand, and approached the bull, which was standing there, head down, looking at him. Gallo returned to the barrera. "You take him, Paco," he told a fellow matador; "I don't like the way he looks at me." So it was with Hooker, perhaps, when he heard that Lee had turned in his direction and was, so to speak, looking at him. Lowe had signaled at noon that the rebels were "considerably diminished" on the heights behind Fredericksburg. Consequently, at 2 o'clock, Fighting Joe wired Butterfield: "From character of information have suspended attack. The enemy may attack me — I will try it. Tell Sedgwick to keep a sharp lookout, and attack if can succeed." In effect, now that Lee had turned his attention westward, Hooker was telling Sedgwick: "You take him, Paco. I don't like the way he looks at me."

None of this perturbation showed in his manner, however, when the returning generals confronted him at the Chancellor house, which he had taken over as his headquarters. "It's all right, Couch; I've got Lee just where I want him," he said expansively. "He must fight me on my own ground." Couch had a cold eye for this blusterous performance. "The retrograde movement had prepared me for something of the kind," he wrote years later, "but to hear from his own lips that the advantages gained by the successive marches of his lieutenants were to culminate in fighting a defensive battle in that nest of thickets was too much. . . . I retired from his presence with the belief that my commanding general was a whipped man."

Whether or not this was the case remained to be seen. For the present, the order was for the army to intrench itself along lines prescribed with the usual attention to detail. On the map they resembled a double-handled dipper. Couch and Slocum, with two divisions each in the vicinity of Chancellorsville — Gibbon had stayed at Falmouth after all — formed the cup, bulging south of the crossroads to include some comparatively high ground known as Fairview. The cup was just over a mile wide at the rim, tapering slightly toward the base, and just under a mile deep. Sickles' three divisions were in reserve, poised for a leap into the cup or a quick march out either of the handles, which were between two and three miles long and extended generally northeast and due west. Meade's three divisions connected the eastern lip of the cup with the Rappahannock, his left resting on a bend of the river south of U.S. Ford, which thus was covered. Howard's three divisions, the dipper's western handle, extended out the turnpike past Wilderness Church, where the plank road came in from the southwest, and thus presumably could block the approach of an enemy moving up from that direction. The troops worked into the night with picks and shovels, intrenching the six-mile line from flank to flank. At 2 a.m. Couch, Slocum, and Howard reported themselves satisfied that their respective sectors could be held against assault. Advantageously disposed along Mineral Spring Run, a small boggy creek that covered his front and rendered his position doubly secure, Meade had reported the same thing earlier. Hooker, with his accustomed thoroughness, seemed to have allowed for all eventualities before he retired to a bedroom in the crossroads mansion to sleep and store up strength for whatever tomorrow was going to bring.

He hoped it would bring an all-out Confederate attack; or so at least he had been saying, all afternoon and evening. "The rebel army is now the legitimate property of the Army of the Potomac," he announced to the officers gathered about him in the May Day sunshine on the Chancellor veranda. The fact that nearly all of his cavalry had ridden well beyond his reach, while nearly all of Lee's was in what Hooker called "my immediate presence," did not seem to him a cause for alarm, but rather an advantage, "which I trust will enable Stoneman to do a land-office business in the interior. I think the enemy in his desperation will be compelled to attack me on my own ground. . . . I am all right." Thus he wired the Washington authorities, thinking that such information, besides relieving the President's concern, might "have an important bearing on movements elsewhere." If the other Union armies would only keep step with this one, the war would soon be over and done with — won.

As the daylight hours wore on and his intrenchments were extended, still with no full-scale rebel assault, his show of confidence reached its zenith. He feared nothing and he wanted it known; not even the artillery of heaven. "The enemy is in my power," he exulted, "and God Almighty cannot deprive me of them." In the late afternoon he issued another circular for the encouragement of subordinates: "The major general commanding trusts that a suspension in the attack today will embolden the enemy to attack him."

★   ★   ★

★

*Federal troops of the Vermont
Brigade prepare to meet an attack by
Jubal Early's Confederates near
Bank's Ford on the Rappahannock
the evening of May 4.*

FIVE

Chancellorsville; Jackson Dies

1863 ★ ★ ★ ★ ★ *L*ee and Jackson met at sundown, on the plank road just over a mile southeast of Chancellorsville, for the purpose of deciding how best to go about giving Hooker what he claimed he wanted. They began their conference on the road itself, at the junction where a trail came in from Catharine Furnace, a rural ironworks on Lewis Creek a mile and a half to the west, but they withdrew presently into a nearby clump of pines when a Federal sharpshooter began ranging in on them from a perch in a tree just up the road, beyond the line along which Anderson's and Slocum's pickets were keeping up a rackety contention. Seated side by side on a log, the two men continued their discussion in the May Day twilight, the gray-bearded elder impeccably dressed as always, his neat gray tunic devoid of trappings except for the three unwreathed stars on each side of the turned-down collar, and the younger wearing the rather gaudy uniform which had provoked such hoots and catcalls on the day of Fredericksburg. Reconnoitering on the right this afternoon, Lee had found the terrain unpromising, hemmed in as it was by a bend of the Rappahannock, and the few heavily wooded approaches well guarded by troops already dug in along the far side of a marsh. To attempt to come to grips with them in that quarter, he said, would be to invite destruction. How about the center and the left? Jackson had not been far to the west, but he had made a long-range

★

examination of the enemy lines in front of Chancellorsville itself and had found the bluecoats disposed three-deep, hard at work with picks and shovels, and supported by many batteries of artillery. However, he was inclined to believe that the question of how to get at Hooker, here in the Wilderness tomorrow, was largely academic. The ease with which he had repulsed the advancing Union columns today made him suspect that their recoil was prelude to a withdrawal. "By tomorrow morning there will not be any of them on this side of the river," he declared.

Lee shook his head. So far he had deferred to Stonewall's judgment, but not in this. Though he too was puzzled by his opponent's sudden, turtle-like reaction to moderate pressure, he was convinced that Hooker was planning to make his main effort right here. Anyhow, even if that were not the case, they must prepare to deal with him tomorrow on even the outside chance that he would still be in his present intrenched position. Without quite giving over his belief that dawn would show the forest empty to their front, Jackson could not disagree with the logic of Lee's contention; besides which, he found the prospect so attractive as to overrule his inclination to think that it would not be offered. For him, as for his commander, to "deal with" Hooker meant to attack him. But how? And where? One possibility was that the Federal center might not appear as stout to a close-up view as it had seemed from a distance. The two generals accordingly dispatched an engineer officer from each of their staffs to go take a look at the intrenchments there and report on what they saw.

While this night reconnaissance was in progress, and while Lee and Jackson continued to speculate on ways of bringing the blue army's current excursion to a violent close, Jeb Stuart came jingling up from Catharine Furnace in fulfillment of his promise to "help all I can when the ball opens." Glad as he was to see his friend Stonewall decked out in the handsome uniform he had given him, he deferred comment in favor of some interesting information which had just come to hand. According to Fitzhugh Lee, who had ridden west to scout it, Hooker's right flank was "in the air" on the Orange Turnpike, wide open to attack from that direction. Though this was news of a kind to set both him and his chief lieutenant on tremble, the southern commander suppressed his excitement to ask whether roads were available for a covered approach to that critical point by troops in large numbers. Stuart replied that he did not know but he would do what he could to find out, and with that he swung back onto his horse and rode off westward, his red-lined cape and cinnamon whiskers glistening in the light of the new-risen moon.

From this time on, Lee and Jackson gave little attention to anything but the possibility of launching the suggested flank attack. When the two engineers returned to announce that the Union center was too strongly intrenched to be assaulted, Lee received the anticlimactic report with a nod and kept peering at a map spread on his knees; he peered so intently, indeed, that he seemed to be trying to make it give him information which it did not contain. "How can we get at those people?" he asked, half to himself and half to Jackson, who replied in an equally distracted manner, as he too searched the map for roads that were not on it: "You know best. Show me what to do, and we will do it." Finally, Lee traced a fingertip westward along the map from their present location, as if to sketch in an ideal route past the front of the enemy position, then northward to intersect the turnpike, where the latter veered abruptly east to address the Union flank end-on. In naval parlance, he was crossing Hooker's T. That would be the movement, he said; Jackson would lead it and Stuart would cover his march. Smiling, Jackson stood erect and saluted. "My troops will move at 4 o'clock," he said. In his eagerness, he not only seemed unable to remain seated, he also seemed to have forgotten his prediction that Hooker would clear out before sunup. Lee checked him with a reminder. If there was

Though he too was puzzled by his opponent's sudden, turtle-like reaction to moderate pressure, he was convinced that Hooker was planning to make his main effort right here.

any doubt about this next morning, he said, Jackson could open from an exposed position with a couple of guns, then judge by the response as to whether the blue army was still behind its Wilderness fortifications.

There was much to be done between now and sunrise: especially by Jackson, to whom Lee had left the choice of a route, the composition of the force to be employed, and the decision as to when and in what manner the flank attack would be delivered. But what both men needed for the present, at the close of a strenuous day and on the eve of what promised to be an even more strenuous morrow, was a few hours' sleep: again especially Jackson, who had demonstrated on several occasions — the Seven Days, for one — that without at least a minimum of profound rest he would be reduced to a state of somnambulism. They lay down where they were, in separate quarters of the grove, spreading their saddle blankets on the pine needles for a bed and using their saddles for a pillow. Both were soon asleep, but Lee was wakened presently by an officer he had sent to look into conditions on the turnpike to the north. "Ah, Captain, you have returned, have you?" he said, and he sat up slowly. "Come here and tell me what you have learned on the right." It was the same young man from

Jackson's staff who had wakened him two mornings ago to tell him Hooker was crossing; J. P. Smith was his name, a divinity student before the war. He hesitated, in awe of the general whose massive features and gray beard looked so imposing in the moonlight, but as he leaned forward the seated man put an arm about his shoulder and drew him down by his side while he finished his report. Lee thanked him and then, still retaining his grip, began to chide him by saying that he regretted that Smith and the other "young men about General Jackson" had not done a better job today of locating and silencing an enemy battery that had held up the advance. Young men nowadays, he declared in the accents of Nestor, were a far remove from the young men of his youth. The captain, seeing, as he later said, that the general "was jesting and disposed to rally me," broke away from the hold Lee tried to retain on his shoulder. As he moved off through the moonlit pines he could hear the Virginian laughing heartily there in the Wilderness where many men now sleeping would be laid in their graves tomorrow and the next day and the next, blue and gray alike, as a result of instructions he had given just before he himself lay down, in apparently excellent spirits, to rest for what he knew was coming with the dawn.

When Lee woke he saw the gaunt figure of Jackson bending over a small fire a courier had built. Rising, he joined him and the two sat on a couple of hardtack boxes the Federals had left behind the day before. It was already past 4 o'clock, the hour set for the column to move out, but Jackson explained that he was awaiting the return of his staff chaplain, who once had had a church hereabouts and was familiar with the region. For this reason he had sent him, together with a skilled cartographer, to explore the roads leading west from Catharine Furnace and then north to the plank road, up which he expected to make his strike. The two sat talking, warming their hands at the meager fire, until the glimmer of dawn showed the staff officers returning from their scout. Major Jedediah Hotchkiss, the cartographer, approached the generals and spread his map on another hardtack box which he placed between them. It was obvious from his manner, before he said a word, that he had found the route he had been seeking, and as he spoke he traced it on the map: first due west to the furnace, then due south, away from the enemy, along a trail that gradually turned back west to enter the Brock Road, which ran northward to the plank road and the turnpike. However, he explained that the column must not turn north at this point, since that would bring it within sight of a Federal signal station at Fairview, but south again for a short distance to another road leading north and paralleling the Brock Road, which it rejoined a couple of miles above in some heavy woods just short of its junction with the plank road. That way, practically the entire route — some ten miles in length from their present position and firm enough throughout to support wagons and artillery — would be screened from the eyes of enemy lookouts. Completing his exposition,

*Generals Lee and Jackson meet to discuss
their plans for the upcoming campaign
at the Battle of Chancellorsville.*

Hotchkiss looked from one to another of the generals, both of whom kept their eyes fixed on the map for what seemed to him an inordinately long time. Finally Lee spoke, raising his head to look at his lieutenant: "General Jackson, what do you propose to do?" Jackson put out his hand and retraced, with a semicircular motion of his wrist, the route just drawn. "Go around here," he said. Lee kept looking at him. "What do you propose to make this movement with?" he asked, and Jackson promptly replied: "With my whole corps."

Now there was a pause while Lee absorbed the shock the words had given him. "What will you leave me?" he asked. The question was rhetorical; he already knew the answer. But Jackson answered it anyhow, as readily as before. "The divisions of Anderson and McLaws." This meant that he would have better than 30,000 soldiers off to the rear and on the flank, necessarily out of contact with the enemy and the rest of his own army for most of the day, while Lee would be left with scarcely half as many troops planted squarely across the path of a greatly superior blue host which might resume its forward movement at any minute. However, having weighed the odds — which had to include the by no means improbable chance that Hooker might learn what was afoot and react accordingly — the southern commander made and announced his decision. "Well, go on," he said.

While they talked the sun had reddened the east, and now it broke clear, fiery above the treetops back toward Fredericksburg, where Early was facing odds almost as long as Lee's would be when the flanking column left. Jackson informed his chief that the march would be led by D. H. Hill's old division, now under Brigadier General Robert Rodes; next would come his own old division, commanded by its senior brigadier, Raleigh Colston; A. P. Hill's division would bring up the rear. He would take all his artillery with him, dispersed along the column, and depend on Stuart to cover his advance. Lee took notes on this, then retired to write the necessary orders while his lieutenant went about making preparations to move out. As Jackson rode past one brigade camp the lounging veterans rose to cheer him, but seeing what one of them later called "battle in his haste and stern looks," they merely gazed at him and wondered what exertion he was about to require of them. The preliminary dispositions were a time-consuming business, involving the extraction of some units already committed, but at last they were completed. Shortly before 8 o'clock, the lead regiment — Georgians who had fought under him in every battle since McDowell, the prologue to the Valley Campaign, which had opened exactly a year ago today with his descent through Brown's Gap to put his troops aboard the cars for Staunton — turned off the plank road and set out westward for Catharine Furnace and Hooker's right. Though he was four hours behind the starting time he had set the night before, Stonewall did not appear to be disturbed by the delay. He was alert but not impatient, one observer remarked, and spoke tersely "as though all were distinctly formed in his mind and beyond all question." Under the lowered bill of his cap, the battle light was already shining fiercely in his pale blue eyes.

Lee came up and joined him at the turn-off where the sniper had tried to draw a bead on them at sunset. Both mounted — Lee on Traveller, a tall dapple gray, and Jackson on stocky, ox-eyed Little Sorrel — they spoke briefly against a background of skirmish fire which had begun to sputter along the two-mile front now occupied exclusively by Anderson and McLaws, with just over 15,000 troops between them. Nothing in Lee's manner showed the strain involved in gambling that his opponent, whether or not he became aware in the meantime of what was happening in his front and on his flank, would not exploit his five-to-one numerical advantage by launching an all-out attack — frontal or otherwise; either would be about equally destructive — before the widely divided Confederate wings were reunited. Moreover, Lee was proceeding not only on the assumption that Jackson could gain and strike the Union flank before the bluecoats recovered from their current puzzling lethargy, here in the Wilderness or back in front of Marye's Heights; he was also proceeding on the belief, or at any rate the hope, that Hooker would be completely unstrung by the explosion on his right. Nothing less would serve. For if Hooker could absorb and then recover from the shock, he might still take the offensive against the outnumbered and divided graybacks to the west and south, or signal eastward for an assault upon the thinly held Fredericksburg ridge in Lee's immediate rear. This was, in short, the longest gamble of a career which had been crowded with risks throughout the eleven months since Lee first took command at Seven Pines. Now, their brief conversation ended, the two men parted, the elder to stay, the other to go. As they did so, the dark-bearded younger general raised his arm and pointed west, in the direction he was headed. Lee nodded, and Stonewall rode off into the forest, out of sight.

★ ★ ★ *F*ighting Joe had been up for hours, conducting a flank-to-flank inspection of his lines. "How strong! How strong!" he marveled as he examined the hastily improvised but elaborate fortifications: particularly those out on the right, where so many of the regiments were composed of foreign-born troops who performed such labor with Germanic thoroughness and a meticulous attention to detail rivaling Hooker's own. Wherever he went this morning, tall in the saddle and rosy-looking, flushed with confidence and trailing a kite tail of staff officers behind his big white high-stepping horse, the soldiers cheered him lustily, delighted to see their commander sharing with them the rigors of the field. His mood was as expansive as before; more so, in fact; and with cause. For he had received, the night before, a report from a trusted operative just in from Richmond, who not only had documentary evidence that Lee was receiving barely 59,000 daily rations, but also reported that the southern commander could hope for no reinforcements except from Longstreet, both of whose divisions — despite the contrary fabrications passed on by yesterday's rebel deserters — were still in front of Suffolk. This last was confirmed by Peck himself, who wired that he had taken prisoners from Hood and Pickett that same day. In reaction, Hooker's last move before retiring had been to direct that Reynolds' corps be detached from Sedgwick and sent to join him here at Chancellorsville. When it arrived — as it should do before long, the summons having been issued at 1.55 this morning — he would have better than 90,000 men on hand to repulse the attack Lee seemed to be preparing to deliver against the bulging center of the Union line. If the old fox really believed what he was rumored to have said the day before, that this "was the only time he should fight equal numbers," he was in for a large surprise. What Fighting Joe was planning was Fredericksburg in reverse, with Lee in the role of Burnside, and himself in the role of Lee: except that this time, when the attackers were exhausted and bled white as a result of their attempts to storm his fortifications, he would be in a position to swing over to the offensive that had been impossible for the Confederates, back in December, because of their numerical inferiority and the guns on Stafford Heights. Hereabouts there were no heights for Lee to mass his guns on, only the blinding and restricting thickets, and Hooker had men aplenty for the delivery of an all-out counterattack and the administration of the windup *coup de grâce* which would end the final spasmodic twitch of the dying rebel army.

He was in excellent spirits when he got back to headquarters at 9 o'clock to find a courier waiting for him from Brigadier General David Birney, commander of a division Sickles had sent out to some unoccupied high ground southwest of Fairview — Hazel Grove, it was called on the map — for a look at what the graybacks might be up to. According to the information brought back by the courier, they were up to a great deal. Hazel Grove afforded a clear but

---

On the off-chance that Lee was attempting at this late date to come up with something out of his bag of tricks, Hooker decided it would be wise to warn Howard of what was going on . . .

---

limited view of Catharine Furnace, less than one mile south, and the advancing bluecoats had spotted a rebel column moving due south of there along a stretch of road that disappeared into the woods. Apparently endless, the column included infantry, artillery, wagons, and ambulances; Birney thought it must signify an important development in the enemy's plans. Hooker agreed. In fact, after referring to his map, which showed that the road in question veered west beyond the screen of trees, he believed he knew just what that development was. The Confederates were in retreat, probably on Gordonsville, where Stoneman must have struck by now, severing one of their two main supply lines. However, on the off-chance that Lee was attempting at this late date to come up with something out of his bag of tricks, Hooker decided it would be wise to warn Howard of what was going on, and he sent him a message advising him to be vigilant in protecting the western flank: "We have good reason to suppose that the enemy is moving to our right. Please advance your pickets for purposes of observation as far as may be safe to obtain timely information of their approach." He might have followed to see for himself that his instructions were carried out, but presently a dispatch arrived from Howard, sent before his own had been received, stating that he too had sighted the rebel column "moving westward on a road parallel with this," and adding, of his own accord: "I am taking measures to resist an attack from the west." It was clear that Howard required no supervision to assure that he did his duty; he had performed it before he was even told what it was, thereby leaving Hooker free to concentrate on the question of pursuit.

In this connection he thought again of Sedgwick, who had been kept by a faulty telegraph connection from getting yesterday's instructions until the hour was too late for an attack. First Sickles and now Reynolds had been detached from the downstream force, but Sedgwick's was the largest corps in the army. With Gibbon's division still available at Falmouth, he had close to 30,000 effectives, plus the support of the long-range guns on Stafford Heights, and though Professor Lowe had reported earlier that a hard wind was bumping him around so much he could not use his telescope, the headquarters intelligence section informed Hooker that only Early's division remained on the Fredericksburg ridge. Accordingly, he directed Butterfield to pass the word along to Sedgwick and authorize him to attack if there was "a reasonable expectation of success." Meanwhile Hooker kept his staff busy preparing orders designed to put the whole army on Lee's trail if he still appeared to be in retreat next morning. A circular issued at 2.30 instructed corps commanders to load up with forage, provisions, and ammunition so as "to be ready to start at an early hour tomorrow." By the time this was distributed, reports had begun to come in from Sickles, who had been given permission at noon to advance with two divisions to investigate the movement Birney had spotted from Hazel Grove. He sent back word that he had pierced the rebel column near Catharine Furnace, capturing men and wagons, but that practically all of it had moved westward beyond his reach by now. Hooker took fire at this, his confidence soaring: Lee was unquestionably in full retreat, intending to follow the heavily escorted train with the Confederate main body. At 4.30 the jubilant Federal commander wired Butterfield to order Sedgwick to throw his entire force across the river, "capture Fredericksburg and everything in it, and vigorously pursue the enemy." Previous instructions had been discretionary, and so were these; but Hooker made it clear that a fine opportunity lay before him. "We know that the enemy is fleeing, trying to save his trains," he added. "Two of Sickles' divisions are among them."

As might have been expected with the rebel column filing through the woods to the army's front, there was a good deal of excitement along the outpost lines. Couriers and even unit commanders began to turn up at the Chancellor house with frantic, sometimes near-hysterical warnings of an impending flank attack. Staff officers had all they could do to keep some of them — especially one persistent artilleryman with the lowly rank of captain, who claimed to have ridden out and seen the graybacks massing — from bothering Hooker himself with their perturbations. When these men finally could be made to understand that the high command was already aware of the alleged danger and had taken steps to meet it in case it developed, they returned to their units, most of them feeling rather sheepish at having presumed to believe they knew more than their superiors. Others, however, remained unconvinced: particularly those through whose ranks the rebel prisoners had been taken rearward after their capture near Catharine Furnace. They were Georgians, hale-looking men in neat butternut clothes, and for the most part they seemed cheerful enough, considering their plight. They had come over, they replied to taunts, to help "eat up them eight-day rations." But some were surly and in no mood to be chided. Told by a bluecoat, "We'll have every mother's son of you before we go away," one snapped back: "You'll catch hell before night." Another was more specific as to how calamity was to be visited upon them, and by whom. "You think you've done a big thing just now," he said, "but wait till Jackson gets around on your flank." This seemed to its hearers well worth passing on to headquarters, but when they went there to report it they were told to return to their outfits; Lee was in retreat, no matter what the butternut captives said, and Hooker was making plans even now for an orderly pursuit.

★ ★ ★ *F*ar out on the right flank, as the shadows lengthened toward 5 o'clock and beyond, Howard's men were taking it easy. They had seen no action so far in the campaign, but that was much as usual; they had seen little real action anywhere in the war, save for a great deal of marching and countermarching, and were in fact a sort of stepchild corps, collectively referred to by the rest of the army as "a bunch of Dutchmen." Indeed, nothing demonstrated more conclusively Hooker's lack of concern for his western flank than the fact that he had posted these men here. Mostly New Yorkers and Pennsylvanians, large numbers of them were immigrants, lately arrived and scarcely able to speak English; "Hessians," their enemies called them, with a contempt dating back to the days of the Revolution. Schurz, Steinwehr, and Schimmelfennig were three of their generals, while their colonels had names such as Von Gilsa, Krzyzanowski, Einsiedel, Dachrodt, and Schluemback. Howard himself was by no means popular with them, despite his sacrifice of an arm to the cause and a record of steady progress up the ladder of command. After his maiming, a year ago at Fair Oaks, he had returned to lead a brigade at Antietam and a division at Fredericksburg, both with such distinction that now — to the considerable displeasure of men whose proudest boast had been "I fights mit Sigel" and who rather illogically put the blame for their hero's departure on his successor — he had a corps. He had had it, in fact, exactly a month today; but in his anxiety to make good he not only had borne down hard on discipline, he also had tried to influence the out-of-hours activities of his troops by distributing religious tracts among them. The latter action was resented even more than the former, for many of the men were freethinkers, lately emerged from countries where the church had played a considerable part in attempting their oppression, and they drew the line somewhere short of being preached at, prayed over, or uplifted. The result of all this, and more, was that army life was not a happy one for them or their commander, whose ill-concealed disappointment at their reaction to his attempt to play the role of Christian Soldier only served to increase their mistrust and dislike of him, empty sleeve and all.

Today was one of the better days, however, with a minimum of work, no drill whatsoever, and a maximum of rest. Extended for more than a mile along the turnpike west of Dowdall's Tavern, an oversized cabin just east of the junction where the plank road came in from the southwest, they lounged behind the elaborate southward-facing breastworks Hooker himself had admired. Like his chief, Howard was convinced that he was onto the rebel strategy, which seemed to him to be designed to cover a retreat with a pretense of strength and boldness. He too rejected various cries of wolf, including those from an outpost major who sent back a stream of frantic messages from beyond the flank, all patterned after the first at 2.45: "A large body of the enemy is massing in my front. For God's sake make disposition to receive him!" At the outer end of the intrenched line, two guns were posted hub-to-hub on the pike itself, facing west, and two regiments of infantry — not over 900 men in all — were disposed at right angles to the road, strung out northward from the point where the guns were posted. These two regiments and guns were all

Union General Oliver O. Howard's pennant flew at his headquarters, which beginning on May 1 was at Dowdall's Tavern on the plank road west of Chancellorsville.

the flank protection Howard had provided after notifying Hooker that he was "taking measures to resist an attack from the west," but he considered them ample, since nothing could approach him from that direction except along the turnpike, covered by the two guns, or through a tangle of second-growth timber and briery underbrush which he had pronounced impenetrable. Moreover, there was a half-mile stretch of unoccupied ground between his left and Slocum's right, marking the former position of his one reserve brigade, which had been detached in the midafternoon and still had not returned from its mission of guarding Sickles' flank in the course of his advance from Hazel Grove. This gap was critical. Though it went unnoticed, or at any rate unfilled, it meant that if anything struck Howard a hard enough blow from the west, he would be in much the same predicament as a man attempting to sit on a chair he did not know had been removed.

That, or something like that, was what happened. Not long after 5 o'clock, with some regiments already eating supper and others lounging about while waiting for it, their rifles neatly stacked, the troops at the far end of the line were alarmed and then amused to see large numbers of deer break out of the thickets to the west and come bounding toward them, accompanied by droves of rabbits darting this way and that in the underbrush, as if pursued by invisible beaters. The men cheered and hallooed, waving their caps at the startled forest creatures, until presently something else they heard and saw froze the laughter in their throats. Long lines of men in gray and butternut, their clothes ripped to tatters by the briers and branches, were running toward them through the "impenetrable" thickets. They were screaming as they came on, jaws agape, and their bayonets caught angry glints from the low-angled sun pouring its beams through the reddened treetops and over their shoulders.

⁂

For all its explosive force, its practically complete surprise, and its rapid gathering of momentum, Stonewall's flank attack was launched with only about two hours of daylight left for the accomplishment of the destruction he intended. One of the two main reasons for this tardiness was that the start itself had been late, and the other was that the finish was delayed by an extension of the march. Between these two untoward extremes, however, all went smoothly, despite attempted enemy interruptions. The roads, described by one of the marchers as "just wet enough to be easy to the feet and free from dust," were narrow but firm, so that the column was elongated but its progress was not impeded. Like his men, who were enthused by a sense of adventure before they had even had time to guess what the adventure was going to be, Jackson was in excellent spirits, and though he did not push them to the limit of their endurance as he had done so often in the past, being concerned for once to conserve their energy for the work that lay ahead, he took care to deal with emergencies in a manner that would not hold up the main body. For instance, when the head of the column came under fire from a section of guns just north of Catharine Furnace, he detached the lead regiment of Georgians, with instructions for them to block a possible infantry probe at that point, and had the remaining units double-time across the clearing, being willing to suffer whatever incidental losses this involved rather than to burn more daylight by taking a roundabout route. Similarly A. P. Hill, whose division did not clear the starting point until well after 11 o'clock, dropped off his two rear brigades to assist the hard-pressed Georgians — forty of them had been captured and most of the rest were about to be captured — in fending off an infantry attack launched by the Federals just as he was approaching the furnace about noon, and forged ahead with his other four brigades. Far in the lead and quite unmindful of his rear, which he left to look out for itself after making the original provision, Jackson kept the main body on the go. "Press forward. Press forward," he urged his subordinate commanders. Including 1500 attached cavalry and 2000 artillerymen in support of his 70 regiments of infantry, Stonewall had better than 31,000 effectives in the column, and his only regret was that he did not have more. "I hear it said that General Hooker has more men than he can handle," he remarked in the course of the march. "I should like to have half as many more as I have today, and I should hurl him into the river!"

His eyes glowed at the thought, and presently they had occasion to blaze even more fiercely, not only at a thought, but also at what was actually spread before them. About 2 o'clock, as he approached the Orange Plank Road — the intended objective, up which he expected to turn the column northeastward for an attack that would strike the Orange Turnpike just west of Dowdall's Tavern, where Hooker's flank presumably was anchored — he was met by Fitz Lee, who approached from the opposite direction, drew rein alongside Little Sorrel, and announced with a barely suppressed excitement that explained his lack of ceremony: "General, if you will ride with me, halting your column here out of sight, I will show you the enemy's right." The two officers, accompanied by a single courier so as not to increase the risk of detection, rode past the plank road intersection, then turned off eastward through the trees to a little hill which they climbed on horseback. From the summit, parting the curtain of leaves, Stonewall saw what had provoked the excitement Lee would still be feeling, years later, when he came to write about it: "What a sight presented itself before me! Below, and but a few hundred yards distant, ran the Federal line of battle . . . with abatis in front and long lines of stacked arms in the rear. Two cannon were visible in the part of the line seen. The soldiers were in groups in the rear, laughing, smoking, probably engaged, here and there, in games of cards and other amusements indulged in while feeling safe and comfortable, awaiting orders. In rear of them were other parties driving up and butchering beeves." As he observed the peaceful scene, Jackson's mind was on a different kind of butchery. According to Lee, "his eyes burned with a brilliant glow, lighting his sad face. His expression was one of intense interest; his face was colored slightly with the paint of the approaching battle, and radiant in the success of his flank movement."

The salient fact was that Hooker's flank was as completely "in the air" as had been reported the night before, but that an attack up the plank road, such as had been intended, would strike it at an angle, about midway, rather than end-on; which would not do. Correction of this, however, called for a two-mile extension of the march in order to get beyond the farthest western reach of the Union intrenchments and approach them on the perpendicular. That meant a further delay of nearly an hour, to which of course would be added the time required to form the three divisions for assault. With the sun already well past the overhead — by now, in fact, the hands of his watch were crowding 2.30 — there might not be enough daylight left for the execution of his plans. But Jackson did not hesitate beyond the few minutes it took him to make a careful examination of what was spread before his eyes. Seeing his lips moving as he looked at the enemy soldiers down below, Lee assumed that he was praying. If this was so, there was no evidence of it in his voice as he turned to the courier and snapped out an order for him to take back to the head of the column, halted on the Brock Road to await instructions: "Tell General Rodes to move across the plank road, halt when he gets to the old turnpike, and I will join him there." The courier took off. Jackson turned for a final look at the lounging bluecoats, disposed as they were for slaughter, then "rode rapidly [back] down the hill, his arms flapping to the motion of his horse, over whose head it seemed, good rider as he was, he would certainly go." Lee saw him thus; then he too turned and followed, somewhat chagrined that he had not received the thanks he had expected in return for making a discovery which not only would save many Confederate lives but also had made possible what gave promise of being the most brilliant tactical stroke of Stonewall's career.

Jackson had already forgotten him, along with practically everything else preceding the moment when his mind became fixed on what he was going to do. Retracing his horse's steps back down the Brock Road he passed Rodes, who had his men slogging northward for the turnpike, and returned to the plank road intersection, where he met and detached Colston's lead brigade — his own old First Manassas outfit, the Stonewall Brigade — to advance a short distance up the plank road and take position at a junction where the road from Germanna Ford came in from the northwest. With his rear and right flank thus

*Robert E. Rodes'
Confederate brigades
were the first to move
eastward along the plank
road toward Oliver O.
Howard's intrenchments
at Dowdall's Tavern.*

screened and protected, he took a moment to scrawl a note briefly explaining the situation to Lee, who he knew must be fretting at the delay. "I hope as soon as practicable to attack," he wrote, and added: "I trust that an ever kind Providence will bless us with great success." The note was headed, "Near 3 p.m."; time was going fast. He hurried northward to the turnpike, overtook Rodes, and gave him the instructions he had promised. Rodes accordingly moved eastward on the pike for about a mile — unopposed and apparently unobserved, although this brought him within 1000 yards of the western knuckle of Howard's intrenchments — then formed his division along a low, north-south ridge. Four brigades were in line, two to the right and two to the left, extending about a mile in each direction from the turnpike, which would be the guide for the assault. The fifth brigade took position behind the extreme right, and Colston's remaining three brigades prolonged this second line northward, 200 yards in rear of the first. Jackson's orders were that the charge would be headlong. Under no circumstances was there to be even a pause in the advance. If a first-line brigade ran into trouble, it was to call for help from the brigade in its immediate rear, without taking time to notify either division commander. The main thing, he emphasized as he spoke to his subordinates in turn, was to keep rolling, to keep up the pressure and the scare.

Maneuvering the stretched-out column off the road and into a compact mass, like a fist clenched for striking, was a time-consuming business, however, especially when it had to be done in woods so dense that visibility scarcely extended beyond the limits of a single regiment. Also there was the problem of fatigue. Though by ordinary standards the march had been neither long nor hard — an average dozen miles in an average eight hours — none of the troops had had anything to eat since breakfast, and many of them had not had even that. Hunger made them trembly. Moreover, there had been a tormenting shortage of water all along the way, and the men were spitting cotton as they filed into position to await the signal that would send them plunging eastward through the thickets to their front. They knew now, for certain, what they had only assumed before: Hooker's flank lay dead ahead and they were about to strike it. But the waiting was long. It was 4.30 by the time Colston had formed in rear of Rodes, and Hill was not yet off the road. Another half hour sufficed to get Little Powell's two leading brigades into position in rear of Colston's left, while the center two were coming forward on the turnpike; but the last two were miles back down the road, delayed by their rear-guard action at Catharine Furnace. Jackson waited as long as he could, watch in hand. Rodes stood beside him, waiting too; he was a V.M.I. graduate, just past his thirty-fourth birthday, and like his chief a former professor of mathematics. Tall and slender, a Virginia-born Alabamian with a tawny mustache that drooped below the corners of his mouth, he had fought well in almost every major battle since First Manassas, taking time off only for wounds, but he would be leading a division in combat for the first time today. At 5.15 — an hour and a half before sundown — Jackson looked up from his watch. His proposed third line was not half formed, but he and the sun could wait no longer.

"Are you ready, General Rodes?"

"Yes sir."

"You can go forward then."

He spoke calmly, almost matter-of-factly; yet what followed within the next quarter hour approximated pandemonium. Crashing through the half-mile screen of brush and stunted trees, whose thorns and brittle, low-hanging limbs quickly stripped the trail-blazing skirmishers near-naked, the long lines of Confederates broke suddenly into the clear, where the sight of the enemy brought their rifles to their shoulders and the quavering din of the rebel yell from their throats; "that hellish yell," one bluecoat called it, though Jackson himself had once referred to the caterwaul as "the sweetest music I ever heard." He was getting his fill of such music now. All across the nearly two-mile width of his front, the woods and fields resounded with it as the screaming attackers bore down on the startled Federals, who had just risen to whoop at the frightened deer and driven rabbits. Now it was their turn to be frightened — and driven, too. For the Union regiments facing west gave way in a rush before the onslaught, and as they fled the two guns they had abandoned were turned against them, hastening their departure and increasing the confusion among the troops facing south behind the now useless breastworks they had constructed with such care. These last, looking over their shoulders and seeing the fugitives running close-packed on the turnpike immediately in their rear, took their cue from them and began to pull out too, in rapid succession from right to left down the long line of intrenchments, swelling the throng rushing eastward along the road. Within twenty minutes of the opening shots, Howard's flank division had gone out of military existence, converted that quickly from organization to mob. The adjoining division was sudden to follow the example set. Not even the sight of the corps commander himself, on horseback near Wilderness Church, breasting the surge of retreaters up the turnpike and clamping a stand of abandoned colors under the stump of his amputated arm while attempting to control his skittish horse with the other, served to end or even slow the rout. Bareheaded and with tears in his eyes, Howard was pleading with them to halt and form, halt and form, but they paid him no mind, evidently convinced that his distress, whether for the fate of his country or his career or both, took no precedence over their own distress for their very lives. Some in their haste drew knives from their pockets and cut their knapsack straps as they ran, unburdening themselves for greater speed without taking the time to fumble at buckles, lest they be overtaken

Stonewall Jackson's Confederates, shouting the rebel yell, stormed the breastworks on the plank road at 5.15 on the afternoon of May 2.

by the horde of tatterdemalion demons stretching north and south as far as the eye could follow and screaming with delight at the prospect of carnage.

Jackson was among the pursuers, riding from point to point just in rear of the crest of the wave, exultant. "Push right ahead," he told his brigadiers and colonels, and as he spoke he made a vigorous thrusting gesture, such as a man would make in toppling a wall. When a jubilant young officer cried, "They are running too fast for us. We can't keep up with them!" he replied sternly: "They never run too fast for me, sir. Press them, press them!" It was 6.30 by now; the sun was down behind the rearward treetops. Dowdall's Tavern lay dead ahead, and from the east the answering thunder of guns and clatter of musketry told Stonewall that Lee had heard or learned of the attack and was applying pressure to keep the tottering Union giant off balance, even though he could scarcely hope to break through the endless curve of fortifications south and east of Chancellorsville. Here to the west, on the other hand, whenever a clump of bluecoats more stalwart than their fellows tried to make a stand, they found themselves quickly outflanked on the left and right by the overlapping lines of the attackers, and they had to give way in a scramble to avoid being surrounded. Every time Jackson heard the wild yell of victory that followed such collapses he would lift his head and smile grimly, as if in thanks to the God of battle. Conversely, whenever he came upon the bodies of his own men, lying where panicky shots had dropped them, he would frown, draw rein briefly, and raise one hand as if blessing the slain for their valor. A staff officer later remarked, "I have never seen him so well pleased with the progress and results of a fight."

On through sundown his pleasure was justified by continuing success, and presently it was increased. By 7 o'clock, with darkness settling fast in the clearings and the woods already black, his triumph over Howard was complete as the Federals gave way around Dowdall's Tavern and began their flight across the reserveless gap that yawned between them and the rest of the blue army. On the right, just south of the turnpike, there was a meeting engagement with a column of Union cavalry, which resulted in its repulse, and enemy guns were booming on Fairview Heights, firing blind to discourage pursuit, but Jackson did not believe there was anything substantial between him and the loom of forest screening Chancellorsville itself, just over a mile ahead. The only deterrent beyond his control was the darkness, and soon there was not even that. As if in response to a signal from the southern Joshua, the full moon came up, huge and red through the drifting smoke, then brightened to gold as it rose to light the way for pursuit. Many times in the past Stonewall had ached to launch a night attack; now he not only had the chance, he believed it was downright necessary if he was to prevent the enemy from recovering from the shock and attempting to turn the tables on the still-divided Confederates. Two immediate objectives he had in mind. One was to strike deep in Hooker's rear, cutting him off from U.S.

Ford so as to prevent his escape across the Rappahannock, and the other was to reunite with Lee for a combined assault on the bluecoats who thus would be hemmed in for slaughter. It was more or less obvious by now that Rodes and Colston had done their worst, at least for the present; they would need a breathing spell in which to regain control of their troops, hopelessly mingled in a single wave that was already ebbing because of exhaustion; but Hill's four brigades were still intact, available as a reserve, and Jackson was determined to use them for a moonlight advance along the pike and up the roads leading northeastward to the single river crossing in Hooker's rear. Soon he found Little Powell and gave him his instructions. There was no studied calmness about him now, such as there had been three hours ago when he told Rodes he could go forward. His excitement was evident to everyone he met, and his sense of urgency was communicated with every word he spoke, including those in the orders he gave Hill: "Press them! Cut them off from the United States Ford, Hill. Press them!"

★ ★ ★ **Hooker by then was doing all he could** to avert disaster, but for the better part of an hour after the first wave of attackers struck and crumpled the tip of his western wing — three miles from the Chancellor gallery where he sat chatting amiably with members of his staff — he had been under the tactical disadvantage of not even knowing that he had been surprised. Because of acoustic peculiarities of the terrain and the cushioning effect of brush and trees, the roar of battle reached him but faintly and indirectly. He and his aides supposed that the racket, such as it was, came from down around Catharine Furnace, a couple of miles to the south, and were exchanging conjectures as to the havoc Sickles must be making among Lee's trains in that direction. Just before sundown, however, one of the officers strolled out to the road and casually gazed westward. "My God — here they come!" the others heard him shout. Then they saw for themselves what he meant. A stumbling herd of wild-eyed men, the frantic and apparently unstoppable backwash of Howard's unstrung corps, was rushing eastward, filling the pike from shoulder to shoulder. Fighting Joe reacted fast. At hand was Sickles' third division — his own in the days before his elevation to corps and army command — left in reserve when the other two moved south; Hooker ordered it to wheel right and stem the rout. "Receive them on your bayonets! Receive them on your bayonets!" he cried, not making it clear whether he meant the demoralized Dutchmen or the rebels somewhere in their rear, as he rode westward through the failing light and into the teeth of the storm.

At Hazel Grove, sealed off from the uproar which by now was just over a mile away, a regiment of Pennsylvania cavalry received at about this same time, between sunset and moonrise, orders to join Howard near Wilderness Church. With no suggestion of urgency in the message and no hint that a clash had occurred, let alone a retreat, the troopers mounted and set out northwest-ward on a trail too narrow for anything more than a column of twos. They rode at a walk, talking casually among themselves, their weapons sheathed, until they approached the turnpike: at which point the major in command barely had time to cry, "Draw sabers! Charge!" before they ran spang into a whole Confederate division moving eastward through darkness that all of a sudden was stitched with muzzle flashes and filled with yells and twittering bullets. One side was about as startled as the other. The riders managed to hack their way out of the melee, though by the time they reassembled in the moonlight back near Chancellorsville a good many saddles had been emptied and a number of troopers had been captured, along with their unmanageable horses.

For blue and gray alike, whether mounted or afoot, the meeting engagement had some of the qualities of a nightmare too awful to be remembered except in unavoidable snatches. But for other Union soldiers, east of there, such an experience would have been counted almost mild in comparison with the one they blundered into a few hours later, in which blue was pitted not only against gray, but also against blue. Down around Catharine Furnace, deep in enemy territory, Dan Sickles knew nothing of what had been happening until well past sundown, when he heard the roar of batteries massed on the heights at Hazel Grove and Fairview, far in his rear. Informed at last of the enemy flank attack, which placed his two divisions precariously between the superior halves of the rebel army and thus exposed him to the danger of being pinched off and surrounded, he pulled hurriedly back to Hazel Grove — unhindered, so far, but by no means out of the trap whose jaws seemed likely to snap shut at any moment. By now it was past 9 o'clock, and except for occasional bellows by the 22 guns posted here and the 34 at Fairview, the firing had died to a mutter. Placing one division on the left and the other on the right of a trail leading northward through the forest, Sickles prepared to continue his march to the comparative safety of the turnpike. He had scarcely set out, however, before the two columns lost the trail and drifted apart, one veering east and the other west, with the result that they ran into horrendous trouble in both directions. The division on the left angled into a line of Confederates, alert behind hastily improvised intrenchments, while the one on the right stumbled into a similar line along which one of Slocum's divisions was deployed. Both broke into flames on contact, and a three-sided fight was in progress as suddenly as if someone had thrown a switch. Caught in what a participant called "one vast square of fire," Sickles' troops milled aimlessly, throwing bullets indiscriminately east and west. Shouts of "Don't fire! We're friends!" brought heavier volleys from both sides of the gauntlet, and consternation reached a climax when rival batteries started pumping shell and canister into the frantic mass hemmed thus between the lines. Somehow, though, despite the darkness and confusion, Sickles finally managed

★

to effect a withdrawal southward, in the direction he had come from. By midnight he had what was left of his two divisions back at Hazel Grove, where the men bedded down to wait for daylight, barely four hours off, and restore their jangled nerves as best they could.

Elsewhere along his contracted line — albeit the contraction had been accomplished more by Jackson's efforts than his own — Hooker saw to it that the rest of his army did likewise. He did not know what tomorrow was going to bring, but he intended to be ready for it. And in point of fact he had cause for confidence. Reynolds was over the river by now; his three divisions were available as a reserve. Even Howard's three, or anyhow a good part of them, had managed to reassemble in the vicinity of U.S. Ford, where they were brought to a halt after ricocheting northward off Lee's intrenchments east of Chancellorsville. Meade's three had been unaffected by the turmoil across the way. Couch and Slocum, under cover of the 56-gun barrage from Hazel Grove

For blue and gray alike, whether mounted or afoot, the engagement had some of the qualities of a nightmare too awful to be remembered . . .

and Fairview, had adapted their four divisions to the altered situation, along with the one Sickles had left behind. Moreover, another brigade of cavalry was at hand, Averell having been called in from near Rapidan Station, where Stoneman had dropped him off, ostensibly to check Stuart's pursuit but actually, since there was no pursuit, to play little or no part in the southward raid. His total loss, after three days in enemy country, was 1 man killed and 4 wounded; Hooker was furious and relieved him on the spot. "If the enemy did not come to him, he should have gone to the enemy," Fighting Joe protested with unconscious irony. Apparently he could not see that this applied in his own case. He still depended on Sedgwick for the delivery of any blow that was to be struck, repeating in greater detail at 9 p.m. the instructions sent him earlier in the day. This time they were peremptory; Sedgwick was to "cross the Rappahannock at Fredericksburg on the receipt of this order." Leaving Gibbon to hold the town, he was to march at once on Chancellorsville and "attack and destroy any force he may fall in with on the road." This would bring him promptly into contact with Lee's rear, "and between us we will use him up. . . . Be sure not to fail." The pattern was unchanged. Now as before, Gallo-Hooker was leaving the confrontation of the bull to Paco-Sedgwick, while he himself stood fast behind the barrera to cheer him on.

Lulled by what one insomniac called "the weird, plaintive notes of the whippoorwills," who would not let even a battle the size of this one cancel their serenade to the full, high-sailing moon, the army slept. From point to point the Wilderness was burning — "like a picture of hell," a cavalryman said of the scene as he viewed it from a hilltop — but the screams of the wounded caught earlier by the flames had died away, together with the growl and rumble of the guns. It was midnight and the Army of the Potomac took its rest.

★ ★ ★ Though the Army of Northern Virginia was doing the same, west and south of the now one-handled Union dipper, it did so in an atmosphere of tragedy out of all ratio to the success it had scored today. Not only had Stonewall's plan for continuing the eastward drive by moonlight been abandoned, but Stonewall himself had been taken rearward, first on a stretcher and then in an ambulance, to a hospital tent near Wilderness Tavern, where even now, as midnight came and went, surgeons were laying out the probes and knives and saws they would use in their fight to save his life. Intimations of national tragedy, intensified by a sense of acute personal loss, pervaded the forest bivouacs as the rumor spread that Jackson had been wounded.

After telling Hill to bring his men forward in order to resume the stalled pursuit, he had proceeded east along the turnpike in search of a route that would intercept the expected blue retreat to U.S. Ford. As he and several members of his staff rode past the fringe of Confederate pickets, taking a secondary road that branched off through the woods on the left, they began hearing the sound of axes from up ahead, where the Federals were trimming and notching logs for a new line of breastworks. "General, don't you think this is the wrong place for you?" an officer asked. Jackson did not agree. "The danger is all over," he said. "The enemy is routed. Go back and tell A. P. Hill to press right on." Presently, though, with the ring of axes much nearer at hand, he drew rein and listened carefully. Then he turned and rode back the way he had come, apparently satisfied that the bluecoats, for all their frenzy of preparation, would be unable to resist what he intended to throw at them as soon as Hill got his troops into position. Soon he came upon Little Powell himself, riding forward with his staff to examine the ground over which he expected to advance, and the two parties returned together. To the pickets crouched in the brush ahead — North Carolinians whose apprehensiveness had been aroused by the meeting engagement, a short while ago, with the saber-swinging Pennsylvanians over on the turnpike — the mounted generals and their staffs, amounting in all to nearly a score of horsemen, must have had the sound of a troop of Union cavalry on the prowl or the advance element of a wave of attackers. At any rate that was the premise on which they acted in opening fire. "Cease firing! Cease firing!" Hill shouted, echoed by one of Jackson's officers: "Cease firing! You are firing into your own men!" Fortunately, no one had been hit by the sudden spatter of bullets, but the Tarheel commander believed he saw through a Yankee trick. "Who gave that order?" he cried. "It's a lie! Pour it into them, boys!" The boys did just that. Not only the pickets but the whole front-line battalion opened fire at twenty paces and with such devastating effect that the bodies of no less than fourteen horses were counted later in the immediate area.

Little Sorrel was not among them, having returned by then to the allegiance from which Stonewall had removed him, nearly two years ago, with his capture at Harpers Ferry. Frightened by the abrupt first clatter of fire from the pickets crouched in the brush ahead, he whirled and made a rearward dash through the woods. Jackson managed to turn him, though he could not slow him down, and was coming back west, his right arm raised to protect his face from low-hanging branches, when the second volley crashed. Once more Little Sorrel whirled and scampered toward the enemy lines, completely out of control now because his rider had been struck by three of the bullets, two in the left arm, which hung useless at his side, and one through the palm of the upraised hand, which he lowered and used as before, despite the pain, to turn the fear-crazed animal back toward his own lines. There one of the surviving officers,

This handkerchief was in Stonewall Jackson's pocket when he was wounded by his own men. Jackson's family donated the relic to the Virginia Military Institute after the war.

dismounted by the volley, caught hold of the horse's bridle and brought him to a stop, while another came up and braced the general in the saddle. He seemed dazed. "Wild fire, that, sir; wild fire," he exclaimed as he sat staring into the darkness lately stitched with muzzle flashes. All around them they could hear the groans and screams of injured men and horses. "How do you feel, General?" one of the officers asked, with the simplicity of great alarm, and Jackson replied: "You had better take me down. My arm is broken." They did so, finding him already so weak from shock and bleeding that he could not lift his feet from the stirrups. Freed at last of the restraining weight, Little Sorrel turned and ran for the third time toward the Union lines, and this time he made it. Meanwhile the two staffers laid the general under a tree. While one went off in search of a surgeon and the other was doing what he could to staunch the flow of blood from an artery severed in the left arm, just below the shoulder, Jackson began muttering to himself, as if in disbelief of what had happened. "My own men," he said.

That was about 9.30; the next two hours were a restless extension of the nightmare as Federal batteries at Fairview began firing, the gunners having spotted the moonlit confusion just over half a mile away. Presently the second of Jackson's two attendant staff officers returned through the storm of bursting shells with a regimental surgeon, who administered first aid and ordered the general taken rearward on a stretcher. This had to be done under artillery fire so intense that the bearers were forced to stop and lie flat from time to time, as much for Jackson's protection as their own. On several such occasions they almost dropped him, and once they did, hard on the injured arm, which made him groan with pain for the first time. At last they found an ambulance and got him back to the aid station near Wilderness Tavern, where his medical director, Dr Hunter McGuire, took one look at "the fixed, rigid face and the thin lips, so tightly compressed that the impression of the teeth could be seen through them," and ordered the patient prepared for surgery. "What an infinite blessing . . . blessing . . . blessing," Stonewall murmured as the chloroform blurred his pain. Then McGuire removed the shattered left arm, all but a two-inch stump. Coming out of the anesthetic, half an hour later — it was now about 3 o'clock in the morning — Jackson said that during the operation he had experienced "the most delightful music," which he now supposed had been the singing of the bone-saw. At that point, however, he was interrupted by a staff officer just arrived from the front. Tragedy had succeeded tragedy. Hill had been incapacitated, struck in both legs by shell fragments, and had called on Jeb Stuart to take command instead of Rodes, the senior infantry brigadier, who until today had never led anything larger than a brigade. Stuart had come at a gallop from Ely's Ford, altogether willing. Knowing little of the situation and almost nothing of Stonewall's plans, however, he had sent to him for instructions or advice. Jackson stirred, contracting his brow at the effort. For a moment the light of battle returned to his eyes. Then it faded; his face relaxed. Even the exertion of thought was too much for him in his weakened condition. "I don't know — I can't tell," he stammered. "Say to General Stuart he must do what he thinks best."

Stuart would do that anyhow, of course, and so would Lee, who was informed at about this same time of the progress of the flank attack and the climactic wounding of his chief lieutenant. "Ah, Captain," he said; he shook his head; "Any victory is dearly bought which deprives us of the services of General Jackson, even for a short time." When the officer started to give him further details of the accident Lee stopped him. "Ah, don't talk about it. Thank God it is no worse." He was quick to agree, however, when the young man expressed the opinion that it had been Stonewall's intention to continue the attack. "Those people must be pressed today," Lee said decisively, and he put this into more formal language at once in a note to Stuart: "It is necessary that the glorious victory thus far achieved be prosecuted with the utmost vigor, and the enemy given no time to rally. . . . Endeavor, therefore, to dispossess them of Chancellorsville, which will permit the union of the army."

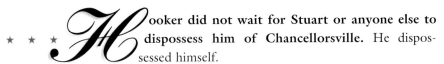

★ ★ ★ ooker did not wait for Stuart or anyone else to dispossess him of Chancellorsville. He dispossessed himself.

After establishing in the predawn darkness a secondary line of defense — a formidable V-shaped affair, with Reynolds deployed along Hunting Run, Meade at the southern apex, where the roads from Ely's and U.S. Fords came together in rear of army headquarters, and the fragments of Howard reassembled in Meade's old position along Mineral Spring Run, so that the flanks were anchored, right and left, on the Rapidan and the Rappahannock — he rode forward at first light, past the works still held by Couch and Slocum around Fairview, to confer in person with Sickles. Despite last night's horrendous experience of being mauled by foes and friends, Sickles had got his nerve back and was all for holding his ground; but Hooker would not hear of it, and ordered him to withdraw at once. It was this well-intentioned readjustment, designed to tidy up his lines and consolidate his defenses south of the vital crossroads, which resulted in his dispossession. Hazel Grove turned out to be the key to the whole advance position, since rebel artillery posted there could enfilade the intrenchments around Fairview, which in turn were all that covered Chancellorsville itself. The result was that everything south of the improvised V came suddenly unglued, and Hooker was left, scarcely twelve hours after his apparent delivery from the first, with a possible second disaster on his hands.

Stuart's advance, south of the turnpike and into the rising sun, coincided with Sickles' withdrawal, the final stages of which became a rout as the graybacks swarmed into Hazel Grove and overran the tail of the blue column. Immediately behind the first wave of attackers came the guns, 30 of them slamming away from the just-won heights at the Federals massed around Fairview, while another 30 assailed the western flank from a position near Howard's former headquarters, back out the pike, and 24 more were roaring from down the plank road to the southeast. Lee's midwinter reorganization of the Confederate long arm, for increased flexibility in close-up support, was paying short-term dividends this morning. Caught in the converging fire of these 84 guns, along with others west and south, the troops of Couch and Slocum were infected by the panic Sickles' men brought out of the smoke at Hazel Grove. North of the pike, sheltered by the breastworks Jackson had heard them constructing the night before, the bluecoats held fast against repeated assaults by the rebel infantry, but they were galled by the crossfire from batteries whose shots were plowing the fields around the crossroads in their rear and smashing their lines of supply and communication. Not even the Chancellor mansion, converted by now into a hospital as well as a headquarters by surgeons who took doors off their hinges and propped them on chairs for use as operating tables, was safe from the bombardment — as Hooker himself discovered presently, in a most emphatic manner. Shortly after 9 o'clock he was standing on the southwest veranda, leaning against one of the squat wooden pillars, when a solid projectile struck and split it lengthwise. He fell heavily to the floor, stunned by the shock. His aides gathered round and took him out into the yard, where they laid him on a blanket and poured a jolt of brandy down his throat. Revived by this first drink in weeks, Fighting Joe got up, rather wobbly still, and walked off a short distance, calling for his horse. It was well that he did, for just after he rose a second cannonball landed directly on the blanket, as if to emphasize the notion suggested by the first that the war had become an intensely personal matter between the Union commander and the rebel gunners who were probing for his life. He mounted awkwardly, suffering from a numbness on the side of his body that had been in contact with the shattered pillar, and rode for the rear, accompanied by his staff.

Despite the fact that he would succeed to command of the army in the event that its present chief was incapacitated, Couch knew nothing of Hooker's precipitate change of base until about 10 o'clock, when he received a summons to join him behind Meade's lines, where the apex of the secondary V came down to within a mile of the Chancellor house. Though he had his hands quite full just then — it was during the past half hour that the lines around Fairview had begun to come unglued in earnest — Couch told Hancock to take charge, and set out rearward in the wake of his chief, whom he found stretched out on a cot in a tent beside the road to U.S. Ford. "Couch, I turn the command

★

George Leo Frankenstein painted this view of the
Chancellor mansion, which served as a hospital
during the Battle of Chancellorsville.

of the army over to you," the injured general said, raising himself on one elbow
as he spoke. However, his next words showed that he did not really mean what
he had said. Whether or not he had control of himself at this point was open to
question, but there was no doubt that he intended to retain control of the army.
"You will withdraw it and place it in the position designated on this map," he
added, indicating a field sketch with the V drawn on it to show where the new
front lines would run. Couch perhaps was relieved to hear that he would not be
given full control, along with full responsibility — "If he is killed, what shall I
do with this disjointed army?" he had asked himself as soon as he heard that
Hooker had been hurt — but others were hoping fervently that he would take
charge; for he was known to be a fighter. "By God, we'll have some fighting
now," a colonel said stoutly as Couch emerged from the tent. Meade looked
inquiringly at his friend, hoping to receive at last the order for which he had

★

been waiting all morning: Go in. Instead, Couch shook his head by way of reply and relayed Hooker's instructions for a withdrawal.

In any event, such instructions were superfluous by now except as they applied to Hancock, whose division was the only one still maintaining, however shakily, its forward position in a state that even approached cohesiveness. The choice, if the army's present disjointed condition allowed for any choice at all, lay not in whether or not to withdraw, as Hooker expressly directed, but in whether or not to counterattack and thus attempt to recover what had been lost by the retreat already in progress; which manifestly would be difficult, if not downright impossible, since the Confederates had just seized the heights at Fairview and with them domination of the open fields across which the troops of Sickles, Couch, and Slocum were streaming to find sanctuary within the line of breastworks to the north. Hancock's rear-guard division was having to back-pedal fast to keep from being cut off or overrun by a horde of butternut pursuers who

---

Never before, perhaps, had the Army of Northern Virginia fought with such frenzy and exaltation, such apparent confidence in its invincibility . . .

---

were screaming as triumphantly now, and with what appeared to be equally good cause, as they had done when they bore down on Howard's startled Dutchmen yesterday. While Stuart pressed eastward, making his largest gains on the south side of the turnpike, Lee had been pushing north and west up the plank road and reaching out simultaneously to the left, past Catharine Furnace, for the anticipated hookup. It was his belief that the best and quickest way to accomplish the reunion of the two wings of his army would be to uncover Chancellorsville, after which it was his intention to launch a full-scale joint assault that would throw Hooker back against the Rappahannock and destroy him.

For a time it looked as if that might indeed be possible in the ten full hours of daylight still remaining. Never before, perhaps, had the Army of Northern Virginia fought with such frenzy and exaltation, such apparent confidence in its invincibility under Lee. Accompanied by the roar of artillery from the dominant heights, McLaws and Anderson moved steadily westward up the turnpike and the plank road, while Rodes, Colston, and Henry Heth — the senior brigadier in Hill's division — plunged eastward along both sides of the turnpike, cheered on by Stuart, who rode among them, jaunty in his red-lined cape, hoicking them up to the firing line and singing at the top of his voice some new words set to a familiar tune: "Old Joe Hooker, won't you come out the

Wilderness?" All advanced rapidly toward the common objective, east and west, as the bluecoats faded back from contact. Shortly before 10.30 the two wings came together with a mighty shout in the hundred-acre clearing around the Chancellor mansion, which had been set afire by the bombardment. Lee rode forward from Hazel Grove, past Fairview, on whose crown two dozen guns had been massed to tear at the rear of the retreating enemy columns, and then into the yard of the burning house, formerly headquarters of the Union army, where the jubilant Confederates, recognizing the gray-bearded author of their victory, tendered him the wildest demonstration of their lives. "The fierce soldiers with their faces blackened with the smoke of battle, the wounded crawling with feeble limbs from the fury of the devouring flames, all seemed possessed with a common impulse," a staff man later wrote. "One long, unbroken cheer, in which the feeble cry of those who lay helpless on the earth blended with the strong voices of those who still fought, rose high above the roar of battle and hailed the presence of the victorious chief. He sat in the full realization of all that soldiers dream of — triumph. . . . As I looked upon him in the complete fruition of the success which his genius, courage, and confidence in his army had won," the officer added, "I thought that it must have been from such a scene that men in ancient times rose to the dignity of gods."

In the midst of this rousing accolade a courier arrived with a dispatch from Jackson, formally reporting that the extent of his wounds had compelled him to relinquish command of his corps. Lee had not known till now of the amputation, and the news shook him profoundly. His elation abruptly replaced by sadness, he dictated in reply an expression of regret. "Could I have directed events," he told his wounded lieutenant, "I would have chosen for the good of the country to be disabled in your stead," and added: "I congratulate you upon the victory, which is due to your skill and energy." This done, he returned to the business at hand. He had, as he said, won a victory; but if it was to amount to much more than the killing, as before, of large numbers of an enemy whose reserves were practically limitless, the present advantage would have to be pressed to the point at which Hooker, caught in the coils of the Rappahannock and with the scare still on him, would have to choose between slaughter and surrender. Before this could be accomplished, however, or even begin to be accomplished by a resumption of the advance, the attackers themselves would have to be reorganized and realigned for the final sweep of the fields and thickets stretching northward to the river. Lee gave instructions for this to be done as quickly as possible, and while waiting got off a dispatch to Davis in Richmond. "We have again to thank Almighty God for a great victory," he announced.

His hope was that he would be sending another announcement of an even greater victory by nightfall. But just as he was about to order the attack, a courier on a lathered horse rode in from the east with news of a disaster. At dawn that morning, with a rush across the pontoon bridge they had thrown under cover of darkness, the Federals had occupied Fredericksburg. Sedgwick then had feinted at the thinly held defenses on the ridge beyond the town, first on the far left and then the right, by way of distracting attention from his main effort against the center. This too had been repulsed, not once but twice, before the weight of numbers told and the bluecoats swarmed up and over Marye's Heights. In accordance with previous instructions designed for such a crisis, Early had withdrawn southward to protect the army's trains at Guiney Station; but Sedgwick had not pursued in that direction. Instead, he had moved — was moving now — due west along the plank road, which lay open in Lee's rear. This was the worst of all possible threats, and the southern commander had no choice except to meet it at this worst of all possible times. Postponing the assault on Hooker, he detached McLaws to head eastward and delay Sedgwick, if possible, while Anderson extended his present right out the River Road to prevent a junction of the two Union forces in case Sedgwick managed to sidestep McLaws or brush him out of the way. By now it was close to 3 o'clock. Holding Rodes and Heth in their jump-off positions, Lee ordered Colston to move up the Ely's Ford Road in order to establish and maintain contact with Hooker, who might be emboldened by this new turn of events. "Don't engage seriously," Lee told Colston, "but keep the enemy in check and prevent him from advancing. Move at once."

Now as before, he was improvising, dividing his badly outnumbered army in order to deal with a two-pronged menace. While McLaws swung east to throw his 7000 soldiers in the teeth of Sedgwick's 20,000 or more, Lee would endeavor to hold Hooker's 80,000 in position with his own 37,000. When and if he managed to stabilize the situation — as Jackson had done, two days ago, with the advance beyond Tabernacle Church — he would decide which of the two enemy wings to leap at, north or east. Meanwhile, as usual, he was prepared to take advantage of any blunder his opponents might commit, and he was determined to recover the initiative. Above all, he kept his head and refused to take counsel of his fears. When an excited officer, alarmed by the threat to the army's rear, arrived with a lurid eyewitness account of the loss of Marye's Heights, Lee cut him short. "We will attend to Mr Sedgwick later," he said calmly.

★ ★ ★ *W*hat with the relentless depletion of his forces, siphoned off westward at the rate of a corps a day for the past two days, and the spate of discretionary orders, generally so delayed in transmission that the conditions under which they had been issued no longer obtained by the time they came to hand, John Sedgwick — "Uncle John" to his troops, a fifty-year-old bachelor New Englander with thirty years of army service, including West Point, the Mexican War, the Kansas border troubles, and frontier Indian uprisings, in all of which he had shown a good deal more of plodding dependability than of flash — had difficulty in maintaining the unruffled disposition for which he was beloved. Even the peremptory dispatch received last night, after the uproar subsided in the thickets across the way, had left him somewhat puzzled. Hooker told him to "cross the Rappahannock at Fredericksburg on receipt of this order," which was clear enough, so far as the words themselves went; but what did it mean? Surely the army commander knew he was already across the Rappahannock, and in fact had been across it for the past three days. . . . Deciding that it meant what it ought to mean, he told Gibbon, whose division was still at Falmouth, to cross the river at dawn and seize the west-bank town, preparatory to joining in the attack Sedgwick was planning to launch against the fortified ridge with his other three divisions. He had not taken part in the December battle, having been laid up with three wounds received at Antietam, but he knew well enough what Burnside had encountered on this ground. For a time, indeed, it appeared that Sedgwick was going to do no better, despite his usual methodical preparations. After feinting on the left and right, he sent ten regiments in mass against the sunken road at the foot of the heights where so many men had come to grief, five months ago, when two of Longstreet's divisions held this section of the line. Now, however, so well had the feints misled the defenders, all that were there were two slim regiments and sixteen guns. Even so, the first two assaults were bloodily repulsed. As the bluecoats dropped back into the swale for a breather, preparatory to giving the thing another try, the colonel of a Wisconsin regiment made a short speech to the men who would lead the third assault. "When the signal *forward* is given you will advance at double-quick," he told them. "You will not fire a gun and you will not stop until you get the order to halt." He paused briefly, then added: "You will never get that order."

The Badgers gulped, absorbing the shock of this, then cheered and went in fast, the other nine regiments following close on their heels. Beyond the stone wall to their front, Barksdale's two Mississippi regiments turned loose with everything they had, attempting to shatter the head of the column of assault, while four batteries of the Washington Artillery, a crack New Orleans outfit, broke into a frenzied roar on the ridge beyond. The attackers took their losses and kept going, over the wall and among the defenders with the bayonet, then across the sunken road and up the slope of Marye's Heights with scarcely a pause, staring directly into the muzzles of the flaming guns on the crest. These too were taken in a rush as the cannoneers got off a final volley and broke for the rear. Within half an hour, and at a cost of no more than 1500 casualties, Sedgwick had his flags aflutter on ground that Burnside had spent 6300 men for no more than a fairly close-up look at, back in December. The bluecoats went into a victory dance, hurrahing and thumping each other on the back in celebration of their triumph; whereas the Confederates, several hundred of whom had been captured, were correspondingly dejected or wrathful, depending on the individual reaction to defeat. One cannoneer, who had managed to get away at the last moment, just as the Union wave broke over his battery, was altogether furious. "Guns be damned!" he replied hotly when a reserve artillerist twitted him by asking where his guns were. "I reckon now the people of the Southern Confederacy are satisfied that Barksdale's Brigade and the Washington Artillery can't whip the whole damned Yankee army!"

Having broken Jubal Early's line and thrown him into retreat, Sedgwick would have enjoyed pursuing his West Point classmate down the Telegraph Road, but another classmate, Hooker himself, had forbidden this by insisting that he push westward without delay, so that between them, as Fighting Joe put it, they could "use up" Lee. Moreover, at 10 o'clock — less than an hour after being stunned by the split pillar, and at about the same time, as it turned out, that his forward defenses began to come unglued — Hooker had his adjutant send Sedgwick a dispatch reminding him of his primary mission: "You will hurry up your column. The enemy's right flank now rests near the plank road at Chancellorsville, all exposed. You will attack at once." This reached Sedgwick at about 11.30, amid the victory celebration on Marye's Heights, and he did what he could to comply. Leaving Gibbon to hold Fredericksburg in his rear, he began to prepare

Smoke rises off Marye's Heights, seen in the distance of this panoramic view of Fredericksburg taken on May 3 from the east bank of the Rappahannock.

his other three divisions for the advance on Lee. It was a time-consuming business, however, to break up the celebration and get the troops into formation for the march. The lead division did not get started until 2 o'clock, and it was brought to a sudden halt within the hour, just over a mile from Marye's Heights, by the sight of Confederate skirmishers in position along a ridge athwart the road. Despite Hooker's assurance that Lee's flank was "all exposed," the graybacks seemed quite vigilant, and what was more they appeared to be present in considerable strength, with guns barking aggressively in support. Sedgwick was obliged to halt and deploy in the face of the resistance, at the cost of burning more daylight.

Slowly the rebels faded back, bristling as they went, leapfrogging their guns from ridge to ridge and flailing the pursuers all the time. Near Salem Church, a mile ahead and a mile short of the junction of the plank road and the turnpike, they stiffened. It was 4 o'clock by now; the day was going fast, and Sedgwick was still a good half-dozen miles from Chancellorsville. Without waiting for the others to come up, he sent the troops of his lead division forward on the run. At first they made headway, driving the graybacks before them, but then they encountered a heavy line of battle. Repulsed, they came streaming back across the fields. The second division was up by now, however, with the third not far behind, and between them they managed to check the pursuit,

though by the time Sedgwick got them rallied and into attack formation the day was too far gone for fighting. Aware by now that he had run into something considerably stronger than a mere rear guard, he set up a perimetrical defense and passed the word for his 22,000 soldiers to bed down.

Today had been a hard day. Tomorrow gave promise of being even harder. He had set out to put the squeeze on Lee, but it had begun to seem to him that he was the one in danger now. All around him, south and east as well as west, he could hear enemy columns moving in the darkness. "Sedgwick scarcely slept that night," an observant soldier later recalled. "From time to time he dictated a dispatch to General Hooker. He would walk for a few paces apart and listen; then returning he would lie down again in the damp grass, with his saddle for a pillow, and try to sleep. The night was inexpressibly gloomy."

★ ★ ★   **T**he night was inexpressibly gloomy, and he was in graver danger than he knew. All that had stood in his way at the outset, when he began his march from Marye's Heights, had been a single brigade of Alabamians, stationed for the past three days on outpost duty at Banks Ford, from which point their commander, Brigadier General Cadmus Wilcox, had shifted them, on his own initiative, when he learned that Early's defenses had been pierced. Determined to do what he could to protect Lee's unguarded rear, he had taken up a position athwart the plank road, spreading his men in the semblance of a stout line of skirmishers, and thus had managed to bluff Sedgwick into caution, delaying his advance until McLaws had had time to post his division near Salem Church and rock the charging bluecoats on their heels. As a result, when darkness ended the fighting here to the east of Chancellorsville, Lee had what he had been hoping for: a more or less stable situation and the opportunity, as he had said, to "attend to Mr Sedgwick." Early, he learned, had retreated only a couple of miles down the Telegraph Road, then had halted on finding that he was unpursued. Lee wrote him, just after sunset, that McLaws was confronting the Federals east of Salem Church; "If . . . you could come upon their left flank, and communicate with General McLaws, I think you would demolish them." A similar message went to McLaws, instructing him to coöperate with Early. "It is necessary to beat the enemy," Lee told him, "and I hope you will do it."

A dawn reconnaissance — Monday now: May 4 — showed Hooker's intrenchments well laid out and greatly strengthened overnight, the flanks securely anchored below and above the U.S. Ford escape hatch, and the whole supported by batteries massed in depth. While this discouraged attack, it also seemed to indicate that the Federals had gone entirely on the defensive in the region north of Chancellorsville. At any rate Lee proceeded on that assumption. Canceling a projected feeling-out of the enemy lines along Mineral Spring Run, he shifted half of Heth's division from the far left, beyond Colston and Rodes, to take up Anderson's position on the right, and ordered Anderson east to join with McLaws and Early in removing the threat to his rear. His plan, if daring, was simple enough. Stuart and the 25,000 survivors of Jackson's flanking column were given the task of keeping Hooker's 80,000 penned in their breastworks, while the remaining 22,000 Confederates disposed of Sedgwick, who had about the same number to the east. This last was now the main effort, and Lee decided to supervise it in person. Riding over to Salem Church at noon, he conferred with McLaws, who was awaiting Anderson's arrival before completing his dispositions for attack, and then proceeded east, skirting the southward bulge of Sedgwick's perimeter, to see Early. He found him on Marye's Heights, which he had reoccupied soon after sunrise, posting the remnant of Barksdale's brigade in the sunken road to resist another possible advance by Gibbon, who had retired into Fredericksburg. The plan of attack, as McLaws and Early had worked it out, was for Anderson to take up a position between them, confronting Sedgwick from the south, while they moved against him, simultaneously, from the east and west. The result, if all went well, would be his destruction. Lee gave his approval, though he saw that this would involve a good deal of maneuvering over difficult terrain, and rode back toward the center.

It was past 2 o'clock by now, and Anderson was not yet in position. Time was running out for Lee today, as it had done the day before for Sedgwick. Already he was finding what it cost him to be deprived even temporarily of the services of Jackson, of whom he would say before the week was over: "He has lost his left arm, but I have lost my right." More hours were spent examining the approaches and correcting the alignment of the columns so as to avoid collisions. While Anderson continued to balk, McLaws was strangely apathetic and Early floundered in the ravines across the way; it was 6 o'clock before all the troops were in position and the signal guns were fired. The fighting was savage at scattered points, especially on Early's front, but McLaws got lost in a

On May 4, Lafayette McLaws advanced his Confederate troops to the east of Salem Church against John Sedgwick's I Corps.

maze of thickets and scarcely made contact, either with the enemy or with Anderson, whose men added to the confusion by firing into each other as they advanced. Fog thickened the dusk and the disjointed movement lurched to a halt within an hour. Sedgwick had been shaken, though hardly demolished. Anxious to exploit his gains, such as they were, before the Federals reintrenched or got away across the river, Lee for the first time in his career ordered a night attack. While the artillery shelled Banks Ford in the darkness, attempting to seal off the exit, the infantry groped about in the fog, dog-tired, and made no progress. At first light, the skirmishers recovered their sense of direction, pushed forward, and found that the works to their front were empty; Sedgwick had escaped. Though his casualties had been heavy — worse than 4600 in all, including the men lost earlier — he had got his three divisions to safety across a bridge the engineers had thrown a mile below Banks Ford, well beyond range of the all-night interdictory fire.

Word came presently from Barksdale that Gibbon too had recrossed the river at Fredericksburg and cut his pontoons loose from the west bank. This meant that for the first time in three days no live, uncaptured bluecoats remained on the Confederate side of the Rappahannock except the ones intrenched above Chancellorsville; Lee had abolished the threat to his rear. Though he was far from satisfied, having failed in another of a lengthening sequence of attempts to destroy a considerable segment of the Union army, he had at least restored — and even improved — the situation that had existed yesterday, when he was preparing to give Hooker his undivided attention. Once more intent on destruction, he allowed the men of McLaws and Anderson no rest, but ordered them to take up the march back to Chancellorsville, intending for them to resume the offensive they had abandoned for Sedgwick's sake the day before. Stuart reported that the Federals, though still present in great strength behind their V, had made no attempt to move against him, either yesterday or so far this morning; yet Lee did what he could to hasten the march westward, not so much out of fear that Hooker would lash out at Stuart, whom he outnumbered better than three to one, as out of fear that he would do as Sedgwick had done and make his escape across the river before the Confederates had time to reconcentrate and crush him.

★ ★ ★ *I*n point of fact, Lee's fears on the latter count were more valid than he had any way of knowing, not having attended a council of war held the night before at his opponent's headquarters. At midnight, while Sedgwick was beginning his withdrawal across the Rappahannock, Hooker had called his other corps commanders together to vote on whether they should do the same. Couch, Reynolds, Meade, Howard, and Sickles reported promptly, but Slocum, who had the farthest to come, did not arrive until after the meeting had broken up. Hooker put the question to them — remarking, as Couch would recall, "that his instructions compelled him to cover Washington, not to jeopardize the army, etc." — then retired to let them talk it over among themselves. Reynolds was much fatigued from loss of sleep; he lay down in one corner of the tent to get some rest, telling Meade to vote his proxy for attack. Meade did so, adding his own vote to that effect. Howard too was for taking the offensive; for unlike Meade and Reynolds, whose two corps had scarcely fired a shot, he had a reputation to retrieve. Couch on the other hand voted to withdraw, but made it clear that he favored such a course only because Hooker was still in charge. Sickles, whose corps had suffered almost as many casualties as any two of the other five combined, was in favor of pulling back at once, Hooker or no Hooker. Fighting Joe returned, was given the three-to-two opinion, and adjourned the council with the announcement that he intended to withdraw the army beyond the river as soon as possible. As the generals left the tent, Reynolds broke out angrily, quite loud enough for Hooker to overhear him: "What was the use of calling us together at this time of night when he intended to retreat anyhow?"

Their instructions were to cut whatever roads were necessary, leading from their present positions back to U.S. Ford, while the army engineers were selecting a strong inner line, anchored a mile above and a mile below the two pontoon bridges, for Meade's corps to occupy in covering the withdrawal. All were hard at work on their various assignments before dawn on the 5th, at which time Hooker crossed in person, accompanied by his staff. Then at noon, with the pull-back to the inner line completed, rain began to fall.

It fell in earnest, developing quickly into what one diarist called "a tremendous cold storm." By midnight the river had risen six feet, endangering the bridges and interrupting the retreat before more than a handful of regiments had reached the opposite bank. Cut off from Hooker, Couch believed he saw his chance. "We will stay where we are and fight it out," he announced. But peremptory orders arrived at 2 a.m. for the movement to be continued. One of the bridges was cannibalized to piece out the other, and the crossing was resumed. By midmorning Wednesday, May 6, it was completed. Except for the dead and missing, who would not be coming back, the army's week-long excursion south of the river had come full circle.

Lee was up by then, after being delayed by the storm the day before, but when his skirmishers pushed forward through the dripping woods they found the enemy gone. He lost his temper at the news and scolded the brigadier who brought it. "That is the way you young men always do," he fumed. "You allow those people to get away. I tell you what to do, but you won't do it!" He gestured impatiently. "Go after them, and damage them all you can!" But no further damage was possible; the bluecoats were well beyond his reach. At a cost of less than 13,000 casualties he had inflicted more than 17,000 and had won

*Oliver O. Howard
was one of several
commanders blamed
by Joseph Hooker for
the Federal defeat at
Chancellorsville.*

what future critics would call the most brilliant victory of his career, but he was by no means satisfied. He had aimed at total capture or annihilation of the foe, and the extent to which he had fallen short of this was, to his mind, the extent to which he had failed. Leaving a few regiments to tend the wounded, bury the dead, and glean the spoils abandoned by the Unionists on the field, he marched the rest of his army back through the rain-drenched Wilderness to Fredericksburg and the comparative comfort of the camps it had left a week ago, when word first came that the enemy was across the Rappahannock.

Back at Falmouth that evening, while his army straggled eastward in his wake, Hooker learned that Stoneman's raid, from which so much had been expected, had been almost a total failure. Intending, as he later reported, to "magnify our small force into overwhelming numbers," the cavalryman had broken up his column into fragments, none of which, as it turned out, had been strong enough to do more than temporary damage to the installations in Lee's rear. According to one disgusted trooper, "Our only accomplishments were the burning of a few canal boats on the upper James River, some bridges, hen roosts, and tobacco houses." Stoneman returned the way he had come, recrossing at Raccoon Ford on the morning of May 7, while other portions of his scattered column turned up as far away as Yorktown. His total losses, in addition to about 1000 horses broken down and abandoned, were 82 men killed and wounded and 307 missing. These figures seemed to Hooker to prove that Stoneman had not been seriously engaged, and it was not long before he removed him from command. However, his own casualties, while quite as heavy as anyone on his own side of the line could have desired — the ultimate total was 17,287, as compared to Lee's 12,821 — were equally condemning, though in a different way, since a breakdown of them indicated the disjointed manner in which he had fought and refrained from fighting the battle. Meade and Reynolds, for example, had lost fewer than 1000 men between them, while Sedgwick and Sickles had lost more than four times that number each. Obviously Lincoln's parting admonition, "Put in all your men," had been ignored. Hooker was quick to place the blame for his defeat on Stoneman, Averell, Howard, and Sedgwick, sometimes singly and at other times collectively. It was only in private, and some weeks later, that he was able to see, or at any rate confess, where the real trouble had lain. "I was not hurt by a shell, and I was not drunk," he told a fellow officer. "For once I lost confidence in Joe Hooker, and that is all there is to it."

In time that would become the registered consensus, but for the present many of his compatriots were hard put to understand how such a disaster had come about. Horace Greeley staggered into the *Tribune* managing editor's office Thursday morning, his face a ghastly color and his lips trembling. "My God, it is horrible," he exclaimed. "Horrible. And to think of it — 130,000 magnificent soldiers so cut to pieces by less than 60,000 half-starved ragamuffins!" An Episcopal clergyman, also in New York, could not reconcile the various reports and rumors he recorded in his diary that night. "It would seem that Hooker has beaten Lee, and that Lee has beaten Hooker; that we have taken Fredericksburg, and that the rebels have taken it also; that we have 4500 prisoners, and the rebels 5400; that Hooker has cut off Lee's retreat, and Lee has cut off Sedgwick's retreat, and Sedgwick has cut off everybody's retreat generally, but has retreated himself although his retreat was cut off. . . . In short, all is utter confusion. Everything seems to be everywhere, and everybody all over, and there is no getting at any truth." Official Washington was similarly confused and dismayed. When Sumner of Massachusetts heard that Hooker had been whipped, he flung up his hands and struck an attitude of despair. "Lost — lost," he groaned. "All is lost!" But the hardest-hit man of them all was Lincoln, whose hopes had had the longest way to fall. Six months ago, on the heels of Emancipation, he had foreseen clear sailing for the ship of state provided the helmsman kept a steady hand on the tiller. "We are like whalers who have been on a long chase," he told a friend. "We have at last got the harpoon into the monster, but we must now look how we steer, or with one flop of his tail he will send us all into eternity." Then had come Fredericksburg, and he had said: "If there is a worse place than Hell, I am in it." Now there was this, a still harder flop of the monster's tail, and Hooker and the Army of the Potomac had gone sprawling. Even before the news arrived, a White House caller had found the President "anxious and harassed beyond any power of description." Yet this was nothing compared to his reaction later in the day, when he reappeared with a telegram in his hand. "News from the army," he said in a trembling voice. The visitor read that Hooker was in retreat, and looking up saw that Lincoln's face, "usually sallow, was ashen in hue. The paper on the wall behind him was of the tint known as 'French gray,' and even in that moment of sorrow . . . I vaguely took in the thought that the complexion of the anguished President's visage was like that of the wall." He walked up and down the room, hands clasped behind his back. "My God, my God," he exclaimed as he paced back and forth. "What will the country say? What will the country say?"

Within the ranks of the army itself, slogging down the muddy roads toward Falmouth, the reaction was not unlike the New York clergy-man's. "No one seems to understand this move," a Pennsylvania private wrote, "but I have no doubt it is all right." He belonged to Meade's corps, which had seen very little fighting, and he could not quite comprehend that what he had been involved in was a defeat. All he knew for certain was that the march back to camp was a hard one. "Most of the way the mud was over shoe, in some places knee deep, and the rain made our loads terrible to tired shoulders." Others knew well enough that they had taken part in a fiasco. "Go boil your shirt!" was their reply to jokes attempted by roadside stragglers. Turning the matter over in their minds, they could see that Hooker had been trounced, but they could not see that this applied to themselves, who had fought as well as ever — except, of course, the unregenerate Dutchmen — whenever and wherever they got the chance. Mostly, though, they preferred to ignore the question of praise or blame. "And thus ends the second attempt on the capture of Fredericksburg," a Maine soldier recorded when he got back to Falmouth. "I have nothing to say about it in any way. I have no opinions to express about the Gen'ls or the men nor do I wish to. I leave it in the hands of God. I don't want to think of it at all."

★   ★   ★   **U**nquestionably, this latest addition to the lengthening roster of Confederate victories was a great one. Indeed, considering the odds that had been faced and overcome, it was perhaps in terms of glory the greatest of them all; *Chancellorsville* would be stitched with pride across the crowded banners of the Army of Northern Virginia. But its ultimate worth, as compared to its cost, depended in large measure on the outcome of Stonewall Jackson's present indisposition. As Lee had said on Sunday morning, when he first learned that his lieutenant had been wounded, "Any victory is dearly bought which deprives us of the services of General Jackson, even for a short time."

★

So far — that is, up to the time when Hooker threw in the sponge and the northern army fell back across the Rappahannock — Dr McGuire's prognosis had been most encouraging and the general himself had been in excellent spirits, despite the loss of his arm. "I am wounded but not depressed," he said when he woke from the sleep that followed the amputation. "I believe it was according to God's will, and I can wait until He makes his object known to me." Presently, when Lee's midday note was brought, congratulating him on the victory, "which is due to your skill and energy," Jackson permitted himself the one criticism he had ever made of his commander. "General Lee is very kind," he said, "but he should give the praise to God." Next day, May 4, with Sedgwick threatening the army's rear, he was removed to safety in an ambulance. The route was south to Todd's Tavern, then southeast, through Spotsylvania Court House, to Guiney Station, where he had met his wife and child, two weeks ago today, to begin the idyl that had ended with the news that Hooker was on the march. All along the way, country people lined the roadside to watch the ambulance go by. They brought with them, and held out for the attendants to accept, such few gifts as their larders afforded in these hard times, cool buttermilk, hot biscuits, and fried chicken. Jackson was pleased by this evidence of their concern, and for much of the 25-mile journey he chatted with an aide, even responding to a question as to what he thought of Hooker's plan for the battle whose guns rumbled fainter as the ambulance rolled south. "It was in the main a good conception, sir; an excellent plan. But he should not have sent away his cavalry. That was his great blunder. It was that which enabled me to turn him, without his being aware of it, and to take him by the rear." Of his own share in frustrating that plan, he added that he believed his flank attack had been "the most successful movement of my life. But I have received more credit for it than I deserve. Most men will think that I had planned it all from the first; but it was not so. I simply took advantage of circumstances as they were presented to me in the providence of God. I feel that His hand led me."

By nightfall he was resting comfortably in a cottage on the Chandler estate near Guiney Station. He slept soundly, apparently free from pain, and woke next morning much refreshed. His wounds seemed to give him little trouble; primary intention and granulation were under way. All that day and the next, Tuesday and Wednesday, he rested easy, talking mainly of religious matters, as had always been his custom in times of relaxation. The doctor foresaw a rapid recovery and an early return to duty. Then — late Wednesday night and early Thursday morning, May 7 — a sudden change occurred. McGuire woke at dawn to find his patient restless and in severe discomfort. Examination showed that the general faced a new and formidable enemy: pneumonia. He was cupped, then given mercury, with antimony and opium, and morphine to ease his pain. From that time on, as the drugs took effect and the pneumonia followed its inexorable course, he drifted in and out of sleep and fuddled consciousness. His wife arrived at midday, having been delayed by Stoneman's raiders, to find him greatly changed from the husband she had left eight days ago. Despite advance warning, she was shocked at the sight of his wounds, especially the mutilated arm. Moreover, his cheeks were flushed, his breathing oppressed, and his senses numbed. At first he scarcely knew her, but presently, in a more lucid moment, he saw her anxiety and told her: "You must not wear a long face. I love cheerfulness and brightness in a sickroom." He lapsed into stupor, then woke again to find her still beside him. "My darling, you are very much loved," he murmured. "You are one of the most precious little wives in the world." Toward evening, he seemed to improve. Once at least, in the course of the night, he appeared to be altogether himself again. "Will you take this, General?" the doctor asked, bending over the bed with a dose of medicine. Stonewall looked at him sternly. "Do your duty," he said. Then, seeing the doctor hesitate, he repeated the words quite firmly: "Do your duty." Still later, those in the room were startled to hear him call out to his adjutant, Alexander Pendleton, who was in Fredericksburg with Lee: "Major Pendleton, send in and see if there is higher ground back of Chancellorsville! I must find out if there is high ground between Chancellorsville and the river. . . . Push up the columns; hasten the columns! Pendleton, you take charge of that. . . . Where is Pendleton? Tell him to push up the columns." In his delirium he was back on the field of battle, doing the one thing he did best in all the world.

All that day and the next, which was Saturday, he grew steadily worse; McGuire sent word to Fredericksburg and Richmond that recovery was doubtful. Lee could not believe a righteous cause would suffer such a blow. "Surely General Jackson will recover," he said. "God will not take him from us now that we need him so much." The editor of the Richmond *Whig* agreed. "We need have no fears for Jackson," he wrote. "He is no accidental manifestation of the powers of faith and courage. He came not by chance in this day and to this generation. He was born for a purpose, and not until that purpose is fulfilled will his great soul take flight." Jackson himself inclined to this belief that he would be spared for a specific purpose. "I am not afraid to die," he said in a lucid moment Friday. "I am willing to abide by the will of my Heavenly Father. But I do not believe I shall die at this time. I am persuaded the Almighty has yet a work for me to perform." On Saturday, when he was asked to name a hymn he would like to hear sung, he requested "Shew Pity, Lord," Isaac Watts's paraphrase of the Fifty-first Psalm:

> *"Shew pity, Lord; O Lord, forgive;*
>
> *Let a repenting rebel live —"*

This seemed to comfort him for a time, but night brought a return of suffering. He tossed sleepless, mumbling battle orders. Though these were mostly unintelligible, it was observed that he called most often on A. P. Hill, his hardest-hitting troop commander, and Wells Hawks, his commissary officer, as if even in delirium he strove to preserve a balance between tactics and logistics.

Sunday, May 10, dawned fair and clear; McGuire informed Anna Jackson that her husband could not last the day. She knelt at the bedside of the unconscious general, telling him over and over that he would "very soon be in heaven." Presently he stirred and opened his eyes. She asked him, "Do you feel willing to acquiesce in God's allotment if He will you to go today?" He watched her. "I prefer it," he said, and she pressed the point: "Well, before this day closes you will be with the blessed Savior in his glory." There was a pause. "I will be the infinite gainer to be translated," Jackson said as he dozed off again. He woke at noon, and once more she broached the subject, telling him that he would be gone before sundown. This time he seemed to understand her better. "Oh no; you are frightened, my child. Death is not so near. I may yet get well." She broke into tears, sobbing that the doctor had said there was no hope. Jackson summoned McGuire. "Doctor, Anna informs me that you have told her I am to die today. Is it so?" When McGuire replied that it was so, the general seemed to ponder. Then he said, "Very good, very good. It is all right." After a time he added, "It is the Lord's day; my wish is fulfilled. I have always desired to die on Sunday."

At 1.30 the doctor told him he had no more than a couple of hours to live. "Very good; it's all right," Jackson replied as before, but more weakly, for his breathing was high in his throat by now. When McGuire offered him brandy to keep up his strength, he shook his head. "It will only delay my departure, and do no good," he protested. "I want to preserve my mind, if possible, to the last." Presently, though, he was back in delirium, alternately praying and giving commands, all of which had to do with the offensive. Shortly after 3 o'clock, a few minutes before he died, he called out: "Order A. P. Hill to prepare for action! Pass the infantry to the front. . . . Tell Major Hawks — " He left the sentence unfinished, seeming thus to have put the war behind him; for he smiled as he spoke his last words, in a tone of calm relief. "Let us cross over the river," he said, "and rest under the shade of the trees."

★   ★   ★

A regiment of Illinois cavalry, possibly part of Colonel Benjamin Grierson's command just arrived from Tennessee, camps outside Baton Rouge in May 1863.

Grant's Plan; The Run; Grierson

1863 ★ ★ ★ ★ ★ While Hooker was crossing the Rappahannock, unaware as yet that he would come to grief within a week, Grant, having caught what he believed was a gleam of victory through the haze of cigar smoke in the former ladies' cabin of the *Magnolia*, was putting the final improvisatorial touches to a plan of campaign that would open, two days later, with a crossing of the greatest river of them all. He too might come to grief, as two of his three chief lieutenants feared and even predicted, but he was willing to risk it for the sake of the prize, which had grown in value with every sore frustration. As spring advanced and the roads emerged from the drowned lands adjacent to the Mississippi — although so far they were little more than trails of slime through the surrounding ooze, not quite firm enough for wagons nor quite wet enough for boats — the Illinois general, with seven failures behind him in the course of the three months he had spent attempting to take or by-pass Vicksburg, reverted in early April to what he had told Halleck in mid-January, before he left Memphis to assume command in person of the expedition four hundred miles downriver: "[I] think our troops must get below the city to be used effectively."

His plan, in essence, was to march his army down the Louisiana bank to a position well south of the fortified bluff, then cross the river and establish a bridgehead from which to assail the Confederate bastion from the rear. The

★

Duckport canal, designed to give his transports access to Walnut and Round-away bayous, and thus allow them to avoid exposure to the plunging fire of the batteries at Vicksburg and Warrenton, had failed; only one small steamer had got through before the water level fell too low for navigation; but exploration of the route had shown that, by bridging those slews that could not be avoided by following the crests of levees flanking the horseshoe curves of the several bayous, it might be practicable to march dry-shod all the way from Milliken's Bend to New Carthage, a west-bank hamlet about midway between Warrenton and Grand Gulf, third of the rebel east-bank strongholds. In late March, by way of preparation, Grant had assigned McClernand the task of putting this route into shape for a march by his own corps as well as the two others, which would follow. This, if it worked, would get the army well south of its objective. Getting the troops across the river was quite another matter, however, depending as it did on the coöperation of the navy, which, as Grant said, "was absolutely essential to the success (even to the contemplation) of such an enterprise." For the navy to get below, in position to ferry the men across and cover the east-bank landing, it would have to run the batteries, and this had been shown in the past to be an expensive proposition even for armored vessels, let alone the brittle-skinned transports which would be required for the ferrying operation. Moreover, Porter was no more under Grant's command than Grant was under Porter's. The most Grant could do was "request" that the run be made. But that was enough, as it turned out. The admiral — who had returned only the week before from the near-disastrous Steele Bayou expedition, considerably the worse for wear and with his boats still being hammered back into shape — expressed an instant willingness to give the thing a try, though not without first warning of what the consequences would be, not only in the event of initial failure but also in the event of initial success, so far at least as the navy was concerned. He could make a downstream run, he said, and in fact had proved it twice already with the ill-fated *Queen of the West* and the equally ill-fated *Indianola*, but his under-powered vessels could never attempt a slow-motion return trip, against the four-knot current, until Vicksburg had been reduced. "You must recollect that when these gunboats once go below we give up all hopes of ever getting them up again," he replied, wanting it understood from the start that this would be an all-or-nothing venture. Moreover: "If I do send vessels below, it will be the best vessels I have, and there will be nothing left to attack Haines Bluff, in case it should be deemed necessary to try it." Grant replied on April 2 that McClernand's men were already at work on the circuitous thirty-mile road down to New Carthage; he had no intention of turning back, even if that had been possible; and in any case Haines Bluff had cost the army blood enough by now. "I would, Admiral, therefore renew my request to prepare for running the blockade at as early a day as possible."

Despite the doubts of others, General Ulysses S. Grant was determined to besiege the Mississippi River stronghold of Confederate Vicksburg from the south.

Two days later he wrote Halleck: "My expectation is for a portion of the naval fleet to run the batteries of Vicksburg, whilst the army moves through by this new route [to New Carthage]. Once there, I will move either to Warrenton or Grand Gulf; most probably the latter. From either of these points there are good roads to Vicksburg, and from Grand Gulf there is a good road to Jackson and the Black River Bridge without crossing the Black River." Much could be said for making the landing at either place. Warrenton, for example, was some fifteen air-line miles closer to his objective. But he knew well enough that a straight line was not always the surest connection between two military points. A Grand Gulf landing, in addition to giving him access to Vicksburg's main artery of supply, would also afford him a chance to supplement his own. By holding the newly established bridgehead with part of his army and sending the balance downstream to assist in the reduction of Port Hudson by Banks, who presumably was working his way upstream at the same time, he then would have an unbroken, all-weather connection with New Orleans and would no longer be exclusively and precariously dependent on what could be brought down from Memphis, first by steamboat, then by wagon over the new road skirting the west-bank complex of bayous across from the fortified bluff, and then again by steamboat in order to get the supplies over the river and into the east-bank bridgehead. Grant pondered the alternatives, and by April 11, a week after the dispatch giving Halleck a brief statement of the problem, he had made his choice: "Grand Gulf is the point at which I expect to strike, and send an army corps to Port Hudson to coöperate with General Banks."

He did not know how Old Brains, whose timidity had been demonstrated in situations far less risky than this one, would react to a plan of campaign that involved 1) exposing the irreplaceable Union fleet to instantaneous destruction by batteries that had been sited on commanding and impregnable heights with just that end in mind, 2) crossing a mile-wide river in order to throw his troops into the immediate rear of a rebel force of unknown strength which, holding as it did the interior lines, presumably could be reinforced more quickly than his own, and 3) remaining dependent all the while, or at least until the problematical capture of Port Hudson, on a supply line that was not only tenuous to the point of inadequacy, but was also subject to being cut by enemy intervention or obliterated by some accident of nature, by no means unusual at this season, such as a week of unrelenting rain, a sudden rise of the river, and a resultant overflow that would re-drown the west-bank lowlands and the improvised road that wound its way around and across the curving bayous and treacherous morasses into which a wagon or a gun could disappear completely, leaving no more trace than a man or a mule whose bones had been picked clean by gars

Every member of Grant's own staff considered the proposed operation not only overrisky and unwise, but also downright unmilitary.

and crawfish. Whether Halleck would approve the taking of all these risks, Grant did not know; but he was left in no such doubt as to the reaction closer at hand. So far, of his three corps commanders, only his archrival McClernand had indicated anything resembling enthusiasm for the plan. Hard at work constructing makeshift bridges from materials found along the designated route to New Carthage, which he reached before mid-April, the former Illinois politician was in high spirits and predicted great results, for both the country and himself, because his corps had been assigned to lead the way. By contrast, though perhaps for the same reason — that is, because the nonprofessional McClernand had the lead — Sherman and McPherson, along with Dana and practically every member of Grant's own staff, considered the proposed operation not only overrisky and unwise, but also downright unmilitary. Sherman in fact was so alarmed at the prospect that he sat down and wrote Grant a long letter, insisting that the proper course would be for the army to return at once to Memphis and resume from there the overland advance along the Mississippi Central, abandoned in December. When his friend and chief replied that he had no intention of canceling his plans, Sherman had no choice except to go along with them, although he still did not approve. "I confess I don't like this roundabout project," he told one of his division commanders, "but we must support Grant in whatever he undertakes." He was loyal and he would remain so, but he also remained glum, writing home even as he ordered his men out of their camps at Milliken's Bend to join the movement: "I feel in its success less confidence than in any similar undertaking of the war."

Porter too had doubts as to the over-all wisdom of Grant's plan, as well as fears in regard to the specific risk the plan required the navy to assume, but he took no counsel of them aside from the more or less normal precautions the prospect of such exposure always prompted, as in the case of a farmer sending eggs to market in a springless wagon over a bumpy road. Unlike Sherman, he wrote no Cassandran letters and made no protest after his initial warning that once the fleet had gone below it could not come back up again until the batteries had been silenced in its rear. Instead, he kept busy preparing his crews and vessels for the passage of bluffs that bristled with 40-odd pieces of artillery, light and heavy, manned by cannoneers whose skill had improved with every chance to show it. By April 16 he was ready. Seven armored gunboats, mounting a total of 79 guns, were assigned to make the run, accompanied by three army transports, loaded with commissary stores instead of troops, and a steam ram captured the year before at Memphis when the Confederate flotilla was abolished in a brief half-morning's fight. At 9.30, two hours after dusk gave way to a starry but moonless night, the column cleared the mouth of the Yazoo, Porter leading aboard the flagship *Benton.*

The "run," so called, was in fact more creep than sprint, however, at least in its early stages; stealth was the watchword up and down the line of eleven boats steaming southward in single file on the dark chocolate surface of what one observer called "the great calm river, more like a long winding lake than a stream." Furnaces had been banked in advance, so as to show a minimum of smoke. All ports were covered and all deck lights doused, except for hooded lanterns visible only from dead astern for guidance. It was hoped that such pre-cautions would hide the column from prying eyes. To reduce the likelihood of noise, which also might give the movement away, low speed was prescribed and exhaust pipes were diverted from the stacks to the paddle boxes, where the hiss of steam would be muffled. Pets and poultry were put ashore, moreover, lest a sudden mewing or cackling alert the rebel sentries. The admiral was leaving as little as possible to chance; but in the event of discovery he was prepared to shift at once from stealth to boldness. Coal-laden barges were lashed to the starboard flanks of the warships, leaving their port-side weapons free to take up any challenge from the high-sited batteries on the Mississippi shore, and water-soaked bales of hay were stacked around the otherwise unprotected boilers and pilot houses of the transports. Instructed to maintain a fifty-yard interval, each helmsman was also told to steer a little to one side of the boat he followed, so as not to have to slow engines or change course to avoid a collision in case of a breakdown up ahead. Thus, though he wanted no trouble he could avoid, Porter was prepared to give as well as receive it in the event that his carefully woven veil of secrecy was ripped away. Passing Young's Point at about 10.30, the dark and silent column swung north as it approached the mouth of Sherman's abandoned canal, then rounded the final turn at 11 sharp, altering course again from north to south, and headed down the straightaway eastern shank of the hairpin bend that led past Vicksburg's dark and silent bluff. Ten minutes later all hell broke loose.

Grant was there to see the show, and he had his two families with him, one military and the other personal, the former consisting of his staff, the latter of his wife and their two sons, who had come downriver from Illinois to afford him a sort of furlough-in-reverse. Both were gathered tonight on the upper deck of the *Magnolia*, which was anchored three miles below Young's Point, just beyond range of the heaviest enemy guns, so that they watched as if from a box in a darkened theater, awaiting the raising of the curtain. The general and Mrs Grant occupied deck chairs near the starboard rail — front row center, as it were — with twelve-year-old Fred beside them; Ulysses Junior, who was ten, sat nearby in young Colonel Wilson's lap. Behind and on both sides of them stood twenty-odd men in uniform, staff officers and two high-ranking observers. One was Dana, who had been sent by Stanton to watch Grant, and the other was no less a personage than Adjutant General Lorenzo Thomas, who had arrived five days ago, five days after Dana, to watch them both. Or so it was said, at any rate, so deep was the supposed mistrust the War Department felt. Just now though, whatever truth there was to the rumored assignment, there was a good deal more to watch than the unimpressive-looking department commander. First there was the passage of the hooded and muffled warships, disappearing northward in the direction of the bend that swung them south toward the rebel batteries; then a long wait in the blackness; then, eastward — across the narrow tongue of land called Vicksburg Point, beyond which the dark loom of bluff reared up to blot out the low-hanging stars — a sudden burgeoning incandescence, exposed as if by a rapid lifting of the awaited curtain. The show was on. It began, so to speak, in midcrescendo as the guns came alive on the bluff and were replied to by those down on the brightly lighted river, growling full-throated, jarring the earth and water for miles around, and adding their muzzle flashes to the vivid illumination of the scene. "Magnificent, but terrible," Grant later called the sight. For the present, however, aside from ordering the younger boy to bed when he heard him whimper and saw him press his face against Wilson's chest in terror at the holocaust of flame and thunder, he said nothing. He merely smoked and watched the fireworks, holding all the while to his wife's hand. After ninety minutes of uproar, during which Dana tallied 525 shots fired by the Confederates, the bluff was once more dark and silent except for the reflection of fires still burning fitfully on the lower level where the boats had been. How much damage had been done and suffered, no one aboard the *Magnolia* could tell, although presently it was clear that some at least of the vessels had got past, for the Warrenton batteries came alive downstream, reproducing in miniature the earlier performance. Finally these too fell silent; which told the watchers exactly nothing, save that the final curtain had come down. Near and far, the fires burned out and the former blackness returned to the bluff and the river.

Unable to wait for word from below — news, perhaps, that the indispensable fleet had gone out of existence — Grant went ashore, got on his horse, and rode south under the paling stars, galloping along the crude and pot-holed road McClernand's corps had spent the past three weeks constructing. This was quite unlike the old Grant, who had never seemed in a hurry about anything at all. Something had come over him, here lately. "None who had known him the previous years could recognize him as being the same man," one officer observed. He had never seen the general ride at even a fast trot, let alone a gallop; but now, he said, "[Grant's] energies seemed to burst forth with new life," with the result that he rode at top speed practically all the time and "seemed wrought up to the last pitch of determination and energy." Shiloh and the long hot unproductive summer of 1862, the ill-wind fiasco near Iuka and the

David Porter's Federal flotilla braved nighttime fire from the batteries at Vicksburg to deliver men and supplies down river.

fruitless victory at Corinth, the period of indecision in Memphis and the recent seven failures above Vicksburg, all were behind him now; he was launched at last on an all-or-nothing effort, a go-for-broke campaign, of which the passage of the batteries by the fleet was the first stage. If this failed, all failed; he would never get his troops across the mile-wide Mississippi. It was no wonder he rode fast.

Near New Carthage about midday he drew rein and breathed a sigh of relief at the sight of the fleet riding at anchor, apparently intact. Closer inspection showed that the boats had been knocked about considerably, however. All were damaged to various degrees, some in their hulls and others in their machinery. One was missing altogether: a transport, as it turned out, set afire by repeated hits and sunk to the accompaniment of cheers from the rebel batteries. But all the rest were seaworthy, or soon would be, after the completion of repairs already under way by bluejackets swarming over their ripped-up decks and pounded bulwarks. Porter and his captains were in excellent spirits, though they were frank to admit that last night's experience had been little short of horrendous. For one thing, all their precautions involving stealth and secrecy had availed them nothing. As they proceeded, dark and silent, down the straightaway eastern shank of the hairpin bend, Confederate sentries posted in skiffs on the river spotted them quickly; whereupon some rowed eastward to give the alarm to the Vicksburg cannoneers, while others, risking capture, crossed to the opposite bank, where they set fire to prepared stacks of pitch-soaked wood, as well as to the abandoned De Soto railroad station midway up the point. Quick-leaping flames floodlighted the approaching Yankee gunboats and the alerted rebel gunners promptly took these well-defined targets under fire. Another difficulty was that the prescribed low speed left the vessels to the mercy of the eddying current, which caught them alternately on the bow and quarter, swinging them broadside to the stream and in some cases even spinning them halfway around, so that they were obliged to come full circle under the plunging fire, as if responding to cruel encores that held them on the brightly lighted stage for further pelting by an irate audience. Clear at last, they played a brief epilogue at Warrenton, then swept on south to anchor above New Carthage in the predawn darkness. Assessing damages, Porter was grateful to discover that, despite a total of 68 hits received, the transport *Henry Clay* was the flotilla's only loss. Not a man had been killed, even aboard the missing boat, and only 13 — in this case a decidedly lucky number — had been wounded. Give him a couple of days in which to complete repairs, he said, and he would be quite ready to coöperate with the army.

Grant returned to Milliken's Bend, much pleased with the outcome, and prepared for another run within the week, this time by transports alone, in order to provide more ferries for the crossing. "If I do not underestimate the enemy," he wrote Halleck on April 21, "my force is abundant, with a foothold once obtained, to do the work." Next night six river steamers, loaded with rations, forage, and medical supplies, attempted the second run under instructions "to drop noiselessly down with the current . . . and not show steam until the enemy's batteries began firing, when the boats were to use all their legs." This was an all-army show, the steamers being army-owned and manned by army volunteers, since the civilian crews had balked at exposing their persons to what they had watched six nights ago from a safe distance. Now as then, Grant was there to see the show; an Illinois private later told how he "saw standing on the upper deck of his headquarters boat a man of iron, his wife by his side. He seemed to me the most immovable figure I ever saw." Then came the fireworks across the way, the sudden illumination and the uproar of the guns on the fuming bluff. Grant took it calmly, the soldier recalled; "No word escaped his lips, no muscle of his earnest face moved." Presently the bat-

Rear Admiral David Dixon Porter's Federal fleet proved crucial to the capture of Vicksburg.

teries fell silent and word arrived from below that, now as before, only a single vessel had failed to survive the run — the steamer *Tigress*, McClernand's former headquarters boat, which Grant had ridden to Shiloh a year ago. Loaded with medicines and surgical equipment, she was hulled a dozen times or more and broke in two and sank, her skeleton crew floating downstream to safety on bits of wreckage. Once more not a man had been killed and the wounded were only a handful. Half the steamers had their engines permanently smashed, but that was no real drawback, since they would hold as many troops as ever and could be pushed or towed across the river as barges. As Grant saw it, this second run had been quite as successful as the first, and he was twice as pleased.

Belittling the loss of the *Tigress* and her cargo, which he said amounted to nothing more than "little extras for the men," he set off southward again on horseback to join Porter for a naval reconnaissance of Grand Gulf, designated as the point where the army would obtain a foothold once the navy had blasted its batteries out of existence. Porter was experiencing misgivings, and Grant, looking the place over from just beyond range of its guns on the 24th, saw that he had indeed given the navy a tough nut to crack. Its batteries were sited high, as at Donelson and Vicksburg, and what was more they seemed altogether ready for whatever came their way. "I foresee great difficulties in our present position," he informed Sherman on his return from the exploratory boat ride, "but it will not do to let these retard any movements." In this connection it seemed to him there might be a chance for an assault to succeed at last up the Yazoo, despite the previous fiasco. "It may possibly happen," he wrote Sherman, "that the enemy may so weaken his forces about Vicksburg and Haines Bluff as to make the latter vulnerable, particularly with a fall of water to give you an extended landing." However: "I leave the management of affairs at your end of the line to you," he added by way of making it clear that he was not definitely ordering an assault.

Monday, April 27, was Grant's forty-first birthday. It also marked the completion of his first-stage preparations for getting his troops across the river in order to come to grips with the rebels on dry ground, which was what he had been after from the start. By now all four divisions of McClernand's corps, having extended their march southward around Bayou Vidal and Lake Saint Joseph, were at Hard Times, Louisiana, the designated point of embarkation for the landing at Grand Gulf, five miles downstream. One of McPherson's divisions was also there and the other two were closing fast, while Sherman's three remained at Young's Point, on call to follow but held in place for the present so as to confuse the lookouts on the Vicksburg bluff. Seven warships and seven transports were available below, and though Porter was still troubled by misgivings — he thought his gunboats could suppress the Grand Gulf batteries, all right, but he warned that they might get so knocked about in the process that they would not be able to provide adequate cover for the crossing that would follow — Grant himself, as usual, expressed no doubt as to the outcome. He foresaw "great difficulties," but he did not admit that they were any occasion for delay. All he asked of the navy was that the rebel guns be silenced, after which there would be no need for cover. Before the anniversary was over, he sent McClernand word to go ahead: "Commence immediately the embarkation of your corps, or so much of it as there is transportation for."

★ ★ ★ The showdown was unquestionably at hand; but Grant was disclosing nothing he could avoid disclosing until the final moment. He had, in fact, devised three separate feints or demonstrations, two of them designed to mislead the enemy as to his chosen point of attack, well downstream, and a third whereby he hoped not only to distract his opponent by diverting his attention from front to rear, but also to add to his confusion, throughout this critical period, by disrupting the lines of supply and communication leading back into the interior of the state whose welfare and defense were the southern commander's assigned concern.

★

Sherman was organically involved in two of these, one of which had already been accomplished during the first ten days of April. Lest Pemberton call in the troops disposed to guard against a penetration of the Delta, and thereby strengthen the Vicksburg garrison in time for the showdown fight now imminent, Fred Steele's division was sent a hundred miles up the Mississippi to Greenville, where the men went ashore and thrashed about for a week in the interior, giving the impression that they were merely the advance contingent for another major drive on the Gibraltar of the West. Having done so — to the extreme alarm of the local planters, who bemoaned the attendant loss of cotton, cattle, and Negroes, and the home-guard commanders, who called loudly for reinforcements — they got back aboard their transports and rejoined Sherman at Young's Point for a share in the second and more important feint, this time against Haines Bluff. Grant had suggested it in his letter of the 24th, after a look at the Grand Gulf defenses, but now on his birthday he returned to the matter in more persuasive terms. "The effect of a heavy demonstration in that direction would be good so far as the enemy are concerned," he wrote Sherman from Hard Times, where McClernand's men were preparing to embark, "but I am loth to order it, because it would be hard to make our own troops understand that only a demonstration was intended and our people at home would characterize it as a repulse. I therefore leave it to you whether to make such a demonstration."

In referring thus to the probable adverse reaction by "our people at home," who of course would get their information from the papers, many of which were hostile — particularly toward Sherman, who returned the hostility in full measure — Grant may or may not have intended to use psychology on his journalist-hating friend. But at any rate it worked. "Does General Grant think I care what the newspapers say?" Sherman exclaimed as soon as he read the letter. And despite his growing antipathy for the strategy his superior had evolved ("I tremble for the result," he wrote his wife that week; "I look upon the whole thing as one of the most hazardous and desperate moves of this or any other war") he replied at once with a pledge of full coöperation. "We will make as strong a demonstration as possible," he declared. "The troops will all understand the purpose and not be hurt by the repulse. The people of the country must find out the truth as best they can; it is none of their business. You are engaged in a hazardous enterprise, and for good reason wish to divert attention; that is sufficient for me, and it shall be done." Warming as he wrote, the red-haired general bristled with contempt for public opinion. "The men have sense, and will trust us. As to the reports in newspapers, we must scorn them, else they will ruin us and our country. They are as much enemies to good government as the secesh, and between the two I like the secesh best, because they are a brave, open enemy and not a set of sneaking, croaking scoundrels."

Accordingly, he spent the next two days in preparation, and on the final day of April — previously designated by Lincoln, at the request of Congress, "as a day of national humiliation, fasting, and prayer" because, in the words of the proclamation, the people had "forgotten God" and become "too proud to pray" — set off up the Yazoo with ten regiments from Frank Blair's division, escorted by the flotilla remnant Porter had left behind, three gunboats, four tinclads, and three mortars, under Lieutenant Commander K. R. Breese. Intent on making the greatest possible show of strength, Sherman spread his troops over the transport decks with orders for "every man [to] look as numerous as possible." Short of Haines Bluff and near the scene of their December repulse, the bluecoats went ashore; marching and countermarching, banners flying and bands playing for all they were worth in the boggy woodland, they demonstrated in sight of the fortified line of hills, while the gunboats closed to within point-blank range of the bluff itself. For three hours the naval attack was pressed, as if in preparation for an infantry assault. However, the defenders clearly had their backs up; nor was there anything wrong with their marksmanship. The overaged *Tyler*, a veteran of all the fights since Henry, retired early with a shot below the water line, and the other two hauled off at 2 p.m. roughly handled, one having taken a total of forty-six hits. Sherman might have let it go at that, but he was determined to play out the game to full advantage. May Day morning he wrote Grant: "At 3 p.m. we will open another cannonade to prolong the diversion, and keep it up till after dark, when we shall drop down to Chickasaw and go on back to camp." The other two divisions, waiting at Young's Point under Steele and Brigadier General James M. Tuttle, were alerted for the long march to Hard Times, while Blair was told to keep up the pretense of attack until darkness afforded cover for withdrawal, at which time he would "let out for home," meaning Milliken's Bend, where he was to shield the rear of the two divisions moving southward to join Grant. Meanwhile, Sherman told him, "I will hammer away this p.m. because Major Rowley [a staff observer], now here, says that our diversion has had perfect success, great activity being seen in Vicksburg, and troops pushing up this way. By prolonging the effort, we give Grant more chance." The infantry continued to mass as if for attack, and the gunboats moved again within range of Haines Bluff, keeping up the action until 8 o'clock that evening. Then Blair's men got back aboard their transports and withdrew, returning to the west bank of the Mississippi, followed by the somewhat battered but undaunted ten-boat flotilla, which dropped anchor off the mouth of the Yazoo. Steele and Tuttle took up the march for Hard Times at first light next morning, accompanied by Sherman himself, who sent a courier ahead with a full account of the two-day affair. Casualties had been negligible, he reported, afloat and ashore. Whether matters had gone as well for Grant, far downriver at Grand Gulf, he did not know; but he was satisfied that the feint from above had held a considerable portion of the Vicksburg garrison in position north of the city, away from the simultaneous main effort to the south. "We will be there as soon as possible," he assured his friend and superior.

Such were the first two of the three diversions intended to confuse and distract the Confederate defenders in the course of this highly critical span of time during which Grant was preparing to launch, and indeed was launching, his main effort a good forty miles downriver from the bluff that was his goal. Though both appeared to have exceeded strategic expectations, the third, while altogether different in scope and composition, was even more successful, and in fact was referred to afterwards by Sherman, who had no direct connection with the venture, as nothing less than "the most brilliant expedition of the war." Grant was as usual more restrained in judgment, qualifying his praise by calling the exploit "one of the most brilliant," but he added that it would "be handed down in history as an example to be imitated."

In point of fact, it was itself an imitation. For two years now, in the West as in the East, the Federal cavalry had suffered from a well-founded inferiority complex; Stuart and Morgan and Forrest had quite literally ridden rings around the awkward blue squadrons and the armies in their charge. Now, perhaps, the time had come for them to emulate the example set by the exuberant gray riders. Hooker thought so, in Virginia, and so did Grant in Mississippi. Back in February he had suggested to Hurlbut, commanding in Memphis, that a cavalry force, "with about 500 picked men, might succeed in making [its] way south and cut the railroad east of Jackson, Miss. The undertaking would be a hazardous one," he added, "but would pay well if carried out. I do not direct that this shall be done, but leave it for a volunteer enterprise." A month later, in mid-March, his instructions were more specific. The conception had been enlarged, tripling the strength of the force to be employed, and the volunteer provision had been removed. Hurlbut was to have all "the available cavalry put in as good condition as possible in the next few weeks for heavy service. . . . The date when the expedition should start will depend upon movements here. You will be informed of the exact time for them to start." In early April the date was set and a leader chosen: Colonel Benjamin H. Grierson, of Grant's home state of Illinois. Hurlbut saw to it that the raiders got away on schedule, April 17, riding south out of La Grange, forty miles east of Memphis, into the dawn that saw Porter's battered gunboats drop anchor near New Carthage after their fiery run past the Vicksburg bluff. "God speed him," Hurlbut said of Grierson, who led the 1700-man column in the direction of the Mississippi line, "for he has started gallantly on a long and perilous ride. I shall anxiously await intelligence of the result."

The wait would necessarily be a long one. Before the raid was over, the blue riders would have covered more than six hundred miles of road and swamp, through hostile territory. At the outset, however, none of the troopers in the three regiments, two from Illinois and one from Iowa, nor of the cannoneers in the attached six-gun battery of 2-pounders, suspected that the warning order, "Oats in the nosebag and five days rations in haversacks, the rations to last ten days," was prelude to so deep a penetration. "We are going on a big scout to Columbus, Mississippi, and play smash with the railroads," one predicted. Only Grierson himself, riding at the head of the column, knew that the true objective was Pemberton's main supply line, the Southern Railroad east of Jackson, connecting Vicksburg with Meridian and thence with Mobile and the arsenals in Georgia and the East. Pennsylvania-born and just short of thirty-seven years of age, with a spade beard and an acquired mistrust of horses dating back to a kick received from a pony in childhood, which smashed one of his cheekbones, split his forehead, and left him scarred for life — he had protested his

Pennsylvania-born and just short of thirty-seven years of age, with a spade beard and an acquired mistrust of horses . . . Grierson eighteen months ago had been a music teacher and bandmaster at Jacksonville, Illinois . . .

assignment to the cavalry in the first place, though to no avail; Halleck, who made the appointment, insisted that he looked "active and wiry enough to make a good cavalryman" — Grierson eighteen months ago had been a music teacher and bandmaster at Jacksonville, Illinois, but all that was left to remind him or anyone else of that now was a jew's-harp he carried inside his blouse, along with a pocket compass and a small-scale map of the region he and his men would be traversing in the course of their strike at the railroad some two hundred air-line miles away. Riding where no bluecoat had ever been before, he could expect to be surrounded en route by small bodies of home guardsmen, who would outnumber him badly if they were consolidated, as well as by sizable detachments of regulars, horse and foot, which Pemberton would certainly send to oppose him, front and rear, once his presence and intention became known. Even if he succeeded in his mission — that is, reached and wrecked an appreciable stretch of the railroad between Jackson and Meridian, temporarily severing the one connection by which reinforcements could reach Vicksburg swiftly from outside Mississippi — he would then be deep in the heart of a land where every man's hand would be raised against him. One suggestion, included in his orders, was that he return to Tennessee by swinging east, then north through Alabama; another was that he plunge on south and west for a hookup with Grant in the vicinity of Grand Gulf, anticipating a successful crossing by McClernand and McPherson at that point, or else take sanctuary within Banks's outpost lines at Baton Rouge, which would give him about as far to go from the railroad south as he would have come already in order to reach it. In any case, whatever escape plan he adopted as a result of the unfolding course of events, the tactical requisites were vigilance, speed, boldness, and deception. Without any one of these four, he and his troopers, in the cavalry slang of the time, would be "gone up."

Across the Mississippi line by sunup, they made thirty miles the first day — a good average march for cavalry, though Grant himself covered nearly as great a distance before noon, galloping south from Milliken's Bend to check on the condition of Porter's gunboats at New Carthage — and called a halt that night just short of Ripley, which they passed through next morning, brushing aside the few startled gray militia they encountered, to camp beyond New Albany at sundown. On the third day, April 19, they continued due south through Pontotoc. Eighty miles from base, with rebel detachments no doubt alerted in his front and rear, Grierson began his fourth day with an inspection, culled out 175 victims of dysentery, chills and fever, and saddle galls — "the Quinine Brigade," the rejected troopers promptly dubbed themselves — and sent them back, under a staff major, with one of the 2-pounders and instructions to "pass through Pontotoc in the night, marching by fours, obliterating our tracks, and producing the impression that we have all returned." He himself continued south with the main body, to Houston and beyond. Deciding to throw a still larger tub to the Confederate whale, he detached Colonel Edward Hatch's regiment of Iowans next morning, along with another of the guns, and gave its commander orders to strike eastward for the Mobile & Ohio, inflicting what damage he could to that vital supply line before heading north in the wake of the Quinine Brigade, thus spreading the scare and increasing the impression that all the raiders were returning. Hatch, a transplanted New Englander hungry for fame and advancement — tomorrow would be his thirty-second birthday — now began a five-day adventure on his own. Though he did not succeed in breaking the well-guarded railroad to the east, he fought two severe skirmishes — one at the outset, a delaying action which allowed Grierson to get away southward, the other near the finish, which allowed his own getaway northward — burned several cotton-stocked warehouses in Okolona, and succeeded handsomely in his primary mission of drawing most of the North Mississippi home guardsmen pell-mell after him and away from Grierson. At a cost of ten men lost en route, he reported that he had inflicted ten times as many casualties on the enemy and "accumulated 600 head of horses and mules, with about 200

★

able-bodied negroes to lead them." Returning to La Grange on Sunday morning, April 26, he brought Hurlbut the first substantial news of the raiders' progress since their departure, nine days back.

The unavailable news was a good deal better; Grierson by then had not only reached his objective, he was already forty hours beyond it, having formulated and put into execution his tactics for escape. Relieved of the threat to his rear on the 21st by Hatch's decoy action south of Houston, he and his 1000 troopers — all Illinoisans now, including the fifty cannoneers with the four remaining guns — rode on past Starkville, where he detached one company for a strike at Macon, twenty-odd miles southeast on the M&O, then took up the march at dawn and cleared Louisville by sundown. Beyond Philadelphia on the 23d he called a halt at nightfall, and made an early start next morning in order to reach the Southern Railroad before noon. Preceded by scouts who seized the telegraph office and thus kept the alarm from being spread — "Butternut Guerillas," these outriders called themselves, for they wore Confederate uniforms, risking hanging for the advantage gained — the raiders burst into Newton Station, a trackside hamlet twenty-five miles west of Meridian and about twice as far east of Jackson, where they at once got down to the work for which they had ridden all this way. Two locomotives were captured and wrecked, along with three dozen freight cars loaded with ordnance and commissary supplies, including artillery ammunition on consignment for Vicksburg, which afforded a rackety fireworks display when set aflame. Meantime other details were ripping up miles of track and crossties, burning trestles and bridges, tearing down telegraph wires all the way to the Chunky River, and setting fire to a government building stocked with 500 small arms and a quantity of new gray uniforms. By 2 o'clock the destruction was complete; Grierson had his bugler sound the rally to assemble the smoke-grimed raiders, some of whom were showing the effects of rebel whiskey they had "rescued" from the flames, then took his accustomed post at the head of the column and led them away from the charred and smoldering evidence of their efficiency as wreckers. Now as before, the march was south. They did not bivouac till near midnight, having covered a good fifty miles of road despite the arduous delay at Newton Station. Next day, April 25, was the easiest of the raid, however, since the blue raiders spent most of it on a plantation in the piny highlands just short of the Leaf River valley, resting their mounts, gorging themselves on smokehouse ham, and presumably nursing their hangovers. Sunday followed, and while Hatch was riding into La Grange at the end of his five-day excursion through North Mississippi, the raiders turned west. In time, according to Grierson's calculations, this would bring them either to Grand Gulf, in case Grant had effected a crossing as planned, or to Natchez, which had been under intermittent Federal occupation for nearly a year.

★

*U*nion raiders pause to burn a depot and rip
up track at one of the three key rail lines they
severed during Grierson's Mississippi foray.

Either place would afford refuge for his saddle-weary troopers if all went as he hoped and planned, but he knew well enough that the most dangerous part of the long ride lay before him. By now, doubtless, every grayback in the state would have learned of the presence of his two regiments at Newton Station two days ago, with the result that a considerable number of them must be hot on his trail or lying in wait for him in all directions. However, this had its compensations as well as its drawbacks. Scarcely less important than the temporary severing of Vicksburg's main supply line was the disruption of its defenses, preventing the hasty concentration of its outlying forces against Grant in the early stages of his river crossing. In point of fact, Grierson was more successful in this regard than he had any way of knowing. Orders flew thick and fast from Pemberton's headquarters in the Mississippi capital, directing all units within possible reach to concentrate on the capture of the ubiquitous blue column. An infantry brigade, en route from Alabama to reinforce Vicksburg, was halted at Meridian to protect that vital intersection of the Southern Railroad and the Mobile & Ohio, while another moved east from Jackson in the direction of the break at Newton Station. Forces at

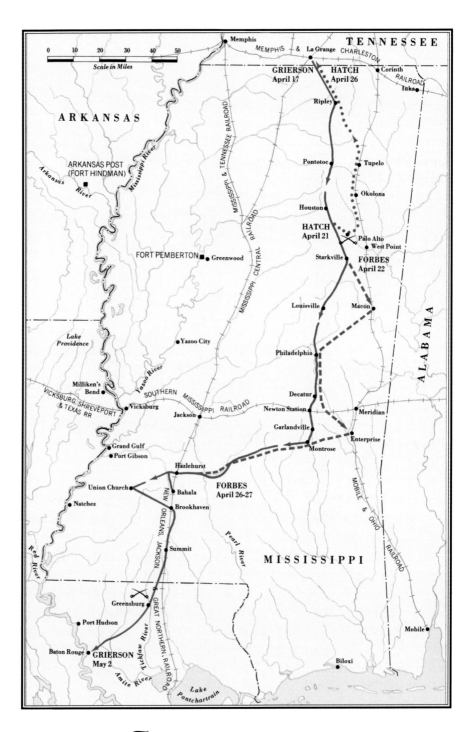

This map of Grierson's raid also shows Colonel Edward Hatch's diversion (dotted line) to decoy the Confederate cavalry.

Panola and Canton, under James Chalmers and Lloyd Tilghman, were shifted to Okolona and Carthage to block the northern escape route. All of these troops, amounting to no less than a full division, not counting the various home-guard units caught up in the swirl, were thus effectively taken out of the play and removed from possible use at this critical time against either Grant or Grierson, who were off in the opposite corner of the map. Not that Pemberton was neglecting matters in that direction, at least so far as Grierson was concerned. Detachments of fast-riding cavalry were ordered eastward from Port Hudson and Port Gibson — the latter a scant half dozen miles from Grant's intended point of landing at Grand Gulf — in case the marauders tried for a getaway to the south or the southwest. In short, Pemberton's reaction to the widespread confusion in his rear and along his lines of supply and communication, while altogether commendable from a limited point of view, amounted to full coöperation with the raiders in the accomplishment of their secondary mission, which was to divert his attention, as well as his reserves, away from the point at which Grant was preparing to hurl two thirds of the blue army.

Grierson wasted no time. Monday, April 27 — Grant's birthday; Sherman prepared for his feint up the Yazoo, and McClernand was told to get his troops aboard the transports at Hard Times — the blue riders pushed westward across Pearl River, aided considerably by the capture of a ferryboat by scouts who masqueraded as Confederates. While the crossing was in progress the company detached five days ago near Starkville rejoined the main body, reporting that in addition to throwing a scare into the defenders of Macon, as instructed, it had also made a feint at Enterprise, twelve miles below Meridian, thus adding to the difficulties of the rebel high command's attempt to pinpoint the location of the invaders. Safely across the Pearl, the reunited 1000-man column pressed on west to Hazlehurst, where a string of boxcars was set afire on a siding of the New Orleans, Jackson & Great Northern Railroad. Flames spreading to a nearby block of buildings, the erstwhile incendiaries turned firemen and worked side by side with the citizens in preventing the loss of the whole town. At dusk, in a driving rain which had helped to contain the fire, the colonel ordered his troopers to remount. The march was west; Grand Gulf was only forty miles away and he hoped to make it there tomorrow, in case Grant had crossed the Mississippi. However, morning brought no indication that any part of the Army of the Tennessee was on this side of the river, so Grierson veered a bit to the south for Natchez, his alternate sanctuary, which was only twenty miles farther away than Grand Gulf. But that too was not to be. Beyond Union Church that afternoon, the raiders were enjoying a rest halt when they were charged by what one of them called "a crowd of graylooking horsemen galloping and shooting in a cloud of dust and smoke." The result at first was panic and the beginning of a rout, but presently they stiffened and repulsed the attackers, who turned out to be nothing more than a couple of understrength companies on the prowl. The colonel prepared to push on next day to Natchez, but was warned that night by one of the Butternut Guerillas, who had ridden ahead and struck up a conversation with a rebel outpost group, that seven companies of cavalry from Grand Gulf were planning to ambush him when he moved westward in the morning. So Grierson once more changed his plans, abandoning Natchez as his destination. Determined now to press on down to Baton Rouge, though this added another hundred miles to the distance his weary men would have to ride, he turned back east at dawn of April 29, avoiding the ambush laid so carefully in what was now his rear.

By early afternoon they were in Brookhaven, twenty-five miles east, astride the railroad they had crossed two days ago, twenty miles to the north, when the march was west. "There was much running and yelling" on the part of the startled citizens, Grierson later reported, "but it soon quieted into almost a welcome." Here, as at Hazlehurst on Monday, sparks from the burning railroad station and another string of boxcars set a section of the town ablaze, and the troopers once more turned firemen to help the natives keep the flames from spreading. Meantime, however, a wrecking crew kept busy tearing up track and burning crossties, thus abolishing the possibility of a locomotive pursuit by troops from Jackson. Back in the saddle, the raiders moved south along the railroad and made camp that night, eight miles below Brookhaven and just over a hundred miles from Baton Rouge. At Summit before sundown of the last day of April, the colonel spared the depot lest his men have to turn firefighters again to save the town, but there was another unfortunate — or fortunate, depending on the point of view — encounter with rebel spirits when the troopers uncovered a cache of rum in fifty-gallon barrels. Grierson broke up the binge, got the revelers mounted at last, drunk or sober, and pressed on south another half dozen miles before stopping for the night. Dawn of May Day completed two full weeks the men had spent in the saddle, with only a half day's rest aside from the minimal halts for sleep and food. Once more the march was west. "A straight line for Baton Rouge, and let speed be our safety," Grierson told his officers as the column was put in motion.

Speed there was — the raiders covered no less than seventy-five miles of road in the following twenty-eight hours — but there was fighting, too, the first and only serious opposition the main body encountered in the course of the long raid. Even so, it was not much. At Wall's Bridge, which spanned the Tickfaw River just north of the Louisiana line, three companies of Confederates from Port Hudson laid a noonday ambush that cost the leading Union company eight casualties. Grierson promptly brought his artillery to the front, shelled the opposite bank, and ordered a charge that not only cleared the bridge but threw the rebels into headlong flight. Riding south all night, with no time out for rest or food, the blue column reached and crossed the Amite River, the last unfordable stream this side of Baton Rouge, before the aroused graybacks could bar the way. Six miles short of the Louisiana capital next morning, his troopers reeling in their saddles from lack of sleep, Grierson called a halt at last. The men tumbled from their mounts and slept where they fell, along the roadside, but the colonel himself, as befitted a former music teacher with an ingrained mistrust of horses, was refreshing himself by playing the piano in the parlor of a nearby plantation house when a picket burst in with news that they were about to be overwhelmed and captured. A rebel force was approaching from the west, he said, with skirmishers out! Grierson, knowing better, rode out to meet the reported enemy, who turned out to be members of the garrison at Baton Rouge, sent to investigate an improbable-sounding rumor "that a brigade of cavalry from General Grant's army had cut their way through

After a two-week, 600-mile sweep through Mississippi, Colonel Benjamin Grierson leads his bedraggled raiders into Baton Rouge on May 2, 1863.

★

the heart of the rebel country, and were then only five miles outside the city." Somewhat restored by their naps, the men remounted and rode into the capital that afternoon. Cheered by spectators, civilians as well as soldiers, the two-mile-long procession of road-worn men and animals, so weathered and dust-caked that they could scarcely be distinguished from the prisoners and Negroes they had gathered along the way, wound slowly around the public square, then south out of town to a grove of magnolias two miles south, where they dismounted, unsaddled, and fell so soundly asleep that they could not be aroused to accept hot coffee.

They had cause for weariness, having covered more than six hundred miles in less than sixteen days, and for thankfulness as well: thankfulness that Pemberton had lost Van Dorn to Bragg three months before, along with nearly all his cavalry, and that it was Abel Streight and not themselves who had been made the prime concern of Bedford Forrest. Streight had left Fort Henry on the day they left La Grange, and was surrendering in East Alabama while Grierson's men, having caught up on their sleep at last, were enjoying their first midday meal in the magnolia grove just south of the Louisiana capital. Different circumstances might well have led to different results, including perhaps a reversal of their current roles as prisoners on the one hand and heroes on the other, but the fact remained that the Illinois troopers had dealt with conditions as they found them. And having done so, they had cause for pride. At a total cost of barely two dozen casualties — "3 killed, 7 wounded, 5 left on the route sick . . . and 9 men missing, supposed to have straggled" — they had "killed and wounded about one hundred of the enemy, captured and paroled over 500 prisoners, many of them officers, destroyed between fifty and sixty miles of railroad and telegraph, captured and destroyed over 3000 stand of arms, and other army stores and government property to an immense amount." So Grierson later reported, adding as if by afterthought, despite his continued mistrust of all equine creatures: "We also captured 1000 horses and mules."

Within three days the colonel was on a steamboat for New Orleans, where he was feted and presented with a horse by the admiring citizenry. "My dear Alice," he wrote his wife that night, "I like Byron have had to wake up one morning and find myself famous. Since I have been here it has been one continuous ovation." In early June, with his picture on the covers of both *Harper's Weekly* and *Leslie's Illustrated*, he was promoted to brigadier general. But perhaps the finest tribute of all came from a man by no means given to using superlatives, on or off the record. Assessing the value of the raid in its relation to the over-all campaign for the taking of Vicksburg, of which it was very much a part, Grant said flatly: "It was Grierson who first set the example of what might be done in the interior of the enemy's country without any base from which to draw supplies."

or the present, however, Grant at Hard Times had no more knowledge of Grierson's progress, across the way, than Grierson had had of Grant's while riding west from Hazlehurst. All the cavalryman learned for certain as he pressed on toward the river was that the army had not crossed as planned, which meant that something must have gone awry. Something had indeed. When the raiders turned back east from Union Church at dawn of April 29, avoiding the ambush laid in what had been their front, they missed hearing the guns of the attackers and defenders at Grand Gulf, less than thirty air-line miles away. It was just as well, for otherwise they might have been lured into what would have been a trap. Except for the rather negative advantage of proving that this was no place to attempt an east-bank landing, the attack was an utter failure, and an expensive one at that.

Porter's doubts had been increasing all week, ever since his April 22 reconnaissance of the stronghold on the bluff across the way. Though he had kept up a show of confidence in his talks with Grant, privately he was airing his misgivings in dispatches to his Washington superiors, not only by way of preparing them for bad news, but also by way of divesting himself in advance of any responsibility for the failure he saw looming. "I am quite depressed with this adventure," he wrote Fox, "which as you know never met with my approval." This last was something less than strictly true, though when he signaled the flotilla captains to move against Grand Gulf at 8 o'clock next morning, April 29, his forebodings soon turned out to have been well founded. The navy's task was to silence the rebel batteries, then cover the crossing by the transports bringing the army over to take the place by storm; but when four of the seven ironclads closed to within pistol shot of the 75-foot bluff — so at least it seemed to Grant, who watched the contest from aboard a tug — they were severely mauled. The flagship *Benton* took 70 hits, the *Tuscumbia* 81; the *Lafayette* took 45, the *Pittsburg* 35. The other three boats, *Carondelet, Mound City,* and *Louisville,* all veterans of the river war from its beginning, did their fighting at long range, lobbing shells into the blufftop works, and consequently suffered little damage. Even so, when Porter hoisted the pennant for the flotilla to drop back out of action at 12.30 — all but the *Tuscumbia,* which had been struck in her machinery and swept powerless downstream until she fetched up short against the Louisiana bank — a total of 75 casualties, including 18 dead, had been subtracted from its crews. By contrast, although time would disclose that they had lost 3 killed and 15 wounded, the defenders seemed unhurt behind their earthwork fortifications. Grand Gulf was as much a failure for the Union navy as Fort Donelson had been, just over a year ago. Porter frankly admitted as much. A crossing might be managed elsewhere, he told Grant, but not here, under the muzzles of those guns across the way.

Grant had not expected a repulse, but he was prepared for what he considered the outside chance of one. Now that a repulse had been encountered, an alternate plan was put into execution without delay. McClernand's men would debark at Hard Times, march south across the point of land to De Shroon's, a plantation landing some four miles downstream, and be ready before dawn to get back aboard the transports, which were to steal past Grand Gulf under cover of darkness, hugging the western bank while the gunboats reëngaged the batteries. All this went as planned, afloat and ashore. The navy lost only one man in its renewal of the duel with the blufftop cannoneers, and the army made its night march unobserved, to find the transports waiting unscathed in the predawn darkness at De Shroon's. "By the time it was light," Grant later wrote, "the enemy saw our whole fleet, ironclads, gunboats, river steamers, and barges, quietly moving down the river three miles below them, black, or rather blue, with National troops."

Accomplishing this he showed the flexibility that would characterize his planning throughout the various stages of the campaign which now was under way in earnest. Other characteristics he also showed. An officer was to remember seeing the general sitting his horse beside the road at a point where a narrow bridge had been thrown across a bog. "Push right along, men," he told the marchers, speaking in almost a conversational tone. "Close up fast and hurry over." The soldiers recognized him and were obviously pleased to see their commander sharing their exertions, but the officer noted that their only reply was to do as he directed. They did not cheer him; they just "hurried over." It was as if, in the course of the long winter of repeated failures, they had caught his quality of quiet confidence. Charles Dana, for one, had begun to think so. He had come down here three weeks ago to report on Grant's alleged bad habits. So far, though, he not only had detected none of these; he had never even heard him curse or seen him lose his temper. Dana was puzzled. "His equanimity was becoming a curious spectacle to me," the former journalist later recalled. Tonight, for example, riding beside the general along the dark road from Hard Times to De Shroon's, he saw Grant's horse stumble. "Now he will swear," he thought, half expecting to see the rider go tumbling over the animal's head; "For an instant his moral status was on trial." But Grant lost neither his balance nor his temper. "Pulling up his horse, he rode on, and, to my utter amazement, without a word or sign of impatience."

Nor did the night march across the point of land, from Hard Times to De Shroon's, put an end to the need for sudden improvisation. Having bypassed Grand Gulf — which he could not allow to remain alive for long, so close in his rear — Grant still was faced with the problem of where to effect a landing on the Mississippi bank, in order to return for a strike at the fortified bluff from its vulnerable landward flank. A look at the map suggested Rodney, another twelve miles downstream. But that would not only give the troops a considerable distance to march, and the defenders time to improve their position and call in reinforcements, it would also place the bluecoats on the far side of Bayou Pierre, which would have to be crossed when they turned back north. Yet to make a landing short of the point where the bayou flowed westward into the river, five miles below, might be to founder the army in some unmapped and unsuspected swamp. What was needed was a guide, a sympathetic native of the region, and Grant sent a detachment of soldiers across the river in a skiff, with instructions to bring back what he wanted. They returned before midnight with an east-bank slave who filled the bill. At first he had been unwilling to come, and in fact had had to be taken by force, but now that he found himself in the lamp-lighted headquarters tent, facing the Union commander across an unrolled chart, he turned coöperative. "Look here," Grant said. "Tell me where this road leads to — starting where you see my finger here on the map and running down that way." The Negro studied the problem, then shook his head. "That road fetches up at Bayou Pierre," he said. "But you can't go that way, 'cause it's plum full of backwater." The thing to do, he replied to further questions, was to go ashore at Bruinsburg, six miles below De Shroon's. This would still be south of Bayou Pierre, but at least it was only half as far as Rodney. Moreover, there was a good road leading from there to Grand Gulf by way of Port Gibson, which lay ten miles inland, well back from the trackless swamps and canebrakes of the river bottoms. At Bruinsburg, the captive slave explained, "you can leave the boats and the men can walk on high ground all the way. The best houses and plantations in all the country are there, sir, all along that road."

So Bruinsburg it was. By midmorning of this last day of April — while Sherman was launching his demonstration against Haines Bluff, fifty air-line miles to the north, and Grierson was pressing southward along the railroad below Brookhaven, the same distance to the east — all four of McClernand's divisions and one of McPherson's, some 23,000 men in all, had completed their debarkation and were slogging inland toward Port Gibson. "When this was effected," Grant declared years later, "I felt a degree of relief scarcely ever equaled since." Then he told why. "I was now in the enemy's country, with a vast river and the stronghold of Vicksburg between me and my base of supplies. But I was on dry ground on the same side of the river with the enemy. All the campaigns, labors, hardships, and exposures from the month of December previous to this time that had been made and endured were for the accomplishment of this one object."

★   ★   ★

Shelby Foote

*On May 14, 1863, Union troops
charged across open ground into
concentrated fire on the
outskirts of Confederate-held
Jackson, Mississippi.*

SEVEN

Eastward, Port Gibson to Jackson

1863 ★ ★ ★ ★ ★ For all his northern birth and starchy manner, which some continued to find personally distasteful, Pemberton by now had either sustained or won the confidence not only of his military superiors but also of the people of Mississippi, who came within his charge. His four-month sequence of successes in the face of threats from all points of the compass far outweighed their original prejudice against him. On May Day, for example — unaware that Sherman was knocking at Vicksburg's upper gate or that Grant, with half his army over the river, already was marching inland from below — an editor in the capital, where the department commander had his headquarters, was taking a sanguine view of the situation. "It would be idle to say that our state and country was not in a position of great peril," he declared. "Yet, strange as it may seem to our readers, we have never felt more secure since the fall of Donelson. The enemy will never reach Jackson; we are satisfied of that. . . . General Pemberton, assisted by vigilant and accomplished officers, is watching the movements of the enemy, and at the proper time will pounce upon him. Let us give the authorities all the assistance we can, and trust their superior and more experienced judgment as to the management of the armies. We know we have a force sufficient, if properly handled, not only to defeat but to rout and annihilate Grant if he ventures far from his river base." As for

★

doubts as to the proper handling of this sufficient force: "Let any man who questions the ability of General Pemberton only think for a moment of the condition the department was in when he was first sent here. No general has evinced a more sleepless vigilance in the discharge of his duty, or accomplished more solid and gratifying results." Nor was this merely the opinion of one uninformed civilian. With reservations, Joe Johnston shared his view. Despite the gloom into which his inspection of the Vicksburg defenses had thrown him, back in December, the Virginian since had warmed to the Pennsylvanian as a result of his apparent skill in fending off the combinations designed for his destruction. In mid-March, reviewing the situation from three hundred miles away in Tennessee, he congratulated him handsomely. "Your activity and vigor in the defense of Mississippi must have secured for you the confidence of the people of Mississippi," he wrote, and added: "I have no apprehension for Port Hudson from Banks. The only fear is that the canal may enable Grant to unite their forces. I believe your arrangements at Vicksburg make it perfectly safe, unless that union should be effected."

Applause was one thing, assistance quite another: as Pemberton soon found out. Despite the denial of help from the vast department across the river, and despite the January transfer of three quarters of his cavalry to Middle Tennessee, he was so encouraged by the flooding of Grant's canal in March that he mistook the subsequent withdrawal of the diggers to Milliken's Bend for an abandonment by the Federals of their entire campaign. On April 11 he notified Johnston that the canal was no longer a danger, that Grant appeared to be pulling back to Memphis, and that he was therefore sending, as requested, a brigade to reinforce Bragg at Tullahoma. Five days later, however, with the blue army still in evidence on the opposite bank and Porter's gunboats preparing for their run past the batteries that night, he recalled the detached brigade, which by then was in northern Mississippi. "[Grant's] movement up the river was a ruse," he wired Johnston. "Certainly no more troops should leave this department." In fact, he said, it was he who stood in gravest need of help. Nothing came of that. Then on April 20, with Porter's ironclads riding at anchor near New Carthage, McClernand moving farther down the Louisiana bank, and Grierson on the rampage east of Grenada — "part and parcel of the formidable invasion preparing before my eyes" — Pemberton stepped up his plea for reinforcements: especially for the return of his 6000 troopers under Van Dorn, the loss of whom had left him three-fourths blind. "Heavy raids are making from Tennessee deep into this state," he warned. "Cavalry is indispensable to meet these expeditions. The little I have is . . . totally inadequate. Could you not make a demonstration with a cavalry force on their rear?" He protested that he had "literally no cavalry from Grand Gulf to Yazoo City, while the enemy is threatening to [cross] the river between Vicksburg and Grand Gulf, having now

The Northern-born John C. Pemberton kept the confidence of his military superiors and the people of Mississippi by staunchly holding Vicksburg despite growing threats from Union forces.

twelve vessels below the former place." Johnston, obliged as he presently was to send Forrest to Alabama after Streight, not only would not agree to make a demonstration against West Tennessee; he also declined to lessen the strength of Bragg's mounted arm, which included Wheeler and Morgan as well as Forrest and Van Dorn, despite the fact that Van Dorn was nominally on loan from Pemberton. It turned out, moreover, that the Pennsylvanian's previous successes worked against him now. Matters had seemed as dark several times before, in the course of the past four months, and he had managed to survive without assistance; apparently Johnston believed he would do as well again. At any rate he was still of his former opinion: "Van Dorn's cavalry is absolutely necessary to enable General Bragg to hold the best part of the country from which he draws supplies."

In effect this amounted to signing Van Dorn's death warrant, since it kept him within range of the Tennessee doctor's wife and her husband's pistol. Pemberton was inclined to think that in the end it might amount to much the same thing for Vicksburg, which Jefferson Davis referred to as "the nailhead that held the South's two halves together." For suddenly now the news grew more alarming. Two nights later, April 22, five unarmored steamboats ran the batteries, obviously to provide the means for a crossing, somewhere below, by the bluecoats slogging down the western bank. Throughout the week that followed, Pemberton sent what little cavalry he had in pursuit of Grierson, whose raiders were disrupting the interior of the state and playing havoc with his lines of supply and communication. Then on April 29 word came from Brigadier General John S. Bowen, commanding at Grand Gulf, that the place was under heavy attack by gunboats attempting to soften him up for an assault by infantry waiting in transports across the river at Hard Times. Scarcely had the news arrived next morning that the ironclads had retired, severely battered, than Pemberton was notified that Haines Bluff was under similar pressure to the north. By the time he learned that this too had been beaten off, a follow-up message from Bowen informed him that the Union fleet had slipped past Grand Gulf in the darkness, transports and all, and was unloading soldiers in large numbers at Bruinsburg, ten miles below. Then came word that the Federals had resumed their pounding of Haines Bluff. Deciding that the downriver threat was the graver of the two, Pemberton resolved to reinforce Bowen, whom he instructed to contest the blue advance on Port Gibson.

On May Day, with the issue still in doubt below — so he thought, though it could scarcely be in doubt for long; the enemy strength was reported at 20,000 men, while Bowen had considerably less than half that many — he appealed once more to Johnston for assistance, bolstering his plea with a wire directly to the President. Davis replied that, in addition to urging Johnston to send help from Tennessee, he was doing all he could to forward troops from southern Alabama. Secretary Seddon, alerted to the danger, informed Pemberton that "heavy reinforcements" would start at once by rail from Beauregard in Charleston. Both messages were gratifying, communicating assurance of assistance from above. But all the harassed Vicksburg commander got from Johnston was advice. "If Grant's army lands on this side of the river," the Virginian replied from Tullahoma, "the safety of Mississippi depends on beating it. For that object you should unite your whole force."

★ ★ ★ A Georgia-born West Pointer, Bowen had left the old army after a single hitch as a lieutenant and had prospered as a St Louis architect before he was thirty, at which age he offered his sword to the newly formed Confederacy. Promoted to brigadier within ten months, he now was thirty-two and eager for further advancement, having spent more than a year in grade because of a long convalescence from a wound taken at Shiloh, where he led his brigade of Missourians with distinction. On the afternoon of April 30, marching his 5500 soldiers out of Grand Gulf and across Bayou Pierre to meet Grant's 23,000 moving inland from Bruinsburg after their downriver creep past his blufftop guns in the darkness, he carried proudly in his pocket a dispatch received last night from Pemberton, congratulating him on the repulse of Porter's ironclads: "In the name of the army, I desire to thank you and your troops for your gallant conduct today. Keep up the good work. . . . Yesterday I warmly recommended you for a major-generalcy. I shall renew it." Bowen had it very much in mind to keep up the good work. Despite the looming four-to-one odds and the changed nature of his task now that he and the blue invaders were on the same bank of the river, he welcomed this

★

opportunity to deal with them ashore today as he had dealt with them afloat the day before. Four miles west of Port Gibson before nightfall, he put his men in a good defensive position astride a wooded ridge just short of a fork in the road leading east from Bruinsburg. Presently the Federals came up and his pickets took them under fire in the moonlight. Artillery deepened the tone of the argument, North and South, but soon after midnight, as if by mutual consent, both sides quieted down to wait for daylight.

McClernand opened the May Day fight soon after sunrise, advancing all four of his divisions under Brigadier Generals Peter Osterhaus, A. J. Smith, Alvin Hovey, and Eugene Carr. The road fork just ahead placed him in something of a quandary, lacking as he did an adequate map, but this was soon resolved by a local Negro who informed him that the two roads came together again on the near side of Port Gibson, his objective. He sent Osterhaus to the left as a diversion in favor of the other three commanders, who were charged with launching the main effort on the right. Grant came up at midmorning to find the battle in full swing and McClernand in some confusion, his heavily engaged columns being out of touch with each other because the two roads that wound along parallel ridges — "This part of Mississippi stands on edge" was how Grant put it — were divided by a timber-choked ravine that made lateral communication impossible. The result was that McClernand's right hand quite literally did not know what his left was doing, though the fact was neither was doing well at all. In his perplexity he called for help from McPherson, who supplied it by sending one brigade of Major General John A. Logan's division to the left and another to the right. "Push right along. Close up fast," the men heard Grant say as they went past the dust-covered general sitting a dust-covered horse beside the road fork. They did as he said, and arrived on the left in time to stall a rebel counterattack that had already thrown Osterhaus off balance, while on the right they added the weight needed for a resumption of the advance. Outflanked and heavily outnumbered on the road to the south, Bowen at last had to pull back to the outskirts of Port Gibson, where he rallied his men along a hastily improvised line and held off the blue attackers until nightfall ended the fighting.

Casualties were about equal on both sides; 832 Confederates and 875 Federals had fallen or were missing. Bowen had done well and he knew it, considering the disparity of numbers, but he also knew that to fight here tomorrow, against lengthened odds and without the advantage of this morning's densely wooded terrain, would be to invite disaster. At sundown he notified Pemberton that he would "have to retire under cover of night to the other side of Bayou Pierre and await reinforcements." Pemberton, who had arrived in Vicksburg from Jackson by now, had already sent word that he was "hurrying reinforcements; also ammunition. Endeavor to hold your own until they arrive, though it may be some time, as the distance is great." At 7.30, having received Bowen's sundown message, he rather wistfully inquired: "Is it not probable that the enemy will himself retire tonight? It is very important, as you know, to retain your present position, if possible. . . . You must, however, of course, be guided by your own judgment. You and your men have done nobly." But Bowen by then had followed up his first dispatch with a second: "I am pulling back across Bayou Pierre. I will endeavor to hold that position until reinforcements arrive." He withdrew skillfully by moonlight, unpursued and unobserved, destroying the three bridges over the bayou and its south fork, northwest and northeast of Port Gibson, and took up a strong position on the opposite bank, covering the wrecked crossing of the railroad to Grand Gulf, which he believed would be Grant's next objective.

But Grant did not come that way, at least not yet. Finding Port Gibson empty at dawn, he pressed on through and gave James Wilson a brigade-sized detail with which to construct a bridge across the south fork of Bayou Pierre, just beyond the town. Wilson was experienced in such work, having built no less than seven such spans in the course of the march from Milliken's Bend, and besides he had plenty of materials at hand, in the form of nearby houses which he tore down and cannibalized. By midafternoon the job was finished, "a

Federal troops slog through Bayou Pierre past a blazing suspension bridge fired by retreating rebels doing all they could to slow the Union pursuit.

★

continuous raft 166 feet long, 12 feet wide, with three rows of large mill-beams lying across the current, and the intervals between them closely filled with buoyant timber; the whole firmly tied together by a cross-floor or deck of 2-inch stuff." So Wilson later described it, not without pride, adding that he had also provided side rails, corduroy approaches over quicksand, and abutments "formed by building a slight crib-work, and filling in with rails covered by sand." Grant was impressed, but he did not linger to admire the young staff colonel's handi-work. The second of McPherson's three divisions having arrived that morning, he was given the lead today, with orders to march eight miles northeast to Grind-stone Ford, which he reached soon after dark. He was prevented from crossing at once because the fine suspension bridge had been destroyed at that point, but Wilson was again at hand and had it repaired by daylight of May 3, when McPherson pressed on over. Near Willow Springs, two miles beyond the stream, he encountered and dislodged a small hostile force which retreated toward Hankinson's Ferry, six miles north, where the main road to Vicksburg crossed the Big Black River. Instructing McPherson to keep up the march northward in pursuit, Grant detached a single brigade to accompany him westward in the direction of Grand Gulf.

McClernand, coming along behind McPherson, whom he was or-dered to follow north, was alarmed to learn what Grant had done, striking off on his own like that, and sent a courier galloping after him with a warning: "Had you not better be careful lest you may personally fall in with the enemy on your way to Grand Gulf?" But Grant was not only anxious to reach that place as soon as possible, and thus reëstablish contact with the navy and with Sherman, who was on the march down the Louisiana bank; he also believed that Bowen, chastened by yesterday's encounter, would fall back beyond the Big Black as soon as he discovered that his position on Bayou Pierre had been turned up-stream. And in this the northern commander was quite right. Reinforcements had reached Bowen from Jackson and Vicksburg by now, but they only increased his force to about 9000, whereas he reckoned the present enemy strength at 30,000, augmented as it was by a full division put ashore at Bruinsburg the night before. When he learned, moreover, that this host had bridged both forks of Bayou Pierre to the east of Port Gibson and was headed for the crossings of the Big Black, deep in his rear, he lost no time in reaching the decision Grant expected. At midnight, finding that his staff advisers "concurred in my belief that I was compelled to abandon the post at Grand Gulf," he "then ordered the evacua-tion, the time for each command to move being so fixed as to avoid any delay or confusion." The retrograde movement went smoothly despite the need for haste. Bringing off all their baggage — which Pemberton, when informed of their predicament, had authorized them to abandon lest it slow their march, but which Bowen declared he was "determined to and did save" — the weary veterans and the newly arrived reinforcements set off northward, leaving the blufftop in-trenchments, which they had defended so ably against the ironclad assault four days ago, yawning empty behind them in the early morning sunlight.

Soon after they disappeared over the northern horizon Porter arrived with four gunboats, intending to launch a new attack. He approached with cau-tion, remembering his previous woes and fearing a rebel trick, but when he found the Grand Gulf works abandoned he did not let that diminish his claim for credit for their reduction. "We had a hard fight for these forts," he wrote Secretary Welles, "and it is with great pleasure that I report that the Navy holds the door to Vicksburg." He announced that his fire had torn the place to pieces, leaving it so covered with earth and debris that no one could tell at a glance what had been there before the bombardment. "Had the enemy succeeded in finishing these fortifications no fleet could have taken them," he declared, quite as if he had subdued the batteries in the nick of time, and added: "I hear nothing of our army as yet; was expecting to hear their guns as we advanced on the forts."

He heard from "our army" presently with the arrival of its com-mander, who had got word of the evacuation while en route from Grindstone Ford and had ridden ahead of the infantry with an escort of twenty troopers. Grant was glad to see the admiral, but most of all — after seven days on a bor-rowed horse, with "no change of underclothing, no meal except such as I could pick up sometimes at other headquarters, and no tent to cover me" — he was glad to avail himself of the admiral's facilities. After a hot bath, a change of underwear borrowed from one of the naval officers, and a square meal aboard the flagship, he got off a full report to Halleck on the events of the past four days. "Our victory has been most complete, and the enemy thor-oughly demoralized," he wrote. Bowen's defense of Port Gibson had been "a very bold one and well carried out. My force, however, was too heavy for his, and composed of well-disciplined and hardy men who know no defeat and are not willing to learn what it is." After this unaccustomed flourish he got down to the matter at hand. "This army is in the finest health and spirits," he declared. "Since leaving Milliken's Bend they have marched as much by night as by day, through mud and rain, without tents or much other baggage, and on irregular rations, without a complaint and with less straggling than I have ever before witnessed. . . . I shall not bring my troops into this place, but immediately follow the enemy, and, if all promises as favorable hereafter as it does now, not stop until Vicksburg is in our possession."

He was on his own, however, in a way he had neither intended nor foreseen. His plan had been to use Grand Gulf as a base, accumulating a reserve of supplies and marking time with Sherman and McPherson, so to speak, while McClernand took his corps downriver to coöperate with Banks in the reduction of Port Hudson, after which the two would join him for a combined assault on

Vicksburg. But he found waiting for him today at Grand Gulf a three-week-old letter from Banks, dated April 10 and headed Brashear City — 75 miles west of New Orleans and equally far south of Port Hudson — informing him of a change in procedure made necessary, according to the Massachusetts general, by unexpected developments in western Louisiana which would threaten his flank and rear, including New Orleans itself, if he moved due north from the Crescent City as originally planned. Instead, he intended to abolish this danger with an advance up the Teche and the Atchafalaya, clearing out the rebels around Opelousas before returning east to Baton Rouge for the operation against Port Hudson with 15,000 men. He hoped to open this new phase of the campaign next day, he wrote, and if all went as planned he would return to the Mississippi within a month — that is, by May 10 — at which time he would be ready to coöperate with Grant in their double venture. . . . Reading the letter, Grant experienced a considerable shock. He had expected Banks to have twice as many

"We had a hard fight for these forts . . . and it is with great pleasure that I report that the Navy holds the door to Vicksburg."

— David Dixon Porter

troops already in position for a quick slash at Port Hudson, to be followed by an equally rapid boat ride north to assist in giving Vicksburg the same treatment. Now all that went glimmering. Some 30,000 men poorer than he had counted on being, he was on his own: which on second thought had its advantages, since the Massachusetts general outranked him and by virtue of his seniority would get the credit, from the public as well as the government, for the reduction of both Confederate strongholds and the resultant clearing of the Mississippi all the way to the Gulf. Grant absorbed the shock and quickly made up his mind that he was better off without him. Banks having left him on his own, he would do the same for Banks. "To wait for his coöperation would have detained me at least a month," he subsequently wrote in explanation of his decision. "The reinforcements would not have reached 10,000 men after deducting casualties and necessary river guards at all high points close to the river for over 300 miles. The enemy would have strengthened his position and been reinforced by more men than Banks could have brought. I therefore determined to move independently of Banks, cut loose from my base, destroy the rebel force in rear of Vicksburg, and invest or capture the city."

★

So much he intended, though he had not yet decided exactly how he would go about it. One thing he knew, however, was that the change of plans called for an immediate speed-up of the accumulation of supplies, preliminary to launching his all-out drive on the rebel citadel two dozen air-line miles to the north. A look at the Central Mississippi interior, with its lush fields, its many grazing cattle, and its well-stocked plantation houses — "of a character equal to some of the finest villas on the Hudson," a provincial New York journalist called these last — had convinced him that the problem was less acute than he had formerly supposed. "This country will supply all the forage required for anything like an active campaign, and the necessary fresh beef," he informed Halleck. "Other supplies will have to be drawn from Milliken's Bend. This is a long and precarious route, but I have every confidence in succeeding in doing it." Accordingly, he ordered this supply line shortened, as soon as the river had fallen a bit, by the construction of a new road from Young's Point to a west-bank landing just below Warrenton. "Everything depends upon the promptitude with which our supplies are forwarded," he warned. He had already directed that two towboats make a third run past the Vicksburg guns with heavy-laden barges. "Do this with all expedition," he told the quartermaster at Milliken's Bend, "in 48 hours from receipt of orders if possible. Time is of immense importance." Hurlbut was ordered to forward substantial reinforcements from Memphis without delay, as well as to lay in a sixty-day surplus of rations, to be kept on hand for shipment downriver at short notice. To Sherman, hurrying south across the way, went instructions to collect 120 wagons en route, load them with 100,000 pounds of bacon, then pile on all the coffee, sugar, salt, and crackers they would hold. "It is unnecessary for me to remind you of the overwhelming importance of celerity in your movements," Grant told him, outlining the situation as he saw it now on this side of the river: "The enemy is badly beaten, greatly demoralized, and exhausted of ammunition. The road to Vicksburg is open. All we want now are men, ammunition, and hard bread. We can subsist our horses on the country, and obtain considerable supplies for our troops."

With all this paper work behind him, he left Grand Gulf at midnight and rode eastward under a full moon to rejoin McPherson, who had reached Hankinson's Ferry that afternoon and had already dispatched cavalry details to probe the opposite bank of the Big Black River. From his new headquarters Grant kept stressing the need for haste. "Every day's delay is worth 2000 men to the enemy," he warned a supply officer, and kept goading him with questions that called for specific answers: "How many teams have been loaded with rations and sent forward? I want to know as near as possible how we stand in every particular for supplies. How many wagons have you ferried over the river? How many are still to bring over? What teams have gone back for rations?" His impatience was such that he had no time for head-shaking or regrets. Learning on May 5 that one

*The staff of U.S. Army's XVII Corps gathers round
its commander, Major General James B. McPherson
(seated second from right), for a portrait.*

of the two towboats and all the barges had been lost the night before in attempting the moonlight run he had ordered, he dismissed the loss with the remark:
"We will risk no more rations to run the Vicksburg batteries," and turned his
attention elsewhere. This touch of bad luck was more than offset the following
day by news that Sherman had reached Hard Times, freeing McPherson's third
division from guard duty along the supply route, and was already in the process of
crossing the river to Grand Gulf. The red-haired general was in excellent spirits,
having learned that four newspaper reporters had been aboard the towboat that
was lost. "They were so deeply laden with weighty matter that they must have
sunk," he remarked happily, and added: "In our affliction we can console ourselves with the pious reflection that there are plenty more of the same sort."

One thing Grant did find time for, though, amid all his exertions at
Hankinson's Ferry. On the 7th he issued a general order congratulating his soldiers
for their May Day victory near Port Gibson, which he said extended "the long
list of those previously won by your valor and endurance." He was proud of
what they had accomplished so far in the campaign, he assured them, and
proudest of all that they had endured their necessary privations without complaint.

Then he closed on a note of exhortation. "A few days' continuance of the same zeal and constancy will secure to this army the crowning victory over the rebellion. More difficulties and privations are before us. Let us endure them manfully. Other battles are to be fought. Let us fight them bravely. A grateful country will rejoice at our success, and history will record it with immortal honor."

★ ★ ★ *P*emberton at this stage was by no means "badly beaten." Neither was he "greatly demoralized," any more than Vicksburg's defenders were "exhausted of ammunition." Nor was the road to the city "open," despite Grant's suppositions in his May 3 note urging Sherman to hurry down to get in on the kill. It was true, on the other hand, that the southern commander had been acutely distressed by the news that the blue invaders were landing in force on the east bank of the river below Grand Gulf, for he saw only too clearly the dangers this involved. "Enemy movement threatens Jackson, and, if successful, cuts off Vicksburg and Port Hudson from the east," he wired Davis on May Day, before he knew the outcome of the battle for Port Gibson, and he followed this up next morning, when he learned that Bowen had withdrawn across Bayou Pierre, with advice to Governor Pettus that the state archives be removed from the capital for safekeeping; Grant most likely would be coming this way soon. Another appeal to Johnston for "large reinforcements" to meet the "completely changed character of defense," now that the Federals were established in strength on this side of the river, brought a repetition of yesterday's advice: "If Grant crosses, unite all your troops to beat him. Success will give back what was abandoned to win it."

If this proposed abandonment included Vicksburg, and presumably it did, Pemberton was not in agreement. He already had ordered all movable ordnance and ammunition sent to that place from all parts of the state, in preparation for a last-ditch fight if necessary, and he arrived in person the following day, about the same time Grant rode into Grand Gulf with a twenty-trooper escort. For all his original alarm, Pemberton felt considerably better now. Davis and Seddon had promised reinforcements from Alabama and South Carolina — 5000 were coming from Charleston by rail at once, the Secretary wired, with another 4000 to follow — and Sherman had withdrawn from in front of Haines Bluff, reducing by half the problem of the city's peripheral defense. Johnston moreover had agreed at last, now that Streight had been disposed of, to send some cavalry under Forrest to guard against future raids across the Tennessee line. Much encouraged, Pemberton telegraphed Davis: "With reinforcements and cavalry promised in North Mississippi, think we will be all right."

His new confidence was based on a reappraisal of the situation confronting him now that Bowen, with his approval, had fallen back across the Big Black River, which curved across his entire right front and center. Not only did this withdrawal make a larger number of troops available for the protection of a much smaller area; it also afforded him the interior lines, so that a direct attack from beyond the arc could be met with maximum strength by defenders fighting from prepared positions. Presumably Grant would avoid that, but Pemberton saw an even greater advantage proceeding from the concentration behind the curved shield of the Big Black. It greatly facilitated what he later called "my great object," which was "to prevent Grant from establishing a base on the Mississippi River, above Vicksburg." Until the invaders accomplished this they would be dependent for supplies on what could be run directly past the gun-bristled bluff, a risky business at best, or freighted down the opposite bank, along a single jerry-built road that was subject to all the ravages of nature. As Pemberton saw it, his opponent's logical course would be to extend his march up the left bank of the Big Black, avoiding the bloodshed that would be involved in attempting a crossing until he was well upstream, in position for an advance on Haines Bluff from the rear and the establishment there of a new base of supplies, assisted and protected by Porter's upper flotilla, which would have returned up the Yazoo to meet him. But the southern commander did not intend to stand idly by, particularly while the latter stages of the movement were in progress. "The farther north [Grant] advanced, toward my left, from his then base below, the weaker he became; the more exposed became his rear and flanks; the more difficult it became to subsist his army and obtain reinforcements." At the moment of greatest Union extension and exposure, the defenders — reinforced by then, their commander hoped, from all quarters of the Confederacy — would strike with all their strength at the enemy's flanks and rear, administering a sudden and stunning defeat to a foe for whom, given the time and place, defeat would mean disaster, perhaps annihilation. Such was the plan. And though there were obvious drawbacks — the region beyond the Big Black, for example, would be exposed to unhindered depredations; critics would doubtless object, moreover, that Grant might adopt a different method of accomplishing his goal — Pemberton considered the possible consummation of his design well worth the risk. Having weighed the odds and assessed his opponent's probable intentions from his actions in the past, he was content to let the outcome test the validity of his insight into the mind of his adversary. "I am a northern man; I know my people," he was to say. Besides, he believed that the Federals, obliged to hold onto one base to the south while reaching out for another to the north, had little choice except to act as he predicted. It was true that in the interim they "might destroy Jackson and ravage the country," he admitted, "but that was a comparatively small matter. To take Vicksburg, to control the valley of the Mississippi, to sever the Confederacy, to ruin our cause, a base upon the eastern bank immediately above was absolutely necessary."

Whatever else was desirable in the conflict now about to be resumed, he knew he would need all the soldiers he could get for the close-up defense of the line on the Big Black. In this connection, at the same time he informed Richmond of the pending evacuation of Grand Gulf he requested permission to bring the so-far unthreatened garrison of Port Hudson north for a share in the coming struggle. "I think Port Hudson and Grand Gulf should be evacuated," he wired Davis on May 2, "and the whole force concentrated for defense of Vicksburg and Jackson." Accordingly, in conformity with Johnston's advice to "unite all your troops," he ordered Major General Franklin Gardner, commanding the lower fortress, to strip the garrison to an absolute minimum and move with all the rest of the men to Jackson; those remaining behind would follow as soon as Richmond confirmed his request for total evacuation. On May 7, however, Davis replied that he approved of the withdrawal from Grand Gulf, but that "to hold both Vicksburg and Port Hudson is necessary to a connection with the Trans-Mississippi." So Pemberton countermanded the order to Gardner. He was to return at once to Port Hudson "and hold it to the last. President says both places must be held."

Such discouragement as this occasioned had been offset in advance, at least in part, by the defeat three nights ago of Grant's third attempt to run supplies downriver past the Vicksburg batteries. The sunken towboat and the flaming barges — not to mention the four Yankee journalists, who had not drowned, as Sherman had so fervently hoped, but had been fished out of the muddy water as prisoners of war — were evidence of improvement in the marksmanship of the gunners on the bluff, although it had to be conceded that the brilliant moonlight gave them an advantage they had lacked before. Another encouragement came soon afterwards from Johnston, who replied on May 8 to a report in which Pemberton explained his preparations for defense: "Disposition of troops, as far as understood, judicious; can be readily concentrated against Grant's army." If this was guarded, it was also approving, which was something altogether new from that direction. Then next day came the best news of all: Johnston himself would

*M*ajor General Franklin Gardner commanded Port Hudson when it was besieged by Federal troops.

be coming soon to Vicksburg to inspirit the men and lend the weight of his genius to the defense of the Gibraltar of the West. Acting under instructions from Davis, Seddon ordered the general to proceed from Tullahoma "at once to Mississippi and take chief command of the forces, giving to those in the field, as far as practicable, the encouragement and benefit of your personal direction." Johnston was suffering at the time from a flare-up of his Seven Pines wound, but he replied without apparent hesitation: "I shall go immediately, although unfit for service." He left Tennessee next morning, May 10, having complied with the Secretary's further instructions to have "3000 good troops" follow him from Bragg's army as reinforcements for Pemberton.

★　★　★　　Pemberton took new hope at the prospect of first-hand assistance from on high; now he could say, with a good deal more assurance than he had felt when he used the words the week before, "Think we will be all right." But there were flaws in the logic of his approach to the central problem, or at any rate errors in the conclusion to which that logic had led him. His assessment of Grant's intention was partly right, but it was also partly wrong: right, that is, in the conviction that what his opponent wanted and needed was a supply base above Vicksburg, but wrong as to how he would go about getting what he wanted. By now Grant had nine of his ten divisions across the Mississippi and had reached the final stage of his week-long build-up for an advance, though not in the direction Pemberton had supposed and planned for.

McPherson had been shifted eight miles east to Rocky Springs, leaving Hankinson's Ferry to be occupied by Sherman, two of whose three divisions were with him, while McClernand was in position along the road between those two points. In connection with the problem of supply, Grant had been collecting all the transportation he could lay hands on, horses, mules, oxen, and whatever rolled on wheels, ever since the Bruinsburg crossing. The result was a weird conglomeration of vehicles, ranging from the finest plantation carriages to ramshackle farm wagons, with surreys and buckboards thrown in for good measure, all piled to the dashboards and tailgates with supplies — mainly crates of ammunition and hardtack, the two great necessities for an army on the move — constantly shuttling back and forth between the Grand Gulf steamboat landing and Rocky Springs, where Grant had established headquarters near McPherson. Sherman, being farthest in the rear, had a close-up view of vehicular confusion that seemed to him to be building up to the greatest traffic snarl in history, despite the fact that there was still not transportation enough to supply more than a fraction of the army's needs. It was his conclusion that Grant's headlong impatience to be up and off was plunging him toward a logistic disaster. By May 9 he could put up with it no longer. "Stop all troops till your army is partially supplied with wagons, and then act as quickly as possible," he advised his chief, "for this road will be jammed as sure as life if you attempt to supply 50,000 men by one single road." The prompt reply from Rocky Springs gave the redhead the shock of his military life. Previously he had known scarcely more of Grant's future plans than Pemberton knew from beyond the Big Black River, but suddenly the veil of secrecy was lifted enough to give him considerably more than a glimmer of what he had never suspected until now. "I do not calculate upon the possibility of supplying the army with full rations from Grand Gulf," Grant told him. "I know it will be impossible without constructing additional roads. What I do expect, however, is to get up what rations of hard bread, coffee, and salt we can, and make the country furnish the balance."

This clearly implied, if it did not actually state, that he intended to launch an invasion, much as Cortez and Scott had done in Mexico, without a base from which to draw supplies. And so he did. Back in December, returning through North Mississippi to Memphis after the destruction of his forward depot at Holly Springs, he had discovered that his troops could live quite easily off the country by the simple expedient of taking what they wanted from the farmers in their path. "This taught me a lesson," he later remarked, and now the lesson was about to be applied. Moreover, the success of Grierson, whose troopers had lacked for nothing in the course of a 600-mile ride that had "knocked the heart out of the state" — so Grant himself declared in passing along to Washington the news of the raid — was a nearer and more recent example of what might be accomplished along those lines. For his own part, in the course of his march from Bruinsburg through Port Gibson to Rocky Springs, he had observed that "beef, mutton, poultry, and forage were found in abundance," along with "quite a quantity of bacon and molasses." What was more, every rural commissary "had a run of stone, propelled by mule power, to grind corn for the owners and their slaves. All these [could be] kept running . . . day and night . . . at all plantations covered by the troops." He felt sure there would be enough food and forage of one sort or another for all his men and animals, leaving room in the makeshift train for ammunition and such hard-to-get items as salt and coffee, provided there were no long halts during which the local supplies would be exhausted. All that was required was that he keep his army moving, and that was precisely what he intended to do, from start to finish, for tactical as well as logistic reasons. His 45,000 effectives were roughly twice as many as Pemberton had behind the curved shield of the Big Black River; he was convinced that he could whip him in short order with a frontal attack. "If Blair were up now," he told Sherman, who was still awaiting the arrival of the division that had feinted at Haines Bluff, "I believe we could be in Vicksburg in seven days." But that would leave some 10,000 rebels alive in his rear at Jackson, which was connected by rail not only to Vicksburg but also to the rest of the Confederacy, so that reinforcements could be hurried there from Bragg and the East until they out-numbered him as severely as he had outnumbered Pemberton, thus turning the tables on him. His solution was to strike both north and east, severing the rail connection between Jackson and Vicksburg near the Big Black crossing, while simultaneously closing in on the capital. He would capture the inferior force at that place, if possible, but at any rate he would knock it out of commission as a transportation hub or a rallying point; after which he would be free to turn on Vicksburg unmolested, approaching it from the east and north, and thus either take the citadel by storm or else establish a base on the Yazoo from which to draw supplies while starving the cut-off defenders into surrender.

Sherman had much of this explained to him when he rode over to Rocky Springs that afternoon, in considerable perturbation, for what he called "a full conversation" with the army commander. But his doubts persisted, much as they had done after he had agreed to stage the Haines Bluff demonstration.

"What I do expect, however, is to get up what rations of hard bread, coffee, and salt we can, and make the country furnish the balance."

— Ulysses S. Grant

"He is satisfied that he will succeed in his plan," he said of Grant in a letter urging Blair to hasten his crossing from Hard Times, "and, of course, we must do our full share." Though he would "of course" coöperate fully in carrying out his chief's design, he wanted it understood from the start — and placed indelibly on the record — that he was doing so with something less than enthusiasm and against his better judgment. Grant by now was accustomed to his lieutenant's mercurial ups and downs, and he did not let them discourage him or influence his thinking. The following day, May 10 — the Sunday Joe Johnston left Tulla-homa for Jackson — he heard again from Banks, who informed him, in a letter written four days ago at Opelousas, that he was making steady progress up the Teche, clearing out the rebels on his flank, and expected to turn east presently for Port Hudson. "By the 25th, probably, and by the 1st certainly, we will be there," he promised. Convinced more than ever that he had done right not to wait for Banks, Grant replied that he was going ahead on his own. Previously he had told him nothing of his plans, not even that he would not be meeting him; but now he did, on the off-chance that Banks might be of assistance. "Many days cannot elapse before the battle will begin which is to decide the fate of

Vicksburg," he wrote, "but it is impossible to predict how long it may last. I would urgently request, therefore, that you join me or send all the force you can spare to coöperate in the great struggle for opening the Mississippi River." Similarly, at this near-final moment, he got off a dispatch to the general-in-chief, announcing that he was leaving Banks to fend for himself against Port Hudson while the Army of the Tennessee cut loose from its base at Grand Gulf and plunged inland in order to come upon Vicksburg from the rear. "I knew well that Halleck's caution would lead him to disapprove of this course," he subsequently explained; "but it was the only one that gave any chance of success." Besides, such messages were necessarily slow in transmission, having to be taken overland from Hard Times to Milliken's Bend, then north by steamboat all the way to Cairo before they could be put on the wire, and Grant saw a certain advantage in this arrangement. "The time it would take to communicate with Washington and get a reply would be so great that I could not be interfered with until it was demonstrated whether my plan was practicable."

This done, he turned to putting the final touches to the plan he had evolved. McClernand would move up the left bank of the Big Black, guarding the crossings as he went, and strike beyond Fourteen Mile Creek at Edwards Station, on the railroad sixteen miles east of Vicksburg. McPherson would move simultaneously against Jackson, and Sherman would be on call to assist either column, depending on which ran into the stiffest resistance. On the 11th, Grant advanced all three to their jump-off positions: McClernand on the left, as near Fourteen Mile Creek as possible "without bringing on a general engagement," Sherman in the center, beyond Cayuga, and McPherson on the right, near Utica. "Move your command tonight to the next crossroads if there is water," Grant told McPherson, "and tomorrow with all activity into Raymond. . . . We must fight the enemy before our rations fail, and we are equally bound to make our rations last as long as possible."

Before dawn the following morning, May 12, they were off. The second phase of the campaign designed for the capture of Vicksburg was under way.

★ ★ ★ *A*dvancing through a rugged and parched region, McClernand's troops found that the only way they could quench their thirst, aggravated by the heat of the day and the dust of the country roads, was to drive the opposing cavalry beyond Fourteen Mile Creek, which was held by a rebel force covering Edwards Station, some four miles to the north. By midafternoon they had done just that. "Our men enjoyed both the skirmish and the water," the commander of the lead division reported. Sherman, coming up on the right, accomplished this same purpose by throwing "a few quick rounds of cannister" at the gray vedettes, who promptly scampered out of range. Pioneers rebuilt a bridge the Confederates had burned as they fell back, and several regiments crossed the creek at dusk, establishing a bridgehead while the two corps went into bivouac on the south bank, prepared to advance on Edwards in the morning.

But that was not to be. McPherson, when within two miles of Raymond at 11 o'clock that morning, had encountered an enemy force of undetermined strength, "judiciously posted, with two batteries of artillery so placed as to sweep the road and a bridge over which it was necessary to pass." This was in fact a single brigade of about 4000 men, recently arrived from Port Hudson under Brigadier General John Gregg, who had come out from Jackson the day before, under orders from Pemberton to cover the southwest approaches to the capital. Informed that the Federals were moving on Edwards, over near the Big Black River, he assumed that the blue column marching toward him from Utica was only "a brigade on a marauding excursion," and he was determined not only to resist but also, if possible, to slaughter the marauders. The result was a sharp and — considering the odds — surprisingly hot contest, in which seven butternut regiments took on a whole Union corps. McPherson threw Logan's division against the wooded enemy position, only to have it bloodily repulsed. While the other two were coming forward, Logan rallied in time to frustrate a determined counterattack and follow it up with one of his own. By now, however, having learned what it was he had challenged — and having suffered 514 casualties, as compared to McPherson's 442 — Gregg had managed to disengage and was withdrawing through Raymond. Five miles to the east, one third of the distance to Jackson, he met Brigadier General W. H. T. Walker, who had marched out to join him with a thousand men just arrived from South Carolina. Gregg halted and faced about, ready to try his hand again; but there was no further action that day. Entering Raymond at 5 o'clock, McPherson decided to stop for the night. "The rough and impracticable nature of the country, filled with ravines and dense undergrowth, prevented anything like an effective use of artillery or a very rapid pursuit," he explained in a sundown dispatch to the army commander.

Grant was seven miles away, at the Dillon plantation on Fourteen Mile Creek with Sherman, and when he learned the outcome of the battle whose guns he had heard booming, five miles off at first, then fading eastward into silence, he revised his over-all plan completely. Edwards could wait. If Jackson was where the enemy was — and the determined resistance at Raymond seemed to indicate as much — he would go after him in strength; he would risk no halfway job in snuffing out a segment of the rebel army concentrated near a rail hub that gave it access to reinforcements from all quarters of the South. Accordingly, at 9.15 he sent orders assigning all three of his corps commanders new objectives for tomorrow and prescribing that each would begin his march "at daylight in the morning." McPherson would move against Clinton, on the railroad nine miles north, then eastward that same distance along the right-of-way to Jackson.

Sherman would turn due east from his present bivouac at Dillon, swinging through Raymond so as to come upon the objective from the south. McClernand, after detaching one division to serve as a rear guard in the event that the Confederates at Vicksburg attempted to interfere by crossing the Big Black, would come along behind Sherman and McPherson, prepared to move in support of either or both as they closed in on the Mississippi capital. Such were Grant's instructions, and presently he had cause to believe that he had improvised aright. Two days ago McPherson had passed along a rumor that "some of the citizens in the vicinity of Utica say Beauregard is at or near Jackson." If the Charleston hero was there it was practically certain he had not come alone. And now there arrived a second dispatch from McPherson, headed 11 p.m. and relaying another rumor that heavy Confederate reinforcements were moving against him out of Jackson, intending to fight again at Raymond soon after sunup. He did not know how much fact there was in this, he added, but he would "try to be prepared for them." Grant had confidence in McPherson, especially when he was forewarned as he was now, and did not bother to reply. Besides, whether it was true or false that the rebels were marching in force to meet him west of their capital, he already had made provisions to counter such a threat by ordering all but one of his ten divisions, some 40,000 men in all, to move toward a convergence on that very objective "at daylight in the morning."

All three columns moved on schedule. By early afternoon McPherson was in Clinton, nine miles from Jackson, and Sherman was six miles beyond Raymond, about the same distance from the Mississippi capital. A lack of determined resistance seemed to indicate that last night's rumor of heavy reinforcements was in error, and this, plus reports from scouts that Pemberton had advanced in force to the vicinity of Edwards, caused Grant to modify his strategy again. McPherson was instructed to spend the rest of the day wrecking the railroad west of Clinton, then resume his eastward march at first light tomorrow, May 14, tearing up more track as he went. Sherman, half a dozen miles to the south, would regulate his progress so that both corps would approach the Jackson defenses simultaneously. McClernand, instead of following along to furnish unneeded support, would turn north at Raymond and march on Bolton Depot, eight miles west of Clinton, occupying a strong position in case Pemberton attempted a farther advance along the railroad toward his threatened capital. There was of course the possibility that the Confederate commander might lunge southward, across Fourteen Mile Creek, with the intention of attacking the Federal army's rear and severing its connection with Grand Gulf: in which case he would be removing himself from the campaign entirely, at least for the period of time required for him to discover that he had plunged into a vacuum. For Grant not only had no supply line; he had no rear, either, in the sense that

Pemberton might suppose. Such rear as Grant had he had brought with him, embodied in McClernand, who now had orders to take up a position at Bolton, astride the railroad about midway between Vicksburg and Jackson, facing west. Moreover, once the capital had fallen and the blue army turned its attention back to its prime objective, the blufftop citadel forty-five miles away, what was now its rear would automatically become its front; McClernand, already in position for an advance, once more would take the lead, with Sherman and McPherson in support. For all the improvisatorial nature of his tactics, Grant, like any good chess player, was keeping a move or two ahead of the game.

By midmorning of May 14, slogging eastward under a torrential rain that quickly turned the dusty roads into troughs of mud, Sherman was within three miles of Jackson. At 10 o'clock, while peering through the steely curtain of the downpour to examine the crude fortifications to his front, he heard the welcome boom of guns off to the north; McPherson was on schedule and in place. While Sherman reconnoitered toward Pearl River for an opening on the flank, McPherson deployed for a time-saving frontal attack, to be launched astride the railroad. He waited an hour in the rain, lest the cartridge boxes of his troops be filled with water, like buckets under a tap, when they lifted the flaps to remove their paper-wrapped ammunition, and then at 11 o'clock, the rain having slacked to a drizzle at last, ordered his lead division forward across fields of shin-deep mud. The rebel pickets faded back to the shelter of their intrenchments, laying down a heavy fire that stopped the bluecoats in their tracks and flung them on their faces in the mud. By now it was noon. McPherson impatiently re-formed his staggered line, having lost an even 300 men, and sent the survivors forward again. This time they found the rebel infantry gone. Only a handful of cannoneers had remained behind to serve the seven guns left on line and be captured by McPherson's jubilant soldiers. Sherman had the same experience, two miles to the south, except that he found ten guns in the abandoned works he had outflanked. Not only were his spoils thus greater than McPherson's; his casualties were fewer, numbering only 32. The Confederates, under Gregg and Walker, who had fallen back from east of Raymond the night before, had lost just over 200 men before pulling out of their trenches to make a hairbreadth getaway to the north. The Battle of Jackson was over, such as it was, and Grant had taken the Mississippi capital at a bargain price of 48 killed, 273 wounded, and 11 missing.

He was there to enjoy in person the first fruits of today's sudden and inexpensive victory. Sherman, riding in from the south — and noting with disapproval some "acts of pillage" already being committed by early arrived bluecoats under the influence "of some bad rum found concealed in the stores of the town" — was summoned by a courier to the Bowman House, Jackson's best hotel, where he found Grant and McPherson celebrating the capture of Jeff

Davis's own home-state capital, the third the South had lost in the past two years. From the lobby they had a view, through a front window, of the State House where the rebel President had predicted, less than six months ago, that his fellow Mississippians would "meet and hurl back these worse than vandal hordes." Quick as the two generals had been to reach the heart of town, riding in ahead of the main body, they were slower than the army commander's young son Fred. His mother and brother had gone back North after the second running of the Vicksburg batteries, but Fred had stayed on to enjoy the fun that followed, wearing his father's dress sword and sash — which the general himself had little use for, and almost never wore — as badges of rank. Grant, an indulgent parent, later explained that the boy "caused no trouble either to me or his mother, who was at home. He looked out for himself and was in every battle of the campaign. His age, then not quite thirteen, enabled him to take in all he saw, and then to retain a recollection of it that would not be possible in more mature years." Fred's recollection of the capture of Jackson was saddened, however, by his failure to get a souvenir he badly wanted. He and a friendly journalist had seen from the

*U*nion officers
watch through a
driving rainstorm
the triumphant
assault of General
Crocker's division on
Jackson, Mississippi.

outskirts of town a large Confederate flag waving from its staff atop the golden dome of the capitol. Mounted, they hurried ahead of the leading infantry column, tethered their horses in front of the big stone building, and raced upstairs — only to meet, on his way down, "a ragged, muddy, begrimed cavalryman" descending with the rebel banner tucked beneath his arm. For Fred, a good measure of the glory of Jackson's capture had departed, then and there.

Grant could sympathize with the boy's disappointment, but he had just been handed something considerably more valuable to him than the lost flag or even the seventeen guns that had been taken in the engagement that served as prelude to the occupation of the capital. Charles Dana arrived in mid-celebration with a dispatch just delivered by a courier from Grand Gulf. Signed by the Secretary of War and dated May 5, it had been sent in response to a letter in which Dana had given him a summation of Grant's plan "to lose no time in pushing his army toward the Big Black and Jackson, threatening both and striking at either, as is most convenient. . . . He will disregard his base and depend on the country for meat and even for bread." Now Stanton replied:

★

General Grant has full and absolute authority to enforce his own commands, to remove any person who, by ignorance, inaction, or any cause, interferes with or delays his operations. He has the full confidence of the Government, is expected to enforce his authority, and will be firmly and heartily supported; but he will be responsible for any failure to exert his powers. You may communicate this to him.

There was more here than met the eye. Stanton of course had authority over Halleck, so that if — or rather, as Grant believed from past experience, *when* — the time came for the general-in-chief to protest that Grant had disobeyed orders by abandoning Banks and striking out on his own, he would find — if indeed he had not found already — that Stanton, and presumably Lincoln as well, had approved in advance the course Grant had adopted. Nor was that all. Dana, having long since taken a position alongside the army commander in his private war against McClernand, had been keeping the Secretary copiously posted on the former congressman's military shortcomings, large and small, and feeling him out as to what the administration's reaction would be when Grant decided the time had come for him to swing the ax. Now the answer was at hand. Grant not only had "full and absolute authority" to sit in judgment; he would in fact be held "responsible for any failure to exert his powers" in all matters pertaining to what he considered his army's welfare and the progress of what Stanton called his "operations," whether against the rebels or McClernand.

It was no wonder then — protected as he now was from the wrath of his immediate superior, as well as from the machinations of his ranking subordinate — that he was in good spirits during the hotel-lobby victory celebration. All around him, meanwhile, the town was in a turmoil. "Many citizens [had] fled at our approach," one Federal witness later recalled, "abandoning houses, stores, and all their personal property, without so much as locking their doors. The Negroes, poor whites, and it must be admitted some stragglers and bummers from the ranks of the Union army, carried off thousands of dollars worth of property from houses, homes, shops and stores, until some excuse was given for the charge of 'northern vandalism,' which was afterwards made by the South. The streets were filled with people, white and black, who were carrying away all the stolen goods they could stagger under, without the slightest attempt at concealment and without let or hindrance from citizens or soldiers. . . . In addition . . . the convicts of the penitentiary, who had been released by their own authorities, set all the buildings connected with that prison on fire, and their lurid flames added to the holocaust elsewhere prevailing." He observed that "many calls were made upon [Grant] by citizens asking for guards to protect their private property, some of which perhaps were granted, but by far the greater number [of these petitioners] were left to the tender mercies of their Confederate friends."

After all, Grant had not brought his army here to protect the private property of men in revolution against the government that army represented; nor, for that matter, had it ever been his custom to deny his soldiers a chance at relaxation they had earned, even though that relaxation sometimes took a rather violent form. His purpose, rather, was to destroy all public property such as might be of possible comfort to the Confederacy. This applied especially to the railroads, the wrecking of which would abolish the Mississippi capital as a transportation hub, at least through the critical period just ahead. But that other facilities were not neglected was observed by a witness who testified that "foundries, machine shops, warehouses, factories, arsenals, and public stores were fired as fast as flames could be kindled." Sherman was the man for this work, Grant decided, and he gave him instructions "to remain in Jackson until he destroyed that place as a railroad center and manufacturing city of military supplies."

Meanwhile there was the campaign to get on with; Pemberton was hovering to the west, already on the near side of the Big Black, and beyond him there was Vicksburg, the true object of all this roundabout marching and such bloodshed as had so far been involved. McPherson was told to get his corps in hand and be prepared to set out for Bolton Depot at first light tomorrow to support McClernand, whose corps was no longer the army's rear guard, but rather its advance. Having attended to this, Grant joined Sherman for a little relaxation of his own; namely, a tour of inspection to determine which of the local business establishments would be spared or burned. In the course of the tour they came upon a cloth factory which, as Grant said later, "had not ceased work on account of the battle nor for the entrance of Yankee troops." Outside the building "an immense amount of cotton" was stacked in bales; inside, the looms were going full tilt, tended by girl operatives, weaving bolts of tent cloth plainly stamped C.S.A. No one seemed to notice the two generals, who watched for some time in amused admiration of such oblivious industry. "Finally," Grant said afterwards, "I told Sherman I thought they had done work enough. The operatives were told they could leave and take with them what cloth they could carry. In a few minutes cotton and factory were in a blaze."

This done, Grant returned to the Bowman House for his first night's sleep on a mattress in two weeks. Joe Johnston, he was told, had occupied the same room the night before.

★   ★   ★

★

*Waving his hat defiantly,
Major General John A. "Black
Jack" Logan rallies the men of the
34th Indiana during the heat of
battle on Champion Hill.*

EIGHT

Westward, Jackson to Vicksburg

Johnston — not Beauregard, as rumor had had it earlier — had arrived at dusk the day before, at the end of a grueling three-day train ride from Tennessee by way of Atlanta, Montgomery, Mobile, and Meridian, only to find the Mississippi capital seething with reports of heavy Union columns advancing from the west. As night closed in, a hard rain began to fall, shrouding the city and deepening the Virginian's gloom still further: as was shown in a wire he got off to Seddon after dark. "I arrived this evening finding the enemy's force between this place and General Pemberton, cutting off communication. I am too late." To Pemberton, still on the far side of the Big Black, he sent a message advising quick action on that general's part. To insure delivery, three copies were forwarded by as many couriers. "I have lately arrived, and learn that Major General Sherman is between us, with four divisions, at Clinton," Johnston wrote. "It is important to reëstablish communications, that you may be reinforced. If practicable, come up in his rear at once. To beat such a detachment would be of immense value. The troops here could co-operate. All the strength you can quickly assemble should be brought. Time is all important."

He had at Jackson, he presently discovered, only two brigades of about 6000 men with which to oppose the 25,000 Federals who were knocking at the western gates next morning. After a sharp, brief skirmish and the sacrifice

★

of seventeen guns to cover a withdrawal, he retreated seven miles up the Canton road to Tugaloo, where he halted at nightfall, unpursued, and sent another message to Pemberton, from whom he had heard nothing since his arrival, informing him that the capital had been evacuated. He was expecting another "12,000 or 13,000" troops from the East, he said, and "as soon as [these] reinforcements are all up, they must be united to the rest of the army. I am anxious to see a force assembled that may be able to inflict a heavy blow upon the enemy. . . . If prisoners tell the truth, the force at Jackson must be half of Grant's army. It would decide the campaign to beat it, which can only be done by concentrating, especially when the remainder of the eastern troops arrive." He himself could do little or nothing until these men reached him, reducing the odds to something within reason, but he did not think that Pemberton should neglect any opportunity Grant afforded meanwhile, particularly in regard to his lines of supply and communication. "Can he supply himself from the Mississippi?" Johnston asked. "Can you not cut him off from it, and above all, should he be compelled to fall back for want of supplies, beat him?"

This last was in accord with Pemberton's own decision, already arrived at before the second message was received. The first, delivered by one of the three couriers that morning at Bovina Station, nine miles east of Vicksburg, had taken him greatly by surprise. He had expected Johnston to come to his assistance in defense of the line along or just in front of the Big Black; yet here that general was, requesting him "if practicable" to come to *his* assistance by marching against the enemy's rear at Clinton, some twenty miles away. Pemberton replied that he would "move at once with the whole available force," explaining however that this included only 17,500 troops at best, since the remaining 9000 under his command were required to man the Warrenton–Vicksburg–Haines Bluff defenses, as well as the principal crossings of the Big Black, which otherwise would remain open in his rear, exposing the Gibraltar of the West to sudden capture by whatever roving segment of the rampant blue host happened to lunge in that direction. "In directing this move," he felt obliged to add, by way of protest, "I do not think you fully comprehend the position Vicksburg will be left in; but I comply at once with your request."

So he said. However, when he rode forward to Edwards, where his mobile force of three divisions under Loring, Stevenson, and Bowen was posted four miles east of the Big Black, he learned that a Union column, reportedly five divisions strong — it was in fact McClernand's corps, with Blair attached as guard for the wagon train — was at Raymond, in position for a northward advance on Bolton. If Pemberton marched on Clinton, as Johnston suggested, ignoring this threat to his right flank as he moved eastward along the railroad, he would not only be leaving Vicksburg and the remaining two divisions under Major Generals M. L. Smith and John H. Forney in grave danger of being gobbled up

William W. Loring's failure to come to the support of Confederate troops holding Champion Hill during a battle on May 16, 1863, led to a rebel rout.

while his back was turned; he would also be exposing his eastbound force to destruction at the hands of the other half of the Northern army. Perplexed by this dilemma, and mindful of some advice received two days ago from Richmond that he "add conciliation to the discharge of duty" — "Patience in listening to suggestions . . . is sometimes rewarded," Davis had added — he decided the time had come for him to call a council of war, something he had never done before in all his thirty years of military service. Assembling the general officers of the three divisions at Edwards Station shortly after noon, he laid Johnston's message before them and outlined the tactical problems it posed. Basically, what he had to deal with was a contradiction of orders from above. As he understood the President's wishes, he was not to risk losing Vicksburg by getting too far from it, whereas Johnston was suggesting a junction of their forces near Jackson, forty miles away, in order to engage what he called a "detachment" of four — in fact, five — divisions, without reference to or apparent knowledge of the five-division column now at Raymond, both of which outnumbered the Confederates at Edwards. Pemberton, on the other hand, did not strictly agree with either of his two superiors, preferring to await attack in a prepared position near or behind the Big Black River, with a chance of following up a repulse with a counterattack designed to cut off and annihilate the foe. These three views could not be reconciled, but neither did he consider that any one of them could be ignored; so that, like the nation at large, this Northerner who sided with the South was torn and divided against himself. That was his particular nightmare in this nightmare interlude of his country's history. According to an officer on his staff, the Pennsylvanian's trouble now and in the future was that he made "the capital mistake of trying to harmonize instructions from his superiors diametrically opposed to each other, and at the same time to bring them into accord with his own judgment, which was averse to the plans of both."

Nor was the council of much assistance to him in finding a way around the impasse. Though a majority of the participants favored complying with Johnston's suggestion that the two forces be united, they were obliged to admit that it could not be accomplished by a direct march on Clinton, which was plainly an invitation to disaster. Meanwhile Pemberton's own views, as he told Johnston later, "were strongly expressed as unfavorable to any advance which would remove me from my base, which was and is Vicksburg." Apparently he limited himself to this negative contention. But finally Loring — known as "Old Blizzards" since his and Tilghman's spirited repulse of the Yankee gunboats above Greenwood — suggested an alternate movement, southeast nine miles to Dillon, which he believed would sever Grant's connection with Grand Gulf and thus force him either to withdraw, for lack of supplies, or else to turn and fight at a disadvantage in a position of Pemberton's choice. Stevenson agreed, along with others, and Pemberton, though he disliked the notion of moving even that much farther from Vicksburg, "did not, however, see fit to put my own judgment and opinions so far in opposition as to prevent a movement altogether." He approved the suggestion, apparently for lack of having anything better to offer, and adjourned the council after giving the generals instructions to be ready to march at dawn. At 5.40, on the heels of the adjournment, he got off a message informing Johnston of his intentions. "I shall move as early tomorrow morning as practicable with a column of 17,000 men," he wrote, explaining the exact location of Dillon so that Johnston would have no trouble finding it on a map which was enclosed. "The object is to cut the enemy's communications and to force him to attack me, as I do not consider my force sufficient to justify an attack on the enemy in position or to attempt to cut my way to Jackson."

Johnston received this at 8.30 next morning, May 15, by which time he had withdrawn another three miles up the Canton road, still farther from the intended point of concentration at Clinton. Though the message showed that Pemberton had anticipated the Virginian's still unreceived suggestion that he attempt to "cut [Grant] off from [the Mississippi]," Johnston no longer favored such a movement. "Our being compelled to leave Jackson makes your plan impracticable," he replied, and repeated — despite Pemberton's objection to being drawn still farther from his base — his preference for an eastward march by the mobile force from Vicksburg: "The only mode by which we can unite is by your moving directly to Clinton, informing me, that [I] may move to that point with about 6000 troops. I have no means of estimating the enemy's force at Jackson. The principal officers here differ very widely, and I fear he will fortify if time is left him. Let me hear from you immediately."

Evidently Johnston believed that Grant was going to hole up in the Mississippi capital and thus allow him time to effect a junction between the Vicksburg troops and his own, including the "12,000 or 13,000" reinforcements expected any day now from the East. If so, he was presently disabused. A reply from Pemberton, written early the following morning but not delivered until after dark, informed him that the advance on Dillon — badly delayed anyhow by the need for building a bridge across a swollen creek — had been abandoned, in accordance with his wishes, and the direction of march reversed. It was Pemberton's intention, as explained in the message, to move north of the railroad, swing wide through Brownsville to avoid the mass of Federals reported to be near Bolton, and converge on Clinton as instructed. "The order of countermarch has been issued," he wrote, and followed a description of his proposed route with the words: "I am thus particular, so that you may be able to make a junction with this army."

The Vicksburg commander at last had abandoned his objections to what Johnston had called "the only mode by which we can unite." He was, or soon would be, moving east toward his appointed destination. But there was an ominous postscript to the message, written in evident haste and perhaps alarm: "Heavy skirmishing is now going on to my front."

★ ★ ★ **W**hat that portended Johnston did not know; but Grant did. Before he retired to the hotel room his adversary had occupied the night before the fall of Jackson, he received from McPherson one of the three copies of Johnston's message urging Pemberton to "come up in [Sherman's] rear at once." This windfall was the result of a ruse worked some months ago by Hurlbut, who banished from Memphis, with considerable fanfare, a citizen found guilty of "uttering disloyal and threatening sentiments," though he was in secret, as Hurlbut knew, a thoroughly loyal Union man. The expulsion, along with his continued expression of secessionist views after his removal to the Mississippi capital, won him the sympathy and admiration of the people there: so much so, indeed, that he was one of the three couriers entrusted with copies of Johnston's urgent message. He delivered it, however, not to Pemberton but to McPherson, who passed it promptly along to Grant. "Time is all important," the Virginian had written. Grant agreed. By first light next morning, May 15, McPherson was marching west from the capital, leaving Sherman to accomplish its destruction while he himself moved toward a junction with McClernand, who had been instructed simultaneously by Grant: "Turn all your forces toward Bolton station, and make all dispatch in getting there. Move troops by the most direct road from wherever they may be on the receipt of this order."

McPherson's three divisions had seventeen miles to go, and McClernand's four — five, including Blair — were variously scattered, from Raymond back to Fourteen Mile Creek. Each corps got one division to Bolton by late afternoon — Hovey and Logan, in that order — while the others camped along the roads at sundown. Carr and Osterhaus were three miles south, with A. J. Smith between them and Raymond, where Blair was. Brigadier Generals John McArthur and Marcellus Crocker, commanding McPherson's other two divisions, were bivouacked beside the railroad leading back to Clinton. Riding out from Jackson to that point before nightfall, Grant ordered McClernand to move on Edwards in the morning, supported by McPherson, but warned him "to watch for the enemy and not bring on an engagement unless he felt very certain of success." The fog of war, gathering again to obscure the Confederate purpose, had provoked this note of caution; but it was dispersed once more at 5 o'clock next morning, when two Union-sympathizing employes of the Vicksburg–Jackson Railroad were brought to Grant at Clinton. They had

Whether his choice of ground was "by accident or design," as Grant ungenerously remarked, there could be no doubt that Pemberton chose well.

passed through Pemberton's army in the night, they said, and could report that it was moving east of Edwards with a strength of about 25,000 men. Though this was in fact some 7500 high, it was still some 10,000 fewer than Grant had on hand. But he was taking no unavoidable chances. Deciding to ignore Johnston, who by now was a day's march north of Jackson at Calhoun Station, he ordered Sherman to "put one division with an ammunition train on the road at once, with directions to its commander to march with all possible speed until he comes upon our rear." The remaining division was to hurry its demolition work and follow along as soon as might be. The orders to McClernand and McPherson were unaltered; all that was changed by this second dispersal of the war fog was the weight of the blow about to be delivered. Now that he knew Pemberton's strength and had him spotted, Grant intended to hit him with everything he had.

At about the time the railroad men were telling all they knew, McClernand started forward in high spirits. "My corps, again, led the advance," he was to say proudly in a letter giving his friend Lincoln an account of the campaign. Such was indeed the case. Three roads led west from the vicinity of Bolton to a junction east of Edwards, and McClernand used all three: Hovey on the one to the north, Osterhaus and Carr on the one in the middle, and Smith on the one to the south. Blair followed Smith, and McPherson's three divisions followed Hovey. Rebel cavalry was soon encountered, gray phantoms who fired and scampered out of range while the blue skirmishers flailed the woods with bullets. Then at 7.30, five miles short of Edwards, Smith came upon a screen of butternut pickets and dislodged them, exposing a four-gun battery, which he silenced. He wanted to plunge on, despite the signs that the high ground ahead was occupied in strength, but McClernand told him to hold what he had till Blair came up to keep his exposed left flank from being turned. Immediately on the heels of this, a rattle of gunfire from the north signified that Osterhaus and Hovey had also come upon johnnies to their front. Mc-Clernand inspected the rebel position as best he could from a distance and, finding it formidable, decided to hang on where he was until the situation could be developed. Having obeyed Grant's instructions "to watch for the enemy," he was also mindful of the injunction "not [to] bring on an engagement unless he felt very certain of success." At this point, with his various columns a mile or two apart and facing a wooded ridge aswarm with graybacks, he was not feeling very certain about anything at all. What he mainly felt was lonely.

Countermarching in obedience to the message received early that morning from Johnston, Pemberton had been warned by his outriders of the Union host advancing westward along the three roads from Bolton and Raymond. When this danger was emphasized by the "heavy skirmishing" mentioned in the postscript to his reply that he was moving north and east toward a junction at Clinton, he knew he had a fight on his hands, wanted or not, and to avoid the risk of being caught in motion, strung out on the road to Brownsville, he hastily put his troops in position for receiving the attack he knew was coming. Whether his choice of ground was "by accident or design," as Grant ungenerously remarked, there could be no doubt that Pemberton chose well. Just south of the railroad and within a broad northward loop of rain-swollen Baker's Creek, a seventy-foot eminence known as Champion Hill — so called because it was on a plantation belonging to a family of that name — caused the due-west road from Bolton to veer south around its flank, joining the middle road in order to cross a timbered ridge that extended southward for three miles, past the lower of the three roads along which the enemy was advancing. Pemberton placed Stevenson's division on the hill itself, overlooking the direct approach from Bolton, and Bowen's and Loring's divisions along the ridge, blocking the other two approaches. Here, in an opportune position of great natural strength, he faced as best he could the consequences of his reluctant and belated compliance with his superior's repeated suggestion that he abandon the security of his prepared lines, along and just in front of the Big Black, for an attack on the Federal "detachment" supposed to be at Clinton. Now, however, as the thing turned out, it was Pemberton who was about to be attacked, a dozen miles short of his assigned objective. And here, precisely midway between Vicksburg and Jackson, both of which were twenty-two miles away, was fought what at least one prominent western-minded historian was to call "the most decisive battle of the Civil War."

Grant did not much like the look of things when he came riding out from Bolton and reached the front, where the road veered south beyond the Champion house, to find Hovey exchanging long-range shots with the enemy on the tall hill just ahead. It seemed to him, as he said later, that the rebels "commanded all the ground in range." However, unlike McClernand on the two roads to the south, he was not content to hold his own while waiting for the situation to develop more or less of its own accord. Logan's division having arrived, he sent it to the right, to prolong the line and feel for an opening in that direction. This was about 10 o'clock; he preferred to wait for Crocker to come up and lend the weight of McPherson's second division to the attack. But Hovey by now was hotly engaged, taking punishment from the batteries on the height and protesting that he must either go forward or fall back. Grant unleashed him. A former Indiana lawyer, of whom it was said that he had taken to

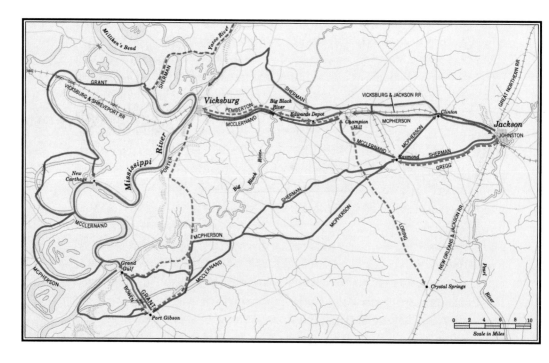

A map of the Vicksburg campaign shows the movements of Federal troops under Grant and Confederate troops under Pemberton in April and May of 1863.

★

the army "just as if he expected to spend his life in it," Hovey drove straight up the steep acclivity to his front, flinging back successive Confederate lines, until he reached and seized the eleven guns that had been pounding him from near the crest. His men were whooping with delight, proud but winded, when they were struck in turn by a powerful counterattack launched from a fringe of woods along the crest. "We ran, and ran manfully," one among them declared, explaining how he and his fellows had been swept back from the captured guns and down the slope they had climbed. Reinforced by Crocker's lead brigade, which had just arrived under Colonel George Boomer, they managed to hang on at the foot of the hill; but only by the hardest. One officer called the fighting there "unequal, terrible, and most sanguinary." For half an hour, he said, the troops "on each side took their turn in driving and being driven."

It was obvious that Hovey, who had left about one third of his division lying dead or wounded on the hillside, could not hold out much longer unassisted. Then one of the survivors looked over his shoulder and saw the army commander speaking to the colonel in charge of Crocker's second brigade, which was coming forward along the road behind them. "I was close enough to see his features," the man was to recall. "Earnest they were, but sign of inward movement there was none." This was the Grant of Belmont, Donelson, and Shiloh, reacting to adversity here as he had reacted there. If the face was "cool and calculating," the soldier observed, it was also "careful and half-cynical." He could not catch the spoken words across the distance, but they were as characteristic as the calm, enigmatic mask or the habitual cigar stump that was wedged between its teeth. "Hovey's division and Boomer's brigade are good troops," Grant was saying. "If the enemy has driven them he is not in good plight himself. If we can go in again here and make a little showing, I think he will give way."

But it developed that a good deal more than this one additional brigade would have to join the melee at the base of Champion Hill if Grant was to make what he called "a little showing." With McPherson's third division still too far away to be of help in time, he had to call on Logan, who had been sent to probe the rebel left. And this, as Grant admitted later, was the salvation of Pemberton today. Logan had ridden around the north end of the hill, where the terrain was more open and gently rolling. He was sitting on horseback, surveying the scene, when a private who had wandered on his own came up to him and remarked laconically, gesturing off to the right: "General, I've been over the rise yonder, and it's my idea that if you'll put a regiment or two over there you'll get on their flank and lick 'em easy." Logan took a look for himself and saw that the man was right; Pemberton's left was "in the air" and the way to his rear was practically unobstructed, including the single bridge over Baker's Creek by which he could fall back. Just then, however, the order to return and support the hard-pressed Hovey was received; Logan had to defer pressing the advantage the amateur tactician had discovered. Learning of this when it was too late to take full advantage of the maneuver, Grant remarked with hindsight: "Had McClernand come up with reasonable promptness, or had I known the ground as I did afterwards, I cannot see how Pemberton could have escaped with any organized force."

The reference to McClernand was something more, this time, than merely another point scored in the private war Grant waged on paper against the former congressman from his home state. Pemberton, observing the lack of enemy aggressiveness to the south, had reinforced his staggered left by shifting troops northward from his center, which was disposed along the ridge. Bowen brought them to Stevenson's assistance on the run, arriving just in time to launch the savage counterattack that drove Hovey's exultant soldiers back down the hill. Like Grant, however, Pemberton was finding that he would need more than this to keep up the pressure or even hold what he had won; so he sent for Loring. That general — referred to as "a scared turkey" by a member of Stonewall Jackson's staff during the Romney controversy, two Christmases ago, which had almost resulted in Jackson's retirement from the army and which had been settled only with Loring's transfer to the West — was already in a state of agitation because Bowen's departure had left him alone on the ridge, with four blue divisions in plain sight. When the summons came for him to follow Bowen he declined. It would be suicidal, he protested. All this time, the pressure against Stevenson was mounting, and when Logan added the weight of his division it became unsupportable. Old Blizzards moved at last, in response to repeated calls from Pemberton; but too late. He was scarcely in motion northward, about 4 o'clock, when the whole Confederate left flank gave way. Stevenson's men fell back in a panic, and though Pemberton managed to rally them with a personal appeal, the damage was done. The eleven retaken guns were lost again, this time for good, and Bowen's division — having, as one officer remarked, "sustained its reputation by making one of its grand old charges, in which it bored a hole through the Federal army" — now found itself unsupported and nearly surrounded; whereupon it "turned around and bored its way back again," following Stevenson's pell-mell flight down to Baker's Creek, where it formed a rear-guard line in an attempt to hold off the bluecoats until Loring too had made his escape across the stream. Darkness fell and there was still no sign of Loring. Bowen waited another two hours, still maintaining his position, then gave it up and crossed in good order, burning the bridge when his last man was safe on the west bank.

Casualties here, after three hours of skirmishing and four of actual battle, had been much the heaviest of the campaign. Grant had lost 2441 men, Pemberton 3624, including prisoners cut off in the retreat — plus 11 guns and, as it turned out, all of Loring's division. Finding his path along the ridge blocked by victorious Federals, he swung west, then back south, and after a brief skirmish in which Lloyd Tilghman was killed by a cannonball while covering the withdrawal, made a rapid getaway around McClernand's open flank. By the following evening he was in Crystal Springs, twenty-five miles south of Jackson, and two days later he was with Johnston at Canton, an equal distance north of the capital. Except for the loss of Tilghman, whose courage and ability had been proved at Fort Henry and Fort Pemberton, Loring's disappearance was more a source of mystery than regret for the army of which he had lately been a part, since he had contributed little to the battle except to assist in the show of strength that immobilized McClernand. Grant felt much the same way about McClernand, whose 15,000-man command — including Blair but not Hovey, who fought beyond McClernand's control and suffered almost half the army's casualties — had lost a total of 17 dead and 141 wounded in the course of what a brigade commander with McPherson called "one of the most obstinate and murderous conflicts of the war." Despite the fact that not a single man had been killed in three of the four divisions to the south, elation over the victory scored by the three divisions to the north was tinged with sorrow at its cost. "I cannot think of this bloody hill without sadness and pride," Hovey was to say, and an Illinois soldier, roaming the field when the fighting was over, was struck by the thought that no moral solution had been arrived at as a result of all the bloodshed. "There they lay," he said of the dead and wounded all around him, "the blue and the gray intermingled; the same rich, young American blood flowing out in little rivulets of crimson; each thinking he was in the right."

Grant was more interested just now in military solutions, and he believed he had reached one. "We were now assured of our position between Johnston and Pemberton," he subsequently declared, "without a possibility of a junction of their forces." Others in his army believed they saw an even more profitable outcome of the struggle on Champion Hill. "Vicksburg must fall now," a participant wrote home that night; "I think a week may find us in possession. It may take longer," he added on second thought, "but the end will be the same."

★ ★ ★   *W*hile Pemberton's depleted army fell back through the darkness to a position covering the Big Black crossing, eight miles to the west, Grant let his soldiers sleep till dawn, by which time Wilson's engineers had the bridge over Baker's Creek rebuilt, then took up the pursuit. McClernand once more had the lead, though Blair was detached to rejoin Sherman, who by now was close at hand with his other two divisions. "We have made good progress today in the work of destruction," he had written Grant the day before, as he prepared to leave the

Mississippi capital. "Jackson will no longer be a point of danger. The land is devastated for thirty miles around." Next morning — Sunday, May 17 — while Grant was crossing Baker's Creek to come to grips with Pemberton again, Sherman passed through Bolton and encountered other signs of devastation. Seeing some soldiers drawing water from a well in front of "a small hewn-log house" beside the road, he turned his horse in at the gate to get a drink. The place had been rifled, its furnishings wrecked and strewn about the yard, and though such acts of vandalism were fairly common at this stage of the campaign — brought on, so to speak, by an excess of skylark energy and delight that things were going so well for the army of invasion — this one appeared to have been committed with an extra measure of glee and satisfaction. When Sherman had one of the men hand him a book he saw lying on the ground beside the well, he found out why. It was a copy of the United States Constitution, with the name Jefferson Davis written on the title page. This was the property the Confederate President's brother had secured for him the year before, when Brierfield was occupied by Butler, and though in the course of his December visit Davis had expressed the hope that he would be spared further depredations, it had not turned out that way. For him, as for his septuagenarian brother, the blue pursuit had been unrelenting. "Joe Davis's plantation was not far off," Sherman later recalled. "One of my staff officers went there, with a few soldiers, and took a pair of carriage horses, without my knowledge at the time. He found Joe Davis at home, an old man, attended by a young and affectionate niece; but they were overwhelmed with grief to see their country overrun and swarming with Federal troops."

Grant meanwhile was pushing west. About 7 o'clock he came upon Pemberton's new position — and found it even stronger, in some respects, than the one the rebels had occupied "by accident or design" the day before. This time, however, it was clearly by design. Not only had the position been prepared overnight for just such an emergency as the Confederates now faced; it was here, in fact, that Pemberton had wanted to do his fighting in the first place. The railroad bridge, which had been floored to provide for passage of his artillery and wagons, was at the apex of a horseshoe bend of the Big Black, whose high west bank afforded the guns emplaced along it an excellent field of fire out over the low-lying eastern bank and the mile-long line of rifle pits already dug across the open end of the horseshoe. Parapeted with bales of cotton brought from surrounding plantations, the line was a strong one, even without the concentric support of the guns emplaced to its rear, its front being protected by a shallow bayou that abutted north on the river and south on an impenetrable cypress brake. Whatever came at the men in these pits would have to come straight up the narrow railroad embankment, a suicidal prospect in the face of all that massed artillery, or across the rain-swollen bayou, beyond which open fields stretched for nearly half a mile, allowing the attackers little or no cover except for a single copse of woods about three hundred yards in front of the far left, where guns were also grouped in expectation. Still unaware that Loring had skedaddled, Pemberton held this intrenched bridgehead in hopes that Old Blizzards would show up in time for a share in the impending fight at the gates of Vicksburg, which was less than a dozen miles back down the road.

What showed up instead was the Yankees. One look at the position his opponent had selected — Pemberton, after all, was a trained engineer, with a reputation for skill in the old army — told Grant that he stood an excellent chance of suffering the bloodiest of repulses if he attempted a frontal attack. Fortunately, though, he had instructed Sherman to swing north of Edwards for a crossing at Bridgeport, five miles upstream; so that all Grant had to do here, for the present, was keep up a show of strength to hold Pemberton in place while Sherman got his three divisions over the river above and came down on his flank. But McClernand had other ideas. Troubled perhaps by his poor showing yesterday — though he would not hesitate presently to claim a lion's share of the credit for the Champion Hill success, on grounds that Hovey's division was from his corps — he moved vigorously today, sending Carr and Osterhaus, the Pea Ridge companions, respectively north and south of the railroad to confront the rebels crouched behind their cotton parapets. An assault was a desperate thing to venture against the dug-in Confederates and all those high-sited batteries in their rear, he knew, but he was quite as determined as Grant to "make a little showing," if not a big one. So was Brigadier General Michael Lawler, commanding Carr's second brigade, which had worked its way into the copse on the far right. A big man, over 250 pounds in weight and so large of girth that he had to wear his sword belt looped over one shoulder, Lawler was Irish, forty-nine years old, and lately an Illinois farmer. His favorite Tipperary maxim, "If you see a head, hit it," was much in his mind as he peered across the chocolate-colored bayou at the rebel intrench-ments three hundred yards away. Many heads were visible there, inviting him to hit them, and at last he could bear it no longer. Stripped to his shirt sleeves because of the midday heat, he stood up, swinging his sword, and ordered his four regiments forward on the double. The bayou was shoulder-deep in places, but the Iowa and Wisconsin soldiers floundered straight across it in what a reporter called "the most perilous and ludicrous charge I witnessed during the war," and came mud-plastered up to the enemy line with a whoop, having suffered 199 casualties in the three minutes that had elapsed since they left the copse. The loss was small compared to the gain, however, for the rebels broke rearward, avoiding contact, only to find that the bridge had been set afire in their rear to keep the close-following bluecoats from surging across in their wake. Lawler's reward was 1200 prisoners — more men, he said, than

*H*arper's Weekly's Theodore Davis drew this sketch of
Federal troops scaling the parapets along the Big Black
River during their advance on Vicksburg.

he himself had brought into action — out of a final total of 1751 Confederates killed and captured, along with 18 guns, when the other brigades took fire from his example and rushed forward, breaking the gray line all down its length. Grant's losses were 276 killed and wounded, plus 3 missing, presumably left at the bottom of the bayou now in his rear.

Across the way, Pemberton had watched the disintegration of his skillfully drawn line and the quick subtraction of a brigade from his dwindling army. Neither was truly catastrophic; he still held the high west bank of the river, and the bridge the Federals might have used for a crossing was burning fiercely in the noonday sunlight; but he was depressed by the failure of his men to hold a position of such strength. If they would not stand fast here, where would they stand fast? Years later, a member of his staff was to say: "The affair of Big Black bridge was one which an ex-Confederate participant naturally dislikes to record." It was unpleasant to remember, and it had been even more unpleasant to observe. Presently, moreover, word came from upstream that Sherman had forced a crossing at Bridgeport, capturing the dozen pickets on duty at that point. There was nothing for it now but to continue the retreat or be out-flanked. Pemberton gave the necessary orders and the westward march got under way, as it had done after yesterday's bloodier action, except that this time there would be no halt until Vicksburg itself was reached. Then what? He did not know how well his troops would fight with their backs to the wall, but this most recent action was not an encouraging example of their mettle. Some thirty hours ago he had had 17,500 effectives in his mobile force, and now he was down to a good deal less than half that many. In fact it was nearer a third, 5375 having been killed, wounded, or captured, while as many more had wandered off with Loring. As he rode westward, accompanied by his chief engineer, young Major Samuel Lockett, Pemberton's distress increased and his confidence touched bottom. "Just thirty years ago," he said at last, breaking a long and painful silence, "I began my military career by receiving my appointment to a cadetship at the U.S. Military Academy, and today — that same date — that career is ended in disaster and disgrace." Lockett tried to reassure the general by reminding him that two fresh divisions stood in the Vicksburg intrench-ments, which had been designed to withstand repeated assaults by almost any number of men. Besides, he said, Joe Johnston would be reinforced at Canton in the event of a siege, and would come to the beleaguered city's relief with all the skill for which he was famous, North and South. "To all of which," the major recalled afterwards, "General Pemberton replied that my youth and hopes were the parents of my judgment; he himself did not believe our troops would stand the first shock of an attack."

A dispatch had already gone to Johnston that morning, announcing the results of yesterday's battle and warning that Haines Bluff would have to be abandoned if the Big Black position was outflanked or overrun. Accordingly, as the retreat got under way, orders were sent for the garrison on the Yazoo to fall back, all but two companies, who were to forward all stores possible and destroy the rest, "making a show of force until the approach of the enemy by land should compel them to retire." Provisions were much on Pemberton's mind, despite his dejection, and he issued instructions that, from Bovina on, "all cattle, sheep, and hogs belonging to private parties, and likely to fall into the hands of the enemy, should be driven within our lines." Similarly, corn was pulled from the fields along the way, "and all disposable wagons applied to this end." If it was to be a siege, food was likely to be as vital a factor as ammunition, and he did all he could in that respect. The march continued, accompanied by the lowing of cows, the bleating of sheep, and the squealing of pigs, steadily westward. For all the Confederates knew, Sherman might have moved fast around their flank and beaten them to the goal. Then up ahead, as Pemberton was to remember it years later, "the outlines of the hill city rose slowly through the heated dust —

★

Vicksburg and security. Passing raddled fields turning colorless from the powdered earth that rose beneath their tramp, the gray soldiers slacked off the turnpikes along the high ground until they came inside the city's breastworks. As word carried down the crooked line of march that the race to Vicksburg had been won, the footsore remnants in the rear flooded down the pike."

Sunset made a red glory over the Louisiana bayous; "The sky faded to a cool green and it was dark." Pemberton and his aides worked through the night, seeing to the comfort of the troops who had fought today and yesterday, bivouacked now in rear of the intrenchments, and inspecting the front-line defenses manned by the two divisions which had remained in the city all this time. Dawn gave light by which to check the overlapping fields of fire commanded by the 102 guns, light and heavy, emplaced along the semicircular landward fortifications. Midmorning brought reports from scouts that the two companies left at Haines Bluff were on their way to Vicksburg, having complied with the order to hold out as long as possible. Heavy columns of Federals were close behind them, while other blue forces were hard on the march from Bovina. Before they arrived — as they presently did, to begin the investment — a messenger came riding in with a reply to yesterday's dispatch to Johnston, who had moved southwest from Canton to a position northeast of Brownsville. Pemberton's spirits had risen considerably since his confession of despair as he fell back from the Big Black the day before, but what his superior had to say was scarcely of a nature to raise them further. For one thing, the Virginian said nothing whatsoever about relief, either now or in the future. As he saw it, the choice had been narrowed to evacuation or surrender.

May 17, 1863.

Lieutenant General Pemberton:

Your dispatch of today . . . was received. If Haines Bluff is untenable, Vicksburg is of no value and cannot be held. If, therefore, you are invested at Vicksburg, you must ultimately surrender. Under such circumstances, instead of losing both troops and place, we must, if possible, save the troops. If it is not too late, evacuate Vicksburg and its dependencies, and march them to the northeast.

Most respectfully, your obedient servant,

J. E. Johnston, General

★

Even if Pemberton had wanted to follow this advice — which he did not, considering it in violation of orders from the Commander in Chief that the place be held at all costs — compliance was altogether beyond his means. Before he had time for more than brief speculation as to what effect these words might have on his chances of survival, Union guns were shelling his outer works. The siege had begun, and Grant was jockeying for positions from which to launch an all-out assault, intending to bring the three-weeks-old campaign, which had opened on his birthday, to the shortest possible end.

Yesterday's rout on the Big Black had seemed to indicate what the result of one hard smash at the rebel lines would be, and Grant's spirits had risen more or less in ratio to the droop of his opponent's. If roads could be found, he said as he watched the enemy abandon the high western bank, he intended to advance in three columns of one corps each, "and have Vicksburg or Haines Bluff tomorrow night." While Wilson and his engineers were collecting materials for replacing the burned railroad bridge, he rode up to Bridgeport and found Sherman hard at work laying India-rubber pontoons for a crossing in force. Soon after dark the first of his three divisions started over, their way lighted by pitch pine bonfires on both banks. Grant and his red-haired lieutenant sat on a log and watched the troops move westward over the Big Black, faces pale in the firelight and gun barrels catching glints from the flames as "the bridge swayed to and fro under the passing feet." Sherman was to remember it so. A water-colorist of some skill back in the days when there had been time for such diversions, he thought the present scene "made a fine war picture."

By daybreak all three divisions were across. Riding south to see whether McClernand and McPherson had done as well, Grant left instructions for Sherman to march northwest in order to interpose between Vicksburg and the forts on the Yazoo. By 10 o'clock this had been done. A detachment sent northward found Haines Bluff unoccupied, its big guns spiked, and made contact with the Union gunboats on the river below, signaling them to steam in close and tie up under the frowning bluff that had defied them for so long. Grant now had the supply base he wanted, north of the city. Presently he came riding up, to find his friend Sherman gazing down from the Walnut Hills at the Chickasaw Bayou region below, from which he had launched his bloody and fruitless assault against these heights five months ago. Up to now, the Ohioan had had his reservations about this eighth attempt to take or by-pass Vicksburg, saying flatly, "I tremble for the result. I look upon the whole thing as one of the most hazardous and desperate moves of this or any other war." But now his doubts were gone, replaced by enthusiasm: as was shown when he turned to Grant, standing quietly by, and abruptly broke the silence.

"Until this moment I never thought your expedition a success," he said; "I never could see the end clearly until now. But this is a campaign. This is a success if we never take the town."

★ ★ ★ Grant shared his friend's enthusiasm, if not his verbal exuberance, with regard to a situation brought about by a combination of careful strategy, flawlessly improvised tactics, sudden marches, and hard blows delivered with such triphammer rapidity that the enemy had never been given a chance to recover the balance he lost when the blue army, feinting coincidentally at Haines Bluff, swarmed ashore at Bruinsburg, forty-five air-line miles away. At no time in the past three weeks, moreover, had the outlook been so bright as it was now. All three corps had crossed the Big Black, the final natural barrier between them and their goal, and were converging swiftly upon the hilltop citadel by three main roads so appropriate to their purpose that they might have been surveyed with this in mind. Sherman advanced from the northeast on the Benton road, McPherson from due east, along the railroad and the Jackson turnpike, and McClernand from the southeast on the Baldwin's Ferry road. By nightfall, after a few brief skirmishes along the ill-organized line of rebel outposts — invariably abandoned at the first suggestion of real pressure — the lead elements of all three columns were in lateral contact with each other and in jump-off positions for tomorrow's assault. Next morning, May 19, while they completed their dispositions, the men were in high spirits. They were in fact, like Sherman, "a little giddy with pride" at the realization of all they had accomplished up to now. In the twenty days since they crossed the Mississippi, they had marched 180 miles to fight and win five battles — Port Gibson, Raymond, Jackson, Champion Hill, Big Black River — occupy a Deep South capital, inflict over 7000 casualties at a cost of less than 4500 of their own, and seize no less than fifty pieces of field artillery, not to mention two dozen larger pieces they found spiked in fortifications they outflanked. In all this time, they had not lost a gun or a stand of colors, and they had never failed to take an assigned objective, usually much more quickly than their commanders expected them to do. And now, just ahead, lay the last and largest of their objectives: Vicksburg itself, the ultimate prize for which the capture of all those others had served as prelude. Their belief that they would carry the place by storm, here and now, was matched by Grant, who issued his final orders before noon. "Corps commanders will push forward carefully, and gain as close position as possible to the enemy's works, until 2 p.m.; at [which] hour they will fire three volleys of artillery from all the pieces in position. This will be the signal for a general charge of all the army corps along the whole line." A closing sentence, intended to forestall the lapse of discipline that would attend a too-informal victory celebration, expressed the measure of his confidence that the assault would be successful, bringing the campaign to a triumphant close today: "When the works are carried, guards will be placed by all division commanders to prevent their men from straggling from their companies."

At the appointed hour, the guns boomed and the blue clots of troops rushed forward, shoulder to shoulder, cheering as they vied for the honor of being first to scale the ridge: whereupon, as if in response to the same signal, a long low cloud of smoke, torn along its bottom edge by the pinkish yellow stabs of muzzle flashes, boiled up with a great clatter from the rebel works ahead. The racket was so tremendous that no man could hear his own shouts or the sudden yelps of the wounded alongside him. What was immediately apparent, however, amid a confusion of sound so uproarious that it was as if the whole mad scene were being played in pantomime, was that the assault had failed almost as soon as it got started. Sherman, watching from a point of vantage near the north end of the line, put it simplest in a letter he wrote home that night: "The heads of the columns have been swept away as chaff thrown from the hand on a windy day." Others, closer up, had a more gritty sense of what had happened. Emerging into the open, an Illinois captain saw "the very sticks and chips, scattered over the ground, jumping under the hot shower of rebel bullets." Startled,

The fine homes of wealthy residents dot the Vicksburg bluff in this photograph taken from the courthouse cupola.

he and his company plunged forward, tumbled into a cane-choked ravine at the base of the enemy ridge, and hugged the earth for cover and concealment. All up and down the line it was much the same for those who had not scattered rearward at the first burst of fire; once within point-blank musket range, there was little the attackers could do but try to stay out of sight until darkness gave them a chance to pull back without inviting a bullet between the shoulder blades. As they lay prone the fire continued, cutting the stalks of cane, one by one, so that "they lopped gently upon us," as if to assist in keeping them hidden. Through the remaining hours of daylight they stayed there, with bullets twittering just above the napes of their necks. Then they returned through the gathering dusk to the jump-off positions they had left five hours ago. Reaching safety after a hard run, the captain and other survivors of his company "stopped and took one long breath, bigger than a pound of wool."

For the first time in history, a major assault was launched by commanders whose eyes were fixed on the hands of watches synchronized the night before.

Pemberton was perhaps as surprised as the bluecoats were at their abrupt repulse. In reporting to the President — the message would have to be smuggled out, of course, before it could be put on the wire for Richmond — that his army was "occupying the trenches around Vicksburg," he added proudly: "Our men have considerably recovered their morale." Meanwhile he strengthened his defenses and improved the disposition of his 20,000 effectives. M. L. Smith's division had the left, Forney's the center, and Stevenson's the right, while Bowen's was held in immediate reserve, under orders to be prepared to rush at a moment's notice to whatever point needed bolstering. There was a crippling shortage of intrenching tools, only about five hundred being on hand. "They were entirely inadequate," an engineer officer later declared, but "the men soon improvised wooden shovels [and used] their bayonets as picks." They had indeed "considerably recovered," now that they had stopped running, and they were hungry for revenge for the humiliations they had been handed, particularly day before yesterday on the Big Black River. If the Yankees would keep coming at them the way they had come this afternoon, the Confederates hoped they would keep it up forever.

In point of fact, that was pretty much what Grant had in mind. He had suffered 942 casualties and inflicted less than 200, thus coming close to reversing the Big Black ratio, but he still thought the ridge could be carried by

★

assault. Conferring next morning with his corps commanders he found them agreed that this first effort had failed, in Sherman's words, "by reason of the natural strength of the position, and because we were forced by the nature of the ground to limit our attacks to the strongest part of the enemy line, viz., where the three principal roads entered the city." Nothing could be done about the first of these two drawbacks, but the second could be corrected by careful reconnaissance. Better artillery preparations would also be of help, it was decided, in softening up the rebel works; moreover, the navy could add the weight of its metal from the opposite side of the ridge, Porter having returned from a two-week expedition up the Red River to Alexandria, where he had met Banks coming north from Opelousas on May 6. Grant told McClernand, Sherman, and McPherson to spend today and tomorrow preparing "for a renewed assault on the 22d, simultaneously, at 10 a.m." Riding his line while the work was being pushed, he found the men undaunted by their repulse the day before, though they were prompt to let him know they were weary of the meat-and-vegetables diet on which they had been subsisting for the past three weeks. Turkey and sweet potatoes were fine as a special treat, it seemed, but such rich food had begun to pall as a regular thing. A private looked up from shoveling, recognized Grant riding by, and said in a pointed but conversational tone: "Hardtack." Others took up the call, on down the line, raising their voices with every repetition of the word, until finally they were shouting with all their might. "Hardtack! Hardtack!" they yelled as the army commander went past. "Hardtack! Hardtack!" Finally he reined in his horse and informed all those within earshot that the engineers were building a road from the Yazoo steamboat landing, "over which to supply them with everything they needed." At this, as he said later, "the cry was instantly changed to cheers." That night there was hardtack for everyone, along with beans, and coffee to wash it down. The soldiers woke next morning strengthened for the work that was now at hand.

For the first time in history, a major assault was launched by commanders whose eyes were fixed on the hands of watches synchronized the night before. This was necessary in the present case because the usual signal guns would not have been heard above the din of the preliminary bombardment, which included the naval weapons on both flanks, upstream and down, and six mortar boats already engaged for the past two days in what one defender contemptuously called "the grand but nearly harmless sport of pitching big shells into Vicksburg." All night the 13-inch mortars kept heaving their 200-pound projectiles into the checkerboard pattern of the city's streets and houses, terrifying citizens huddled under their beds and dining-room tables. ("Vertical fire is never very destructive of life," the same witness remarked. "Yet the howling and bursting shells had a very demoralizing effect on those not accustomed to them.") Then at dawn the 200 guns on the landward side chimed in, raising geysers of dirt on

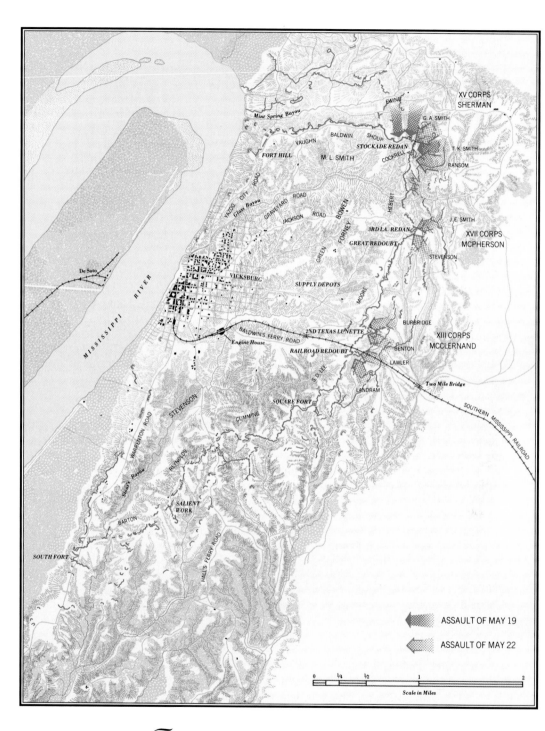

This map depicts Grant's advance on the Stockade Redan on May 19 and his push to the Railroad Redoubt and 3d Louisiana Redan on May 22 during the Vicksburg campaign.

the ridge where the Confederates were intrenched and waiting. At 9.30, in compliance with Grant's request, Porter closed the range with four gunboats from below and took the lower water batteries under fire. He was supposed to keep this up until 10.30, half an hour past the scheduled time for the infantry assault to open, but since he could see no indication that the army had been successful in its storming attempt, he kept up the fire for an extra hour before dropping back downriver and out of range. One ironclad, the *Tuscumbia*, was severely battered and forced to retire before the others. Otherwise, though he reported that this was altogether the hottest fire his boats had yet endured, Porter suffered little damage in the bows-on fight, aside from a few men wounded. He could not see, however, that he had accomplished much in the way of punishing the defenders. Nor was there any evidence that the army had done any better.

As a matter of fact, the army had done a good deal worse, though not for lack of trying. At the appointed hour the men of all three corps rushed forward, the advance waves equipped with twenty-foot scaling ladders to be used against steep-walled strongpoints, of which there were many along the ridge ahead. "The rebel line, concealed by the parapet, showed no sign of unusual activity," Sherman observed from his point of vantage to the north, "but as our troops came in fair view, the enemy rose behind their parapet and poured a furious fire upon our lines. . . . For about two hours we had a severe and bloody battle, but at every point we were repulsed." It was much the same with McPherson and McClernand, to the south, who also lost heavily as a result of these whites-of-their-eyes tactics employed by the Confederates. At several points, left and right and center, individual groups managed to effect shallow penetrations, despite what an Illinois colonel called "the most murderous fire I ever saw," but were quickly expelled or captured by superior forces the enemy promptly brought to bear from his mobile reserve. Those bluecoats who crouched in the ravines and ditches at the base of the ridge, taking shelter there as they had done three days ago, were dislodged by the explosion in their midst of 12-inch shells which the defenders rolled downhill after lighting the fuzes. On McClernand's front a heavier lodgment was effected at one point, and the general, taking fire at the sight of his troops flaunting their banners on the rebel works, sent word to Grant that he had "part possession of two forts, and the stars and stripes are floating over them." If the other two corps "would make a diversion in my favor," he thought he could enlarge his gains and perhaps score an absolute breakthrough. At any rate, he earnestly declared, "a vigorous push ought to be made all along the line."

Grant was with Sherman when the message reached him. "I don't believe a word of it," he said. Sherman protested that the note was official and must be credited. Though he had just called off his own attack, admitting failure, he offered to renew it at once in the light of this appeal from McClernand. Grant thought the matter over, then told the redhead he "might try it again" at

3 o'clock, if no contrary orders reached him before that time. Riding south, he detached one of McPherson's divisions to support McClernand and authorized a resumption of the attack on the center as well. Promptly at 3, Sherman launched his promised second assault, but found it "a repetition of the first, equally unsuccessful and bloody." McPherson had the same unpleasant experience. McClernand, still afire with hope, threw the borrowed division into the fray — though not in time to maintain, much less widen or deepen, the penetration of which he had been so proud. A whooping counterattack by Colonel T. N. Waul's Texas Legion killed or captured all but a handful of Federals at that point. By sundown the firing had died to a sputter, and at nightfall the survivors crept back across the corpse-pocked fields to the safety of the lines they had left with such high hopes that morning. Some measure of their determination and valor was shown by a comparison of their losses today with those of three days ago. The previous assault had ended with two stands of colors left on the forward slope of the enemy ridge; this time there were five. Moreover, the casualties exceeded this five-two ratio. Less than a thousand men had fallen the time before, including 165 killed or missing, whereas this time the figures went above three thousand — 3199, to be exact — with 649 in the killed-or-missing category. In other words, Grant had lost in the past three days almost as many soldiers as he had lost in the past three weeks of nearly continuous battle and maneuver which had brought him within sight of the ramparts of Vicksburg only to be repulsed.

He was furious. "This last attack only served to increase our casualties without giving any benefit whatever," he wrote some twenty years later, still chagrined. Quick as ever to shift the blame for any setback or evidence of short-coming — at Belmont it had been overexcited "higher officers"; at Donelson it had been McClernand; at Shiloh it had been Prentiss and Lew Wallace, although the former most likely had saved him from defeat; at Iuka it had been Rosecrans and the wind — he notified Halleck, two days after the second Vicksburg repulse: "The whole loss for the day will probably reach 1500 killed and wounded. General McClernand's dispatches misled me as to the real state of facts, and caused much of this loss. He is entirely unfit for the position of corps commander, both on the march and on the battlefield. Looking after his corps gives me more labor and infinitely more uneasiness than all the remainder of my department." And yet, on the day of battle itself, he included that general's misleading claims in his own dispatch informing Halleck of the outcome. "Vicksburg is now completely invested," he declared. "I have possession of Haines Bluff and the Yazoo; consequently have supplies. Today an attempt was made to carry the city by assault, but was not entirely successful. We hold possession, however, of two of the enemy's forts, and have skirmishers close under all of them. Our loss was not severe." As he wrote, his optimism grew; for that was the reverse of the coin. He would no more admit discouragement than he would entertain self-blame.

"The nature of the ground about Vicksburg is such that it can only be taken by a siege," he judged, but added: "It is entirely safe to us in time, I would say one week if the enemy do not send a large army upon my rear."

He did not regret having made the assaults; he only regretted that they had failed. Besides, he subsequently explained, his high-spirited troops had approached the gates of Vicksburg with a three-week cluster of victories to their credit; they would never have settled down willingly to the tedium of siege operations unless they had first been given the chance to prove that the place could not be taken by storm. Now that this had been demonstrated, though at the rather excessive price of 4141 casualties, they took to spadework with a will, constructing their own complex system of intrenchments roughly parallel to those of the rebels, which in a few places were not much more than fifty yards away. As they delved in the sandy yellow clay of the hillsides or drew their beads on such heads as appeared above the enemy parapets, they were encouraged by news of tangential victories, particularly on the part of the navy, which was on a rampage now that the outlying Confederate defenses had been abandoned. An expedition made up of the *DeKalb* and three tinclads, all under Lieutenant Commander John Walker, had been sent up the Yazoo on May 20, the day after the first assault, and returned on the 23d, the day after the second, to report that the rebels had set their Yazoo City navy yard afire at the approach of the Union vessels, the flames consuming three warships under construction on the stocks, for an estimated loss of $3,000,000. This meant that there would be no successor to the *Arkansas*, which was welcome news indeed. But Porter was unsatisfied; he sent the expedition back upriver the next morning. This time Walker steamed to within a dozen miles of Fort Pemberton, destroying steamboats and sawmills as he went, then came back downstream to push 180 miles up the winding Sunflower River, where he caught and burned still more fugitive rebel steamboats. Returning this second time, he could report that these streams were no longer arteries of supply for the Confederates below the confluence of the Tallahatchie and the Yalobusha, nearly one hundred air-line miles from the beleaguered Vicksburg bluff.

Pemberton took the news of this without undue distress. After all, the Yazoo and the Sunflower were no longer of much interest to him; the Father of Waters was now his sole concern, and only about a dozen miles of that. "I have decided to hold Vicksburg as long as possible," he had replied to Johnston's last-minute dispatch urging evacuation, "with the firm hope that the Government may yet be able to assist me in keeping this obstruction to the enemy's free navigation of the Mississippi River. I still conceive it to be the most important point in the Confederacy." His outlook improved with the repulse of the first Federal assault, and on the eve of the second he was asking: "Am I to expect reinforcements? From what direction, and how soon? . . . The men credit and are encouraged by a report that you are near with a large force. They are fighting in good spirits, and the reorganization is complete."

After the second repulse, however, the defenders were faced with an unpleasant problem. For three days — six, in the case of those who had fallen in the first assault — Grant's dead and injured lay in the fields and ditches at the base of the Confederate ridge, exposed to the fierce heat of the early Mississippi summer. The stench of the dead, whose bodies were swollen grotesquely, and the cries of the wounded, who suffered the added torment of thirst, were intolerable to the men who had shot them down; yet Grant would not ask for a truce for burial or treatment of these unfortunates, evidently thinking that such a request would be an admission of weakness on his part. Finally Pemberton could bear it no longer. On the morning of May 25 he sent a message through the lines to the Union commander: "Two days having elapsed since your dead and wounded have been lying in our front, and as yet no disposition on your part of a desire to remove them being exhibited, in the name of humanity I have the honor to propose a cessation of hostilities for two hours and a half, that you may be enabled to remove your dead and dying men." To Pemberton's relief, Grant at last "acceded" to this proposal. At 6 p.m. all firing was suspended while the Federals came forward to bury the dead where they lay and bring comfort to such few men as had survived the three-day torture. This done, they returned through the darkness to their lines and the firing was resumed with as much fury as before.

In nothing was Grant more "unpronounceable" than in this. He would berate, and in at least one case attack with his fists, any man he saw abusing a dumb animal; he had, it was said to his credit, no stomach for suffering; he disliked above all to ride over a field where there had been recent heavy fighting; he would not eat a piece of meat until it had been cooked to a char, past any sign of blood or even pinkness. Yet this he could do to his own men, this abomination perhaps beyond all others of the war, without expressed regret or apparent concern. However, this too was the reverse of a coin, the other side of which was his singleness of purpose, his quality of intense preoccupation with what he called "the business," meaning combat. He took his losses as they came — they had, in fact, about been made up already with the arrival that week of a division of reinforcements from Memphis, and would be more than made up with the arrival, early the following week, of a second such division, while four more were being alerted even now for the trip downriver from Tennessee, Missouri, and Kentucky to bring his mid-June total to 71,000 effectives — for the sake of getting on with the job to which he had set his hand. Long ago in Mexico, during a lull in the war, he had written home to the girl he was to marry: "If we have to fight, I would like to do it all at once and then make friends." He felt that way about it still, and now that he was calling the turn, he wanted no interludes or delays; he wanted it finished, and he believed the finish was in sight. "The enemy are now undoubtedly in our grasp," he told Halleck the day before the burial truce. "The fall of Vicksburg and the capture of most of the garrison can only be a question of time."

This was not to say there would be no more setbacks and frustrations. There would indeed, war being the chancy thing it was, and Grant knew it: which perhaps was why he had dropped his prediction, made two days before, that the fall of the city would be accomplished within "I would say one week." And in fact there was one such mishap three days later, two days after the burial truce, this time involving the navy. In the course of drawing his lines for the siege, Sherman had begun to suspect, from the amount of artillery fire he drew, that the Confederates were shifting guns from their upper water batteries to cover the landward approaches, particularly on their far left. Requested by Grant to test the facts of the case, Porter on May 27 sent the *Cincinnati* to draw the fire of the guns "if still there," covering her movements with four other ironclads at long range. She started downriver at 7 o'clock in the morning, commanded by Lieutenant G. M. Bache, and by 10 the matter had been settled beyond doubt. Not only were the guns still there, but they sank the *Cincinnati*. Rounding to in order to open fire, she took a pair of solids in her shell room and a third in her magazine. As she tried to make an upstream escape, a heavy shot drove through her pilot house and her starboard tiller was carried away, along with all three flagstaffs. Hulled repeatedly by plunging fire, she began filling rapidly. Bache, with five of his guns disabled in short order, tried to get beyond range and tie the vessel up to the east bank before she sank, but could not make it. She went down in three fathoms of water, still within range of the enemy guns, and what remained of her crew had to swim for their lives. The total loss, aside from the *Cincinnati* herself, was 5 killed, 14 wounded, and 15 missing, presumed drowned.

Convinced that Bache and his crew had done their best under disadvantageous circumstances, Porter accepted the loss of the ironclad — the third since his arrival in early December — as one of the accidents of war, and did not relax on that account his pressure against the rebels beleaguered on their bluff. He already had the approval of Grant for his conduct of naval affairs. Replying to a message in which the admiral informed him that Banks, although he had wound up his West Louisiana campaign at last, would "not [be] coming here with his men. He is going to occupy the attention of Port Hudson, and has landed at Bayou Sara, using your transports for the purpose," Grant told Porter: "I am satisfied that you are doing all that can be done in aid of the reduction of Vicksburg. There is no doubt of the fall of the place ultimately, but how long it will be is a matter of doubt. I intend to lose no more men, but to force the enemy from one position to another without exposing my troops."

★ ★ ★

★

Gun emplacements such as this, sitting high above the Mississippi atop a craggy 800-foot bluff, made Port Hudson unassailable from the river.

Port Hudson:
Banks and Gardner

1863 ★ ★ ★ ★ ★ ★

Banks had done a good deal **more by now** than merely "occupy the attention of Port Hudson." Crossing the Mississippi on the day after Grant's second repulse at Vicksburg, he completed his investment of the Louisiana stronghold on May 26, and next morning — simultaneous with the sinking of the *Cincinnati*, 240 winding miles upriver — launched his own all-out assault, designed to bring to a sudden and victorious end a campaign even more circuitous than Grant's. That general had covered some 180 miles by land and water before returning to his approximate starting point and placing his objective under siege, whereas Banks had marched or ridden about three times that far, as the thing turned out, to accomplish the same result. However, not only was the distance greater; the numerical odds had been tougher, at least at the start. Back in mid-March, when Farragut ran two ships past the fuming hundred-foot bluff, Banks had maneuvered on the landward side, only to discover that the defenders had more men inside the works than he had on the outside. This gave him pause, as well it might, and while he pondered the problem he learned that Grant, whom he had expected to join him in reducing Port Hudson as a prelude to their combined movement against Vicksburg, was stymied north of the latter place, involved in a series of canal and bayou experiments which seemed likely to delay him for

★

some time. Thinking it over, Banks decided to accomplish his assignment on his own. If he could not take Port Hudson, he would do as Grant was trying to do upriver. He would go around it.

It was not only that he was disinclined to wait and share the glory, politically ambitious though he was. He also believed he could not, and with cause. Nearly half of the 35,000 troops in his department were nine-month volunteers whose enlistments would be expiring between May and August; they would have to be used before summer or not at all. However, there was about as much need for caution as there was for haste, since more than half of this total, long- and short-term men alike, were required to garrison Baton Rouge, New Orleans, and various other points along the Mississippi and the Gulf. As a result of these necessary smaller detachments, his five divisions were reduced to about 5000 men each. Three of the five were with him near Port Hudson, under Major General C. C. Augur and Brigadier Generals William Emory and Cuvier Grover, while the fourth was at New Orleans under Brigadier General Thomas W. Sherman. Leaving Augur to hold Baton Rouge, Banks set out downriver with the other two on March 25 to join Godfrey Weitzel, commanding his fifth division at Brashear City, near Grand Lake and the junction of the Atchafalaya River and Bayou Teche. Back in January, Weitzel had ascended the former stream for a few miles, intending to establish an alternate route, well removed from the guns of Port Hudson, from the mouth of Red River to the Gulf. In this he had failed, not so much because of interference from Richard Taylor's scratch command of swamp-bound rebels, which he had thrown into precipitate retreat, but mainly because he had found the Atchafalaya choked with brush at that season of the year. Banks believed that this time he would succeed, and he hoped to abolish Taylor as a continuing threat. He intended in fact to capture him, bag and baggage, having worked out his plans with that in mind.

Taylor had about 4000 troops between the Teche and the Atchafalaya, his flanks protected right and left by two captured Union warships, the gunboat *Diana* and the armed ram *Queen of the West*, the former having been ambushed and seized that week near Pattersonville, when she imprudently ventured up the bayou, and the latter having been brought down from the Red River the week before to prevent her destruction or recapture by Farragut after his run past Port Hudson. Banks had four Gulf Squadron gunboats with which he planned to neutralize these two turncoat vessels, and he intended to bag Taylor's entire land force by sending one division from his 15,000-man command across Grand Lake to land in the rear of the rebels while he engaged them in front with his other two divisions. Hemmed in and outnumbered nearly four to one, Taylor would have to choose between surrender and annihilation. On April 11, in accordance with his design, Banks moved Emory and Weitzel from Brashear across the Atchafalaya to Berwick, and while they were advancing up the left bank of the Teche next day,

Federal troops storm ashore off transports in the Atchafalaya River to force a small detachment of Confederates to withdraw from near Irish Bend in the mid-April action at Bayou Teche.

skirmishing as they went, Grover put his troops aboard transports, escorted by the quartet of gunboats, and set out across the lake for a landing on the western shore within a mile of Irish Bend, an eastward loop of the Teche, control of which would place him squarely athwart the only Confederate line of retreat. Despite some irritating delays, the maneuver seemed to be going as planned; the skirmishing continued in front and Grover got his division ashore six miles in the enemy rear; Banks anticipated a Cannae. But Taylor got wind of what was up and reacted fast. Leaving a handful of men to put up a show of resistance to the two blue divisions in his front, he swung rearward with the rest to attack Grover and if possible drive him into the lake. On the 13th heavy fighting ensued. The shoestring force managed to delude and delay Emory and Weitzel while the main body fell on Grover. Though the latter was not driven into the lake, he was held in check while Taylor withdrew up the Teche in the darkness, foiling the plans so carefully laid for his destruction. In three days of intermittent action the Federals had lost 577 killed and wounded, the Confederates somewhat less, although there was considerable disagreement between the two commanders, then and later, as to the number of prisoners taken on each side, Taylor afterwards protesting that Banks had claimed the capture of more men than had actually opposed him.

Whatever the truth of his claims in this regard, and despite his failure to bring off the Cannae he intended, there could be no doubt that Banks, after a season of rather spectacular defeats in Virginia at the hands of Stonewall Jackson, had won his first clear-cut victory in the field. And next day, when he received word that the *Diana* and the *Queen* had been destroyed — the former burned by the rebels, who could not take her with them up the narrow Teche, and the latter sunk by the four Union gunboats, who blew her almost literally out of the water as soon as she entered Grand Lake and came within their range — his elation knew no bounds. Moreover, two of the gunboats steamed forthwith up the Atchafalaya and found it open to navigation all the way to the mouth of the Red, fifty miles above Port Hudson. This meant that Banks had the by-pass he had been seeking, though of course it would be of small practical use until Vicksburg had likewise been by-passed or reduced. Since there was no news that Grant had succeeded in any of his experimental projects in that direction, the Massachusetts general decided to explore some vistas he saw opening before him as a result of Taylor's defeat and withdrawal. Within two weeks New Orleans would have been returned to Federal control a solid year, and yet this principal seaport of the South had even less commerce with the outside world today than she had enjoyed in the days of the blockade runners, mainly because the rebel land forces had her cut off from those regions that normally supplied her with goods for shipment. One of the richest of these lay before him now: the Teche. Return of the Teche country to Union control, along with its vast supplies of cotton, salt, lumber, and foodstuffs, would restore New Orleans to her rightful place among the world's great ports and would demonstrate effectively, as one observer pointed out, "that the conquests of the national armies instead of destroying trade were calculated to instill new life into it." There was one drawback. Such a movement up the long riverlike bayou stretching north almost to Alexandria, even though un-opposed, might throw him off his previously announced schedule, which called for a meeting with Grant at Baton Rouge on May 10 for a combined attack, first on Port Hudson and then on Vicksburg. But Banks decided the probable gains were worth the risk. Besides, May 10 was nearly a month away, and he hoped to have completed his conquest of the region before then. If not, then Grant could wait, just as he had kept Banks waiting all this time.

Eager for more victories now that he had caught the flavor, the former Bay State governor put his three divisions on the march up the right bank of the Teche without delay. Two days later — April 16: Porter's bluejackets were steeling themselves for their run past the Vicksburg batteries that night, and Grierson's troopers would ride out of La Grange the following morning — he entered New Iberia and pushed on next day to the Vermilion River, which branched south-ward from the Teche near Vermilionville. Finding Taylor's rear guard drawn up on the opposite bank to contest a crossing, the bluecoats forced it with a brief skirmish, rebuilt the wrecked bridge, and on April 20 marched into Opelousas, evacuated two days earlier by the Louisiana government which had moved there a year ago when Farragut steamed upriver from New Orleans and trained his guns on Baton Rouge. Taylor did not challenge the occupation of this alternate capital, but continued to fall back toward Alexandria, having received from Kirby

Smith at Shreveport, his Transmississippi headquarters, a message expressing "gratification at the conduct of the troops under your command" and congratulating Taylor for the skill he had shown "in extricating them from a position of great peril." Banks called a halt in order to rest his men for a few days and consolidate his gains, which were considerable. Conquest of the Teche had brought within his grasp large quantities of lumber, 5000 bales of cotton, many hogsheads of sugar, an inexhaustible supply of salt, and an estimated 20,000 head of cattle, mules, and horses. He later calculated the value of these spoils to have been perhaps as high as $5,000,000 and pointed out that even this liberal figure should be doubled, since the goods it represented had not only come into Federal hands but had also been kept from the Confederates beyond the Mississippi, for whom they had been in a large part intended. Nor was that all. There were human spoils as well. Back in New Orleans the year before, Ben Butler had begun to enlist freedmen and fugitive slaves in what he called his Corps d'Afrique; now Banks

Return of the Teche country to Union control, along with its vast supplies of cotton, salt, lumber, and foodstuffs, would restore New Orleans to her rightful place among the world's great ports . . .

continued this recruitment in the Teche. Two such regiments were organized at Opelousas, with about 500 men in each. Styled the 1st and 3d Louisiana Native Guards, the former was composed of "free Negroes of means and intelligence," with colored line officers and a white lieutenant colonel in command, while the latter was made up largely of ex-slaves whose officers were all white. There was considerable speculation, in the army of which they were now a part, as to how they would behave in combat — when and if they were exposed to it, which many of their fellow soldiers thought inadvisable — but Banks was willing to abide the issue until it had been settled incontrovertibly under fire.

Taylor by now had reached the Red at Gordon's Landing, where the *Queen of the West* had been blasted and captured back in February, thirty miles below Alexandria. Renamed Fort De Russy, the triple-casemated battery had held the low bluff against all comers, and on May 4 its staunchness was proved again when it was attacked by the two gunboats that had come up the Atchafalaya from Grand Lake after sinking the *Queen*. Leading the way, however, was the *Albatross*, which had got past Port Hudson with Farragut in mid-March. She closed the range to five hundred yards and kept up a forty-minute bombardment, supported by the other two ships at longer range, before dropping back with eleven holes punched in her hull and most of her spars and rigging shot away. Fifty miles downriver next morning, having given up hope of reducing the fort on their own, the three ships met Porter — who, after completing the ferrying of Grant's two lead divisions across the Mississippi, had taken possession of Grand Gulf three days ago — coming up the Red with three of his ironclads, a steam ram, and a tug. This seemed quite enough for the task of reduction, but when he reached Fort De Russy late that afternoon, prepared to throw all he had at the place, he found it abandoned, its casemates yawning empty. Threatened from the rear by Banks, who had ended his Opelousas rest halt and resumed his northward march beyond the headwaters of the Teche, the garrison had retreated to avoid capture. Porter continued on to Alexandria next day, May 6, to find that Taylor had also fallen back from there. A couple of hours later, Banks marched in at the head of his three-division column. He was in fine spirits, still wearing his three-week-old aura of victory, and Porter was impressed — particularly by the outward contrast between this new general and the one he had been working alongside for the past four months around Vicksburg. "A handsome, soldierly-looking man," the admiral called the former Speaker of the House, "though rather theatrical in his style of dress." The impression was one of nattiness and sartorial elegance; Banks in fact was something of a military dude. "He wore yellow gauntlets high upon his wrists, looking as clean as if they had just come from the glove-maker; his hat was picturesque, his long boots and spurs were faultless, and his air was that of one used to command. In short, I never saw a more faultless-looking soldier."

General Nathaniel Banks engaged African-American troops in the fight against the Confederacy. Here, a black sentry stands guard near C. C. Augur, seated left.

Banks was about as proud as he was dapper, and with cause. His Negro recruits more than made up — in numbers at any rate, though it was true their combat value was untested — for the casualties he had suffered in the course of his profitable campaign up the Teche, and his present position at Alexandria gave him access to the entire Red River Valley, a region quite as rich as the one he had just traversed, and far more extensive. With elements already on the march for Natchitoches, fifty air-line miles upriver, and Taylor still fading back from contact, he saw more vistas opening out before him. He also realized, however, that they were unattainable just yet. "The decisive battle of the West must soon be fought near Vicksburg," Kirby Smith was telling a subordinate even now. "The fate of the Trans-Mississippi Department depends on it, and Banks, by operating here, is thrown out of the campaign on the Mississippi." The Massachusetts general agreed, although unwillingly, that he must first turn back east to resume his collaboration with Grant for the reduction of Vicksburg and Port Hudson. Then perhaps, with the Mississippi unshackled throughout its length, he would return up the Red to explore those new vistas stretching all the way to Texas. Grant meanwhile, having won the Battle of Port Gibson, crossed Bayou Pierre, and put his three divisions into jump-off positions for the advance on Jackson, was calling urgently for Banks to join him at once in front of Vicksburg; "But I must say, without qualifications," the latter replied on May 12, "that the means at my disposal do not leave me a shadow of a chance to accomplish it." Though he was "dying with a kind of vanishing hope to see [our] two armies acting together against the strong places of the enemy," he had "neither water nor land transportation to make the movement by the river or by land. The utmost I can accomplish," he told Grant, "is to cross for the purpose of operating with you against Port Hudson."

Once more having reached a decision he wasted no time. Two days later, ending a week's occupation in the course of which he sent no less than 2000 spoils-laden wagons groaning south, he began his withdrawal from Alexandria. The march prescribed was via Simmesport for a crossing at Bayou Sara, a dozen miles above Port Hudson, but Banks himself did not accompany the three divisions on their overland trek; he went instead by boat, first down the Red, then down the Atchafalaya to Brashear City, where he caught a train for New Orleans. With him rode the fifty-two-year-old Emory, whose health had failed in the field and who had been succeeded by Brigadier General Halbert Paine, fifteen years his junior and the only non-West Pointer in Banks's army with so much rank — aside from Banks himself, of course — though he could claim the distinction of having shared a law office with Lincoln's friend Carl Schurz before the war. In New Orleans, Banks gave Emory the task of defending the city with a stripped-down garrison left behind by Thomas Sherman, who was instructed to put most of his men aboard transports bound for Baton Rouge to join Augur for an advance on Port Hudson. As Banks planned it, the two divisions marching north from Baton Rouge would converge on the objective at the same time as the three marching south from Bayou Sara. For all the omnivorous reading he had done since his days as a bobbin boy in his home-state spinning mills, he may or may not have known that in thus intending to unite two widely divided columns on the field of battle he was attempting what Napoleon had called the most difficult maneuver in the book. If so, nonprofessional though he was, he showed no qualms beyond those normally involved in getting some 20,000 troops from one place — or in this case two places — to another. What was more, he brought it off. Advancing simultaneously north and south, the two bodies converged on schedule, May 25. Next day they completed their investment, and the following morning they launched an all-out assault on the 7000 rebels penned up inside Port Hudson.

★ ★ ★ Like Pemberton, who was nine years his senior, Franklin Gardner was a northern-born professional who married South — his father-in-law was ex-Governor Alexander Mouton, who presided over the legislative body that voted Louisiana out of the Union — then went with his wife's people when the national crisis forced a choice. New York born and Iowa raised, the son of a regular army colonel who had been Adjutant General during the War of 1812, he had graduated from West Point in the class of '43, four places above Ulysses Grant and one below Christopher Augur, whose division was part of the blue cordon now drawn around the bastion Gardner was defending. A brigadier at Shiloh and with Bragg in Kentucky, he had been promoted to major general in December, shortly before his fortieth birthday, and sent to command the stronghold Breckinridge had established at Port Hudson after being repulsed at Baton Rouge in August. By early April his strength had risen beyond 15,000 men, but it had since been whittled down to less than half that as a result of levies by the department commander, reacting to upriver pressure from Grant while Banks was off in the Teche. On May 4, in response to what turned out to be Pemberton's final call, Gardner set out for Jackson with all but a single brigade, only to receive on May 9 at Osyka, just north of the Mississippi line, a dispatch instructing him to return at once to Port Hudson and hold it "to the last," this being Pemberton's interpretation of the President's warning that "both Vicksburg and Port Hudson [are] necessary to a connection with Trans-Mississippi." Gardner did as he was told, and got back there barely ahead of Banks. His strength report of May 19 — the date of Grant's first assault on the Vicksburg intrenchments, 120 air-line miles to the north — showed an "aggregate present" of 5715 in his three brigades, plus about one thousand artillerists in the permanent garrison. That was also the date on a message Joe Johnston addressed to Gardner from north of the Mississippi capital, which had

★

fallen on the day after his arrival the week before: "Evacuate Port Hudson forth-with, and move with your troops toward Jackson to join other troops which I am uniting. Bring all the fieldpieces that you have, with their ammunition and the means of transportation. Heavy guns and their ammunition had better be destroyed, as well as the other property you may be unable to remove." By the time the courier got there, however, he found a ring of Federal steel drawn tightly around the blufftop fortress. He could only report back to Johnston that Port Hudson — like Vicksburg, 240 roundabout miles upriver — was besieged.

The Union navy had reappeared ahead of the Union army. On May 4, meeting Porter at the mouth of the Red, Farragut gave over his blockade duties from that point north and steamed back down the Mississippi to Port Hudson. For three days, May 8-10, he bombarded the bluff from above and below, doing all he could to soften it up for Banks, who was still at Alexandria. Upstream were the *Hartford* and the *Albatross,* patched up since her recent misfortune at Fort De Russy, while the downstream batteries were engaged by the screw sloops *Monongahela* and *Richmond,* the gunboat *Genesee,* and the orphaned ironclad *Essex,* which had been downriver ever since her run past Vicksburg the summer before. Coming overland down the western bank, Farragut conferred with Banks on his arrival from New Orleans, May 22. The rebels had given him shell for shell, he said, and shown no sign of weakening under fire, but he assured the general that the navy would continue to do its share until the place had been reduced. Banks thanked him and proceeded to invest the bluff on its landward side, north and east and south, depending on the fleet to see that the beleaguered garrison made no westward escape across the river and received no reinforcements or supplies from that direction. Assisted meanwhile by Grierson's well-rested troopers, who had ridden up from Baton Rouge with the column from the south, he drew his lines closer about the rebel fortifications. On May 26, with ninety guns in position opposing Gardner's thirty-one, he issued orders for a full-scale assault designed to take the place by storm next morning. Weitzel, Grover, and Paine were north of the Clinton railroad, which entered the works about midway, Augur and Sherman to the south. The artillery preparation would begin at daybreak, he explained, augmented by high-angle fire from the navy, and the five division commanders would "dispose their troops so as to annoy the enemy as much as possible during the cannonade by advancing skirmishers to kill the enemy's cannoneers and to cover the advance of the assaulting column." This was somewhat hasty and Banks knew it, but he had reasons for not wanting to delay the attempt for the sake of more extensive preparations. First, like Grant eight days ago at Vicksburg, he believed the rebels were demoralized and unlikely to stand up under a determined blow if it were delivered before they had time to recover their balance. Second, and more important still, he was anxious to wind up the campaign and return to New

Orleans; Emory was already complaining that he was in danger of being swamped by an attack from Mobile, where the Confederates had some 5000 men — twice as many as he himself had for the defense of the South's first city — or from Brashear, to which Taylor was free to return now that Banks had left the Teche. This was indeed a two-pronged danger; in fact, despite the cited lack of transportation, it had been the real basis for the Massachusetts general's refusal to join Grant in front of Vicksburg. However, for all his haste, the special orders he distributed on the 26th for the guidance of his subordinates in next day's operation were meticulous and full. Attempting to forestall confusion by assigning particular duties, he included no less than eleven numbered paragraphs in the order, all of them fairly long except the last, which contained a scant half-dozen words: "Port Hudson must be taken tomorrow."

At first it appeared that the order would be carried out, final paragraph and all; but around midmorning, when the thunder of the preliminary bombardment subsided and Weitzel went forward according to plan, driving the rebel skirmishers handsomely before him, he found that this unmasked their artillery, which opened point-blank on his troops with murderous effect. The bluecoats promptly hit the dirt and hugged it while their own batteries came up just behind them and unlimbered, returning the deluge of grape and canister at a range of two hundred and fifty yards. Crouched under all that hurtling iron

and lead from front and rear, the men were badly confused and lost what little sense of direction they had retained during their advance through a maze of obstructions, both natural and man-made. "The whole fight took place in a dense forest of magnolias, mostly amid a thick undergrowth, and among ravines choked with felled and fallen timber, so that it was difficult not only to move but even to see," a participant was to recall, adding that what he had been involved in was not so much a battle or a charge as it was "a gigantic bush-whack." Paine and Grover, moving out in support of Weitzel, ran into the same maelstrom of resistance, with the same result. So did Augur, somewhat later, when his turn came to strike the Confederate center just south of the railroad. But all was strangely quiet all this while on the far left. At noon Banks rode over to look into the cause of this inaction, and found to his amazement that Tom Sherman had "failed utterly and criminally to bring his men into the field." The fifty-two-year-old Rhode Islander was at lunch, surrounded by "staff officers all with their horses unsaddled." As usual, despite the multiparagraphed directive, someone — in this case about 3500 someones, from the division commander down to the youngest drummer — had not got the word. Nettled by the dressing-down Banks gave him along with peremptory orders to "carry the works at all hazards," Sherman got his two brigades aligned at last and took them forward shortly after 2 o'clock. He rode at their head, old army style; but

Federal infantry clamber over fallen timbers during one of Nathaniel Banks's two attacks on Port Hudson, which cost him a total of 4000 dead and wounded.

not for long. A conspicuous target, he soon tumbled off his horse, and the surgeons had to remove what was left of the leg he had been shot in.

Command of the division passed to Brigadier General William Dwight, who had resigned as a West Point cadet ten years ago to go into manufacturing in his native Massachusetts at the age of twenty-one, but had returned to military life on the outbreak of the war. However, for all the youth and vigor which had enabled him to survive three wounds and a period of captivity after being left for dead on the field of Williamsburg a year ago next month, Dwight could do no more than Sherman had done already. His pinned-down men knew only too well that to attempt to rise, with all those guns and rifles trained on them from behind the red clay parapets ahead, would mean at best a trip back to the surgery where the doctors by now were sawing off their former commander's leg. To attempt a farther advance, either here or on the east, was clearly hopeless; yet Banks was unwilling to call it a day until he had made at least one more effort.

They had settled one other matter effectively: the question of whether Negroes would stand up under fire and take their losses as well as white men.

Weitzel's division, which had opened the action that morning around to the north, had gained more ground than any of the other four, causing one observer to remark that if he had "continued to press his attack a few minutes longer he would probably have broken through the Confederate defense and taken their whole line in reverse." Now that the defenders were alert and had the attackers zeroed in, that extra pressure would be a good deal harder to exert, but Banks at any rate thought it worth a try. Orders were sent to the far right for a resumption of the assault, and were passed along to the colonel commanding the two regiments lately recruited in the Teche, the 1st and 3d Louisiana Native Guards. Held in reserve till now, they were about to receive their baptism of fire: a baptism which, as it turned out, amounted to total immersion. A Union staff officer who watched them form for the attack described what happened. "They had hardly done so," he said, "when the extreme left of the Confederate line opened on them, in an exposed position, with artillery and musketry and forced them to abandon the attempt with great loss." However, that was only part of the story. Of the 1080 men in ranks, 271 were hit, or one out of every four. They had accomplished little except to prove, with a series of disjointed rushes and repulses over broken ground and through a tangle of obstructions, that the rebel position could not be carried in this fashion. And yet they had settled one other matter effectively: the question of whether Negroes would stand up under fire and take their losses as well as white men. "It gives me pleasure to report that they answered every expectation," Banks wrote Halleck. "In many respects their conduct was heroic. No troops could be more determined or more daring."

Yet this was but a fraction of the day-long butcher's bill, which was especially high by contrast; 1995 Federals had fallen, and only 235 Confederates. In reaction, Banks told Farragut next day that Port Hudson was "the strongest position there is in the United States." Though he frankly admitted, "No man on either side can show himself without being shot," he was no less determined than he had been before the assault was launched. "We shall hold on today," he said, "and make careful examinations with reference to future operations." That morning — unlike Grant after his second repulse, five days earlier at Vicksburg — he had requested "a suspension of hostilities until 2 o'clock this afternoon, in order that the dead and wounded may be brought off the field." Gardner consented, not only to this but also to a five-hour extension of the truce when it was found that the grisly harvest required a longer time for gleaning. Meanwhile Banks was writing to Grant, bringing him up to date on events and outlining the problem as he saw it now. "The garrison of the enemy is 5000 or 6000 men," he wrote. "The works are what would ordinarily be styled 'impregnable.' They are surrounded by ravines, woods, valleys, and bayous of the most intricate and labyrinthic character, that make the works themselves almost inaccessible. It requires time even to understand the geography of the position. [The rebels] fight with determination, and our men, after a march of some 500 or 600 miles, have done all that could be expected or required of any similar force." A postscript added an urgent request: "If it be possible, I beg you to send me at least one brigade of 4000 or 5000 men. This will be of vital importance to us. We may have to abandon these operations without it." No such reinforcements would be coming either now or later from Grant, who had his hands quite full upriver; but Banks had no real intention of abandoning the siege. "We mean to harass the enemy night and day, and to give him no rest," he declared in a message to Farragut that same day, and he followed this up with another next morning: "Everything looks well for us. The rebels attempted a sortie upon our right last evening upon the cessation of the armistice, but were smartly and quickly repulsed." Two days later, May 31, when the admiral informed him that three Confederate deserters had stated that "unless reinforcements arrive they cannot hold out three days longer," Banks replied: "Thanks for your note and the cheering report of the deserters. We are closing in upon the enemy, and will have him in a day or two."

So he said. But presently a dispatch arrived from Halleck, dated June 3, which threatened to cut the ground from under the besieging army's feet. Like Grant, and perhaps for the same reasons, Banks had kept the general-in-chief in the dark as to his intentions until it was too late for interference, and Old Brains expressed incredulity at the secondhand reports of what had happened. "The newspapers state that your forces are moving on Port Hudson instead of coöperating with General Grant, leaving the latter to fight both Johnston and Pemberton. As this is so contrary to all your instructions, and so opposed to military principles, I can hardly believe it true." That it was true, however, was shown by a bundle of letters he received that same day from Banks, announcing his intention to move southeast from Alexandria. "These fully account for your movement on Port Hudson, which before seemed so unaccountable," Halleck wrote next morning. But he still did not approve, and he said so in a message advising Banks to get his army back on what the general-in-chief considered the right track. "I hope that you have ere this given up your attempt on Port Hudson and sent all your spare forces to Grant. . . . If I have been over-urgent in this matter, it has arisen from my extreme anxiety lest the enemy should concentrate all his strength on one of your armies before you could unite, whereas if you act together you certainly will be able to defeat him." Banks bristled at being thus lectured to. It irked him, moreover, that the authorities did not seem to take into account the fact that he was the senior general on the river. If any reproach for noncoöperation was called for, it seemed to him that it should have been aimed at Grant. "Since I have been in the army," he replied in mid-June, when the second message reached him, "I have done all in my power to comply with my orders. It is so in the position I now occupy. I came here not only for the purpose of coöperating with General Grant, but by his own suggestion and appointment." In time Halleck came round. "The reasons given by you for moving against Port Hudson are satisfactory," he conceded in late June. "It was presumed that you had good and sufficient reasons for the course pursued, although at this distance it seemed contrary to principles and likely to prove unfortunate." If this was not altogether gracious, Banks did not mind too much. He considered that he had already disposed of Halleck's bookish June 4 argument with a logical rebuttal, written by coincidence on the same day: "If I defend New Orleans and its adjacent territory, the enemy will go against Grant. If I go with a force sufficient to aid him, [by-passing Port Hudson,] my rear will be seriously threatened. My force is not large enough to do both. Under these circumstances, my only course seems to be to carry this post as soon as possible, and then to join General Grant. . . . I have now my heavy artillery in position, and am confident of success in the course of a week."

Here again he underestimated the rebel garrison's powers of resistance; Port Hudson was not going to fall within a month, much less a week. Gardner had drawn his semicircular lines with care, anchoring both extremities to the lip of the hundred-foot bluff overlooking the river, and had posted his troops for maximum effect, whatever the odds. North of the railroad there were two main forts, one square, the other pentagonal, with a small redoubt between them, all three surrounded and tied together by a network of trenches, occupied by two brigades under Colonels I. G. W. Steedman and W. R. Miles. Brigadier General William Beall, a Kentucky-born West Pointer, had his brigade, which was as big as the other two combined, disposed to the south along a double line of bastions, the largest of which surmounted the crest of a ridge and was called the Citadel because it dominated all the ground in that direction. These various major works, together with their redans, parapets, ditches, and gun emplacements, were mutually supporting, so that an advance on one invited fire from those adjoining it. Banks had discovered this first, to his regret, while launching the May 27 assault. Since then, he had limited his activities mainly to long-range bombardments and the digging of lines of contravallation, designed to prevent a breakout and to protect his troops from sorties. After two weeks of this, in the course of which a considerable number of his men were dropped by snipers, he grew impatient and ordered a probing night action which he characterized as an endeavor "to get within attacking distance of the works in order to avoid the terrible losses incurred in moving over the ground in front." Informed that the sudden lunge was to be preceded by a twenty-hour bombardment, Farragut, whose ships by now were getting low on ammunition, protested mildly that he did not think the constant shelling did much good. "After people have been harassed to a certain extent, they become indifferent to danger, I think," he said. But he added: "We will do all in our power to aid you." That power was not enough, as it turned out. At 3 o'clock in the morning, June 11, the blue infantry crept quietly forward under cover of darkness — and found the defenders very much on the alert. Though some men got through the abatis and up to the hostile lines, once the alarm was sounded they were quickly driven back, while those who chose not to run the gauntlet to regain their jump-off positions were taken captive. Except for lengthening the Federal casualty lists and increasing Confederate vigilance in the future, the action had no effect on anything whatsoever, so far as Banks and his shovel-weary, sniper-harassed men could discern: least of all on the siege, which continued as before.

His spirits were revived, however, by a message received two days later from Dwight, who reported that he had interrogated a quartet of Confederate deserters and had learned from them that the garrison, reduced by sickness to 3200 infantry and 800 artillerymen, was down to "about five days' beef." There were "plenty of peas, plenty of corn," but "no more meal." Starvation was staring the rebels in the face. In fact, a Mississippi regiment was said to be in such low spirits that it "drove about 50 head of cattle out of the works about a week ago," intending thereby to hasten the inevitable end. In short, Dwight wrote, "The troops generally wish to surrender, and despair of relief." Next morning, June 13, Banks decided to test the validity of this report. His plan, as he explained it to

Farragut, whose coöperation was requested, was to "open a vigorous bombardment at exactly a quarter past eleven this morning, and continue it for exactly
one hour. . . . The bombardment will be immediately followed by a summons to
surrender. If that is not listened to, I shall probably attack tomorrow." The guns
roared on schedule, then stopped at the appointed time, and Banks sent forward
under a white flag his demand for instant capitulation. "Respect for the usages of
war, and a desire to avoid unnecessary sacrifice of life, impose on me the necessity
of formally demanding the surrender of the garrison of Port Hudson." That was
the opening sentence of the page-long "summons," and it was balanced by another
very like it at the close: "I desire to avoid unnecessary slaughter, and I therefore
demand the immediate surrender of the garrison, subject to such conditions only
as are imposed by the usages of civilized warfare. I have the honor to be, sir, very
respectfully, your most obedient servant, *N. P. Banks,* Major General, Commanding." The Confederate reply was prompt and a good deal briefer. "Your
note of this date has just been handed to me, and in reply I have to state that my
duty requires me to defend this position, and therefore I decline to surrender. I
have the honor to be, sir, very respectfully, your most obedient servant, *Frank.
Gardner,* Major General, Commanding C. S. Forces."

Banks had said that if his demands were not "listened to" he probably
would launch a second full-scale assault next morning, all along the line. At daybreak, following a vigorous one-hour cannonade which apparently served little
purpose except to warn the Confederates he was coming, he did just that. When
the smoke cleared it was found that he had suffered the worst drubbing of the
war, so far at least as a comparison of the casualties was concerned. On the far
left, Dwight was misdirected by his guides, with the result that he was blasted
into retreat before he even knew he was exposed. In the center, Augur and
Paine attacked with vigor and were bloodily repulsed when they struck what
turned out to be the strongest point of the enemy line, the priest-cap near the
Jackson road; Paine himself fell, badly wounded, and was carried off the field.
On the right, Grover and Weitzel were stopped in midcareer when it was
demonstrated that no man could clear the fire-swept ridge along their front and
live. "In examining the position afterward," a Union officer declared, "I found
[one] grass-covered knoll shaved bald, every blade cut down to the roots as by a
hoe." By noon it was apparent that the assault had failed in every sector. All that
had been accomplished was a reduction of the range for the deadly snipers
across the way, and the price exacted was far beyond the worth of a few yards of
shell-torn earth. There was hollow mockery, too, in the respective losses, North
and South. The Federals had 1792 killed, wounded, and missing subtracted from
their ranks, while the Confederates had lost an over-all total of 47.

Four weeks of siege, highlighted by two full-scale assaults and one
abortive night attack, had cost Banks more than 4000 casualties along his seven

*J*ust outside Port Hudson, an emplacement for
Battery F, 1st U.S. Artillery, is fortified with
logs, cotton bales, and other material.

concave miles of front. His men, suspecting that they had inflicted scarcely more than one tenth as many casualties on the enemy, were so discouraged that the best he could say of them, in a note to Farragut that evening, was that they were "in tolerable good spirits." Presently, though, even this was more than he could claim. "The heat, especially in the trenches, became almost insupportable, the stenches quite so," a staff major later recalled. "The brooks dried up, the creek lost itself in the pestilential swamp, the springs gave out, and the river fell, exposing to the tropical sun a wide margin of festering ooze. The illness and mortality were enormous." Counting noses four days after the second decisive repulse, Banks reported that he was down to 14,000 effectives, including the nine-month volunteers whose enlistments were expiring. This too was a source of discontent, which reached the stage of outright mutiny in at least one Bay State regiment, and the reaction was corrosive. Men whose time was nearly up did not "feel like desperate service," Banks told Halleck, while those who had signed on for the duration did not "like to lead where the rest will not follow." Old Brains had a prescription for that, however. "When a column of attack is formed of doubtful troops," he answered, "the proper mode of curing their defection is to place

★

artillery in their rear, loaded with grape and canister, in the hands of reliable men, with orders to fire at the first moment of disaffection. A knowledge of such orders will probably prevent any wavering, and, if not, one such punishment will prevent any repetition of it in your army."

This was perhaps reassuring, though in an unpleasant sort of way, since it showed the general-in-chief to be considerably more savage where blue rebels were concerned than he had ever been when his opponents wore butternut or gray. However, Banks had even larger problems than mutiny on his hands by then. Emory was crying havoc in New Orleans, which he protested was in grave danger of being retaken by the rebels any day now. "The railroad track at Terre Bonne is torn up. Communication with Brashear cut off," he notified Banks on June 20, adding: "I have but 400 men in the city, and I consider the city and the public property very unsafe. The secessionists here profess to have certain information that their forces are to make an attempt on the city." Five days later — by which date Port Hudson had been under siege a month — he declared that the rebels bearing down on him were "known and ascertained to be at least 9000, and may be more. . . . The city is quiet on the surface, but the undercurrent is in a ferment." "Something must be done for this city, and that quickly," he insisted four days later. His anxiety continued to mount in ratio to his estimate of the number of graybacks moving against him, until finally he said flatly: "It is a choice between Port Hudson and New Orleans. . . . My information is as nearly positive as human testimony can make it that the enemy are 13,000 strong, and they are fortifying the whole country as they march from Brashear to this place, and are steadily advancing. I respectfully suggest that, unless Port Hudson is already taken, you can only save this city by sending me reinforcements immediately and at any cost." What was more, he said, the danger was not only from outside New Orleans. "There are at least 10,000 fighting men in this city (citizens) and I do not doubt, from what I see, that these men will, at the first appearance of the enemy within view of the city, be against us to a man. I have the honor to be &c. *W. H. Emory*, Brigadier General, Commanding."

But Banks had no intention of loosening his grip on the upriver fortress, which he believed — despite the nonfulfillment of all his earlier predictions — could not hold out much longer. Emory would have to take his chances. If it came to the worst and New Orleans fell, Farragut would steam down and retake it with the fleet that would be freed for action on the day Port Hudson ran up the white flag. Meanwhile the signs were good. On June 29, no less than thirty deserters stole out of the rebel intrenchments and into the Union lines, and though by now Banks knew better than to judge the temper of the garrison by that of such defectors, he was pleased to learn from those who arrived in the afternoon that their dinner had been meatless. In the future, they had been told, the only meat they would get would be that of mules. Judging by the adverse reaction of his own troops to a far more palatable diet, Banks did not think the johnnies would be likely to sustain their morale for long on that. However, one of the butternut scarecrows brought with him a copy of yesterday's *Port Hudson Herald*, which featured a general order issued the day before by Gardner, "assuring the garrison that General Johnston will soon relieve Vicksburg, and then send reinforcements here." The southern commander declared as well, Banks pointed out in passing the news along to Halleck, "his purpose to defend the place to the last extremity."

Confident none the less "of a speedy and favorable result" — so at least he assured the general-in-chief — Banks kept his long-range batteries at work around the clock, determined to give the Confederates no rest. The fire at night was necessarily blind, but that by day was skillfully directed by an observer perched on a lofty yardarm of the *Richmond*, tied up across the river from the bluff. He communicated by wigwag with a battery ashore, which also had a signalman, and the two kept up a running colloquy, not only to improve the marksmanship, but also to relieve the tedium of the siege.

"Your fifth gun has hit the breastwork of the big rifle four times. Its fire is splendid. Can dismount it soon."

"You say our fifth gun?"

"Yes, from the left." But the next salvo brought a shift of attention. "Your sixth gun just made a glorious shot. . . . Let the sixth gun fire 10 feet more to the left."

"How now about the fifth and sixth guns?"

"The sixth gun is the bully boy."

"Can you give it any directions to make it more bully?"

"Last shot was little to the right."

Just then, however, the cannoneers were forced to call a halt. "Fearfully hot here," the battery signalman explained. "Several men sunstruck. Bullets whiz like fun. Have ceased firing for a while, the guns are so hot. Will profit by your directions afterward." Presently they resumed firing, though with much less satisfactory results, according to the observer high in the rigging of the *Richmond*.

"Howitzer shell goes 6 feet over the guns every shot; last was too low, little too high again." Exasperated, he added: "Can't they, or won't they, depress that gun?"

"Won't, I guess. . . . Was that shot any better, and that?"

"Both and forever too high."

"We will vamose now. Come again tomorrow."

"Nine a.m. will do, will it not?"

"Yes; cease signaling."

★　★　★

★

Shelby Foote

*Advancing on Vicksburg, Federal
sappers construct a shielded
approach, roofed with bundles of
wood called fascines and strong
enough to withstand artillery fire.*

TEN

Vicksburg Siege, Through June

1863 ★ ★ ★ ★ ★ ★ he forces threatening New Orleans were no such host as Emory
envisioned, but they were under the
determined and resourceful Richard Taylor, who earlier, though much against his
will, had struck at Grant's supposedly vital supply line opposite Vicksburg. "To
break this would render a most important service," Pemberton had told Kirby
Smith in early May, in one of his several urgent appeals for help across the way.
Returning to Alexandria as soon as Banks pulled out, Taylor prepared to move at
once back down the Teche, threaten New Orleans, and thereby "raise such a
storm as to bring General Banks from Port Hudson, the garrison of which could
then unite with General Joseph Johnston in the rear of General Grant." On May
20, however, before he could translate his plan into action, he received instructions from Smith directing him to march in the opposite direction. "Grant's
army is now supplied from Milliken's Bend by Richmond, down the Roundaway
and Bayou Vidal to New Carthage," the department commander explained, and
if Taylor could interrupt the flow of supplies along this route, the Federal drive
on Vicksburg would be "checked, if not frustrated." He sympathized with Taylor's
desire "to recover what you have lost in Lower Louisiana and to push on toward
New Orleans," Smith added, "but the stake contended for near Vicksburg is the
Valley of the Mississippi and the Trans-Mississippi Department; the defeat of

★

General Grant is the *terminus ad quem* of all operations in the West this summer; to its attainment all minor advantages should be sacrificed." Taylor agreed as to the object, but not as to the method, much preferring his own. However, as he said later, "remonstrances were of no avail." He turned his back on New Orleans, at least for the present, and set out up the Tensas, where he was joined by a division of about 4000 men under Major General John G. Walker, a Missourian lately returned from Virginia, where he had commanded a division in Lee's army and was one of the many who could fairly be said to have saved the day at Sharpsburg.

Debarking June 5 on the east bank of the Tensas, some twenty-five miles west of Grant's former Young's Point headquarters, Taylor sent his unarmed transports back downstream to avoid losing them in his absence. Next day he surprised and captured a small party of Federals at Richmond, midway between the Tensas and the Mississippi, only to learn that Grant had established a new base up the Yazoo, well beyond the reach of any west-bank forces, and was no longer dependent on the one at Milliken's Bend. "Our movement resulted, and could result, in nothing," Taylor later admitted. All the same, he carried out his instructions by attacking, at dawn of the 7th, both Young's Point and Milliken's Bend, sending a full brigade against each. Like Banks, Grant had been recruiting Negroes, but since he intended to use them as laborers rather than as soldiers,

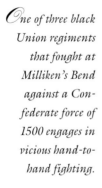

One of three black Union regiments that fought at Milliken's Bend against a Confederate force of 1500 engages in vicious hand-to-hand fighting.

he had given them little if any military training apart from the rudiments of drill. Surprised in their camps by the dawn attacks, they panicked and fled eastward over the levee to the protection of Porter's upstream flotilla. The gunboats promptly took up the quarrel, blasting away at the exultant rebels, and Taylor, observing that the panic was now on the side of the pursuers, ordered Walker to retire on Monroe, terminus of the railroad west of Vicksburg, while he himself went back down the Tensas and up the Red to Alexandria. Once there, he returned his attention to Banks and New Orleans, glad to have done with what he called "these absurd movements" against a supposedly vital supply line which in fact had been abandoned for nearly a month before he struck it.

Though the losses had been unequal — 652 Federals had fallen or were missing, as compared to 185 Confederates — Grant was not disposed to be critical of the outcome. Agreeing with Porter that the rebels had got "nothing but hard knocks," he was more laconic than reproachful in his mid-June report of the affair: "In this battle most of the troops engaged were Africans, who had little experience in the use of firearms. Their conduct is said, however, to have been most gallant, and I doubt not but with good officers they will make good troops." Anyhow, this was beyond the circle of his immediate attention, which was fixed on the close-up siege of Vicksburg itself. Six divisions had been added by now to his original ten, giving him a total of 71,000 effectives disposed along

two lines, back to back, one snuggled up to the semicircular defenses and the other facing rearward in case Joe Johnston got up enough strength and nerve to risk an attack from the east. Three divisions arrived in late May and early June from Memphis, the first of which, commanded by Brigadier General Jacob Lauman, was used to extend the investment southward, while the other two, under Brigadier Generals Nathan Kimball and William Sooy Smith, made up a fourth corps under Washburn, now a major general, and were sent to join Oster-haus, who had been left behind to guard the Big Black crossings while the two assaults were being launched. Frank Herron, who at twenty-five had won his two stars at Prairie Grove to become the Union's youngest major general, arrived from Missouri with his division on June 11 and extended the line still farther southward to the river, completing Grant's nine-division bear hug on Pemberton's beleaguered garrison. The final two were sent by Burnside from his Department of the Ohio. Commanded by Brigadier Generals Thomas Welsh and Robert Potter, they constituted a fifth corps under Major General John G. Parke and raised the strength of the rearward-facing force to seven divisions. "Our situation is for the first time in the entire western campaign what it should be," Grant had written Banks in the course of the build-up. And now that it was complete, so was his confidence as to the outcome of the siege, which he expressed not only in official correspondence but also in informal talks with his officers and men. "Gen. Grant came along the line last night," an Illinois private wrote home. "He had on his old clothes and was alone. He sat on the ground and talked with the boys with less reserve than many a little puppy of a lieutenant. He told us that he had got as good a thing as he wanted here."

One item he would have liked more of was trained engineers. Only two such officers were serving in that capacity now in his whole army. However, as one of them afterwards declared, this problem was solved by the "native good sense and ingenuity" of the troops, Middle Western farm boys for the most part, who showed as much aptitude for such complicated work as they had shown for throwing bridges over creeks and bayous during the march that brought them here. According to the same officer, "Whether a battery was to be constructed by men who had never built one before, [or] a sap-roller made by those who had never heard the name . . . it was done, and after a few trials well done." Before long, a later observer remarked, "those who had cut wood only for stoves would be speaking fluently of gabions and fascines; men who had patiently smoothed earth so that radishes might grow better would be talking affectionately of terrepleins for guns." In all of this they were inspired by the same bustling energy and quick adaptability on the part of the generals who led them; for one thing that characterized Grant's army was the youth of its commanders. McCler-nand, who was fifty-one, was the only general officer past fifty. Of the twenty-one corps and division commanders assigned to the Army of the Tennessee

★

in the course of the campaign, the average age was under forty. And that promotion had been based on merit was indicated by the fact that the average age of the nine major generals was as low as that of the dozen brigadiers; indeed, excepting McClernand, it was better than one year lower. Moreover, nine of these twenty-one men were older than Grant himself, and this too was part of the reason for his confidence in himself and in the army which had come of age, so to speak, under his care and tutelage. He considered it more than a match for anything the Confederates could bring against him — even under Joe Johnston, whose abilities he respected highly. One day a staff officer expressed the fear that Johnston was planning to fight his way into Vicksburg in order to help Pemberton stage a breakout; but Grant did not agree. "No," he said. "We are the only fellows who want to get in there. The rebels who are in now want to get out, and those who are out want to stay out. If Johnston tries to cut his way in we will let him do it, and then see that he don't get out. You say he has 30,000 men with him? That will give us 30,000 more prisoners than we now have."

"I have since seen the position at Sevastopol, and without hesitation I declare that at Vicksburg to have been the more difficult of the two."

— William Tecumseh Sherman

This was not to say that the two repulsed assaults had taught him nothing. They had indeed, if only by way of confirming a first impression that the rebel works were formidable. One officer, riding west on the Jackson road, had found himself confronted by "a long line of high, rugged, irregular bluffs, clearly cut against the sky, crowned with cannon which peered ominously from embrasures to the right and left as far as the eye could see." Beyond an almost impenetrable tangle of timber felled on the forward slopes, "lines of heavy rifle pits, surmounted with head-logs, ran along the bluffs, connecting fort with fort, and filled with veteran infantry." The approaches, he said, "were frightful enough to appall the stoutest heart." Sherman agreed, especially after the two assaults which had cost the army more than four thousand casualties. "I have since seen the position at Sevastopol," he wrote years later, "and without hesitation I declare that at Vicksburg to have been the more difficult of the two." Skillfully constructed, well sited, and prepared for a year against the day of investment, the fortifications extended for seven miles along commanding ridges and were anchored at both extremities to the lip of the sheer 200-foot bluff, north and south of the beleaguered city. Forts, redoubts, salients, redans, lunets, and bastions had been erected or dug at irregular intervals along the line, protected by overlapping fields of fire and connected by a complex of trenches, which in turn were mutually supporting. There simply was no easy way to get at the defenders. Moreover, Grant's three-to-one numerical advantage was considerably offset, not only by the necessity for protecting his rear from possible attacks by the army Johnston was assembling to the east, but also by the fact that, because of the vagaries of the up-ended terrain, his line of contravallation had to be more than twice the length of the line he was attempting to confront. "There is only one way to account for the hills of Vicksburg," a Confederate soldier had said a year ago, while helping to survey the present works. "After the Lord of Creation had made all the big mountains and ranges of hills, He had left on His hands a large lot of scraps. These were all dumped at Vicksburg in a waste heap." One of Grant's two professional engineers was altogether in agreement, pronouncing the Confederate position "rather an intrenched camp than a fortified place, owing much of its strength to the difficult ground, obstructed by fallen trees to its front, which rendered rapidity of movement and *ensemble* in an assault impossible."

Yet even this ruggedness had its compensations. Although the hillsides, as one who climbed them said, "were often so steep that their ascent was difficult to a footman unless he aided himself with his hands," the many ravines provided excellent cover for the besiegers, and Grant had specified in his investment order: "Every advantage will be taken of the natural inequalities of the ground to gain positions from which to start mines, trenches, or advance batteries." With the memory of slaughter fresh in their minds as a result of their two repulses, the men dug with a will. Knowing little or nothing at the outset of the five formal stages of a siege — the investment, the artillery attack, the construction of parallels and approaches, the breaching by artillery or mines, and the final assault — they told one another that Grant, having failed to go over the rebel works, had decided to go under them instead. Fortunately the enemy used his artillery sparingly, apparently conserving ammunition for use in repelling major assaults, but snipers were quick to shoot at targets of opportunity: in which connection a Federal major was to recall that "a favorite amusement of the soldiers was to place a cap on the end of a ramrod and raise it just above the head-logs, betting on the number of bullets which would pass through it within a given time." Few things on earth appealed to them more, as humor, than the notion of some butternut marksman flaunting his skill when the target was something less than flesh and blood. Mostly, though, they dug and took what rest they could, sweating in their wool uniforms and cursing the heat even more than they did the snipers. Soon they were old hands at siege warfare. "The excitement . . . has worn away," a lieutenant wrote home from the trenches in early

This "Ketchum" hand grenade was discovered unexploded at Vicksburg after the siege ended.

June, "and we have settled down to our work as quietly and as regularly as if we were hoeing corn or drawing bills in chancery."

Life in the trenches across the way — though the occupants did not call them that; they called them "ditches" — was at once more sedentary and more active. With their own 102 guns mostly silent and Grant's opposing 220 roaring practically all the time, they did nearly as much digging as the bluecoats, the difference being that they did it mainly in the same place, time after time, repairing damages inflicted by the steady rain of shells. Nor were they any less inventive. "Thunder barrels," for example — powder-filled hogsheads, fuzed at the bung — were found to be quite effective when rolled downhill into the enemy parallels and approaches. Similarly, such large naval projectiles as failed to detonate, either in the air or on contact with the ground, could be dug up, re-fuzed, and used in the same fashion to discourage the blue diggers on the slopes. However, despite such violent distractions, after a couple of weeks of spadework the two lines were within clod-tossing distance of each other at several points, and this resulted in an edgy sort of existence for the soldiers of both sides, as if they were spending their days and nights at the wrong end of a shooting gallery or in a testing chamber for explosives. "Fighting by hand grenades was all that was possible at such close quarters," a Confederate was to recall. "As the Federals had the hand grenades and we had none, we obtained our supply by using such of theirs as failed to explode, or by catching them as they came over the parapet and hurling them back."

Resistance under these circumstances implied a high state of morale, and such was indeed the case. Grant's heavy losses in his two assaults — inflicted at so little cost to the defenders that, until they looked out through the lifting smoke and saw the opposite hillsides strewn with the rag-doll shapes of the Union dead, they could scarcely believe a major effort had been made — convinced them that the Yankees could never take the place by storm. What was more, they had faith in "Old Joe" Johnston, believing that he would raise the siege as soon as he got his troops assembled off beyond the blue horizon, whereupon the two gray forces would combine and turn the tables on the besiegers. Until then, as they saw it, all that was needed was firmness against the odds, and they stood firm. Thanks to Pemberton's foresight, which included pulling corn along the roadside and driving livestock ahead of the army during its march from the Big Black, food so far was more plentiful inside the Confederate lines than it was beyond them. The people there were the first to feel the pinch of hunger; for the Federals, coming along behind the retreating graybacks, had consumed what little remained while waiting for roads to be opened to their new base on the Yazoo. "The soldiers ate up everything the folks had for ten miles around," a Union private wrote home. "They are now of necessity compelled to come here

Union troops riddled the grounds of the stately Shirley House with bombproofs to protect themselves from Confederate artillery after the Vicksburg siege began.

and ask for something to live upon, and they have discovered that they have the best success when the youngest and best-looking one in the family comes to plead their case, and they have some very handsome women here." This humbling of their pride did not displease him; it seemed to him no more than they deserved. "They were well educated and rich before their niggers ran away," he added, but adversity had brought them down in the world. "If I was to meet them in Illinois I should think they were born and brought up there."

Whether this last was meant as a compliment, and if so to whom, he did not say. But at least these people beyond the city's bristling limits were not being shot at; which was a great deal more than could be said of those within the gun-studded belt that girdled the bluff Vicksburg had been founded on, forty-odd years ago, by provision of the last will and testament of the pioneer farmer and Methodist parson Newitt Vick. In a sense, however, the bluff was returning to an earlier destiny. All that had been here when Vick arrived were the weed-choked ruins of a Spanish fort, around which the settlement had grown in less than two generations into a bustling town of some 4500 souls, mostly devoted to trade with planters in the lower Yazoo delta but also plagued by flatboat men on the way downriver from Memphis, who found it a convenient place for letting off what they called "a load of steam" that would not wait for New Orleans. As it turned out, though, the ham-fisted boatmen with knives in their boots and the gamblers with aces and derringers up their sleeves were mild indeed compared to what was visited upon them by the blue-clad host sent against them by what had lately been their government. Now the bluff was a fort again, on a scale beyond the most flamboyant dreams of the long-departed Spaniards, and the residents spent much of their time, as one of them said, watching the incoming shells "rising steadily and shiningly in great parabolic curves, descending with ever-increasing swiftness, and falling with deafening shrieks and explosions." The "ponderous fragments" flew everywhere, he added, thickening the atmosphere of terror until "even the dogs seemed to share the general fear. On hearing the descent of a shell, they would dart aside [and] then, as it exploded, sit down and howl in a pitiful manner." Children, on the other hand, observed the uproar with wide-eyed evident pleasure, accepting it as a natural phenomenon, like rain or lightning, unable to comprehend — as the dogs, for example, so obviously did — that men could do such things to one another and to them. "How is it possible you live here?" a woman who had arrived to visit her soldier husband just before the siege lines tightened asked a citizen, and was told: "After one is accustomed to the change, we do not mind it. But becoming accustomed: that is the trial." Some took it better than others, in or out of uniform. There was for instance a Frenchman, "a gallant officer who had distinguished himself in several severe engagements," who was "almost unmanned" whenever one of the huge mortar projectiles fell anywhere near him. Chided by friends for this reaction, he would

Two women and a rebel soldier in a Vicksburg lane shrink in terror at the sight of a Federal shell with a sputtering fuze.

reply: "I no like ze bomb: I cannot fight him back!" Neither could anyone else "fight him back," least of all the civilians, many of whom took refuge in caves dug into the hillsides. Some of these were quite commodious, with several rooms, and the occupants brought in chairs and beds and even carpets to add to the comfort, sleeping soundly or taking dinner unperturbed while the world outside seemed turned to flame and thunder. "Prairie Dog Village," the blue cannoneers renamed the city on the bluff, while from the decks of ironclads and mortar rafts on the great brown river, above and below, and from the semicircular curve of eighty-nine sand-bagged battery emplacements on the landward side, they continued to pump their steel-packaged explosives into the checkerboard pattern of its streets and houses.

Like the men in the trenches, civilians of both sexes and all ages were convinced that their tormentors could never take Vicksburg by storm, and whatever their fright they had no intention of knuckling under to what they called the bombs. For them, too, Johnston was the one bright hope of deliverance. Old Joe would be coming soon, they assured each other; all that was needed was to hold on till he completed his arrangements; then, with all the resources of the Confederacy at his command, he would come swooping over the eastern horizon and down on the Yankee rear. But presently, as time wore on and Johnston did not come, they were made aware of a new enemy. Hunger. By mid-June, though the garrison had been put first on half and then on quarter rations of meat, the livestock driven into the works ahead of the army back in May had been consumed, and Pemberton had his foragers impress all the cattle in the city. This struck nearer home than even the Union shells had done, for it was no easy thing for a family with milk-thirsty children to watch its one cow being led away to slaughter by a squad of ragged strangers. Moreover, the army's supply of bread was running low by now, and the commissary was directed to issue instead equal portions of rice and flour, four ounces of each per man per day, supplementing a quarter-pound of meat that was generally stringy or rancid or both. When these grains ran low, as they soon did, the experiment was tried of baking bread from dough composed of equal parts of corn and dried peas, ground up together until they achieved a gritty consistency not unlike cannon powder. "It made a nauseous composition," one who survived the diet was to recall with a shudder, "as the corn meal cooked in half the time the peas meal did, so the stuff was half raw. . . . It had the properties of india-rubber, and was worse than leather to digest." Soon afterwards came the crowning indignity. With the last cow and hog gone lowing and squealing under the sledge and cleaver, still another experiment was tried: the substitution of mule meat for beef and bacon. Though it was issued, out of respect for religious and folk preju-dices, "only to those who desired it," Pemberton was gratified to report that both officers and men considered it "not only nutritious, but very palatable, and in every way preferable to poor beef." So he said; but soldiers and civilians alike found something humiliating, not to say degrading, about the practice. "The rebels don't starve with success," a Federal infantryman observed jokingly from beyond the lines about this time. "I think that if I had nothing to eat I'd starve better than they do." Vicksburg's residents and defenders might well have agreed, especially when mule meat was concerned. Even if a man refused to eat such stuff himself, he found it disturbing to live among companions who did not. It was enough to diminish even their faith in Joe Johnston, who seemed in point of fact a long time coming.

Though at the outset the Virginian had sounded vigorous and pur-poseful in his assurance of assistance, Pemberton himself by now had begun to doubt the outcome of the race between starvation and delivery. "I am trying to gather a force which may attempt to relieve you. Hold out," Johnston wrote on May 19, and six days later he made this more specific: "Bragg is sending a divi-sion. When it comes, I will move to you. Which do you think is the best route?

How and where is the enemy encamped? What is your force?" Receiving this last on May 29 — the delay was not extreme, considering that couriers to and from the city had to creep by darkness through the Federal lines, risking capture every foot of the way — the Vicksburg commander replied as best he could to his superior's questions as to Grant's dispositions and strength. "My men are in good spirits, awaiting your arrival," he added. "You may depend on my holding the place as long as possible." After waiting nine days and receiving no answer, he asked: "When may I expect you to move, and in what direction?" Three more days he waited, and still there was no reply. "I am waiting most anxiously to know your intentions," he repeated. "I have heard nothing from you since [your dispatch of] May 25. I shall endeavor to hold out as long as we have anything to eat." Three days more went by, and then on June 13 — two weeks and a day since any word had reached him from the world outside — he received a message dated May 29. "I am too weak to save Vicksburg," Johnston told him. "Can do no more than attempt to save you and your garrison. It will be impossible to extricate you unless you coöperate and we make mutually supporting movements. Communicate your plans and suggestions, if possible." This was not only considerably less than had been expected in the way of help; it also seemed to indicate that Johnston did not realize how tightly the Union cordon was drawn about Vicksburg's bluff. In effect, the meager trickle of dispatches left Pemberton in a position not unlike that of a man who calls on a friend to make a strangler turn loose of his throat, only to have the friend inquire as to the strangler's strength, the position of his thumbs, the condition of the sufferer's windpipe, and just what kind of help he had in mind. So instead of "plans and suggestions," Vicksburg's defender tried to communicate some measure of the desperation he and his soldiers were feeling. "The enemy has placed several heavy guns in position against our works," he replied on June 15, "and is approaching them very nearly by sap. His fire is almost continuous. Our men have no relief; are becoming much fatigued, but are still in pretty good spirits. I think your movement should be made as soon as possible. The enemy is receiving reinforcements. We are living on greatly reduced rations, but I think sufficient for twenty days yet."

Having thus placed the limit of Vicksburg's endurance only one day beyond the Fourth of July — now strictly a Yankee holiday — Pemberton followed this up, lest Johnston fail to sense the desperation implied, with a more outspoken message four days later; "I hope you will advance with the least possible delay. My men have been thirty-four days and nights in the trenches, without relief, and the enemy within conversation distance. We are living on very reduced rations, and, as you know, are entirely isolated." He closed by asking bluntly, "What aid am I to expect from you?" This time the answer, if vague, was prompt. On June 23 a courier arrived with a dispatch written only the day before. "Scouts report the enemy fortifying toward us and the roads blocked," Johnston declared. "If I can do nothing to relieve you, rather than surrender the garrison, endeavor to cross the river at the last moment if you and General Taylor communicate." To Pemberton this seemed little short of madness. Taylor had made his gesture against Young's Point and Milliken's Bend more than two weeks ago; by now he was all the way down the Teche, intent on menacing New Orleans. But that was by no means the worst of Johnston's oversights, which was to ignore the presence of the Union navy. The bluejacket gun crews would have liked nothing better than a chance to try their marksmanship on a makeshift flotilla of skiffs, canoes, and rowboats manned by the half-starved tatterdemalions they had been probing for at long range all these weeks. Besides, even if the boats required had been available, which they were not, there was the question of whether the men in the trenches were in any condition for such a strenuous effort. They looked well enough to a casual eye, for all their rags and hollow-eyed gauntness, but it was observed that they tired easily under the mildest exertion and could serve only brief shifts when shovel work was called for. The meager diet was beginning to tell. A Texas colonel reported that many of his men had "swollen ankles and symptoms of incipient scurvy." By late June, nearly half the garrison was on the sick list or in hospital. If Pemberton could not see what this meant, a letter he received at this time — June 28: exactly one week short of the date he had set, two weeks ago, as the limit of Vicksburg's endurance — presumed to define it for him in unmistakable terms. Signed "Many Soldiers," the letter called attention to the fact that the ration now had been reduced to "one biscuit and a small bit of bacon per day," and continued:

> The emergency of the case demands prompt and decided action on your part. If you can't feed us, you had better surrender us, horrible as the idea is, than suffer this noble army to disgrace themselves by desertion. I tell you plainly, men are not going to lie here and perish, if they do love their country dearly. Self-preservation is the first law of nature, and hunger will compel a man to do almost anything. . . . This army is now ripe for mutiny, unless it can be fed. Just think of one small biscuit and one or two mouthfuls of bacon per day. General, please direct your inquiries in the proper channel, and see if I have not stated the stubborn facts, which had better be heeded before we are disgraced.

★

"rant is now deservedly the hero," Sherman wrote

★ ★ ★ home in early June, adding characteristically — for his dislike of reporters was not tempered by any evidence of affection on their part, either for himself or for Grant, with whom, as he presently said, "I am a second self" — that his friend was being "belabored with praise by those who a month ago accused him of all the sins in the calendar, and who next will turn against him if so blows the popular breeze. Vox populi, vox humbug."

In point of fact, however, once the encompassing lines had been drawn, the journalists could find little else to write about that had not been covered during the first week of the siege. And it was much the same for the soldiers, whose only diversion was firing some fifty to one hundred rounds of ammunition a day, as required by orders. Across the way — though the Confederates lacked even this distraction, being under instructions to burn no powder needlessly — the main problem, or at any rate the most constant one, was hunger; whereas for the Federals it was boredom. "The history of a single day was the history of all the others," an officer was to recall. Different men had different ways of trying to hasten the slow drag of time. Sherman, for instance, took horseback rides and paid off-duty visits to points of interest roundabout, at least one of which resulted in a scene he found discomforting, even painful. Learning that the mother of one of his former Louisiana Academy cadets was refugeeing in the neighborhood — she had come all the way from Plaquemine Parish to escape the attentions of Butler and Banks, only to run spang into Grant and Sherman — he rode over to tender his respects and found her sitting on her gallery with about a dozen women visitors. He introduced himself, inquired politely after her son, and was told that the young man was besieged in Vicksburg, a lieutenant of artillery. When the general went on to ask for news of her husband, whom he had known in the days before the war, the woman suddenly burst into tears and cried out in anguish: "You killed him at Bull Run, where he was fighting for his country!" Sherman hastily denied that he had "killed anybody at Bull Run," which was literally true, but by now all the other women had joined the chorus of abuse and lamentation. This, he said long afterwards, "made it most uncomfortable for me, and I rode away."

Other men had other spare-time diversions. Grant's, it was said, was whiskey. Some denied this vehemently, protesting that he was a teetotaler, while some asserted that this only appeared to be the case because of his low tolerance for the stuff; a single glass unsteadied him, and a second gave him the glassy-eyed look of a man with a heavy load on. He himself seemed to recognize the problem from the outset, if only by the appointment and retention of John A. Rawlins as his assistant adjutant general. A frail but vigorous young man, with a "marble pallor" to his face and "large, lustrous eyes of a deep black,"

★

As Grant's chief of staff, John A. Rawlins kept watch over the general's drinking, once pledging to resign his commission if his commander became "an intemperate man."

Rawlins at first had wanted to be a preacher, but had become instead a lawyer in Galena, where Grant first knew him. His wife had died of tuberculosis soon after the start of the war, and he himself would die of the same disease before he was forty, but the death that seemed to have affected him most had been that of his father, an improvident charcoal burner who had died at last of the alcoholism that had kept him and his large family in poverty all his life. Rawlins, a staff captain at thirty and now a lieutenant colonel at thirty-two, was rabid on the subject of drink. He was in fact blunt in most things, including his relationship with Grant. "He bossed everything at Grant's headquarters," Charles Dana later wrote, adding: "I have heard him curse at Grant when, according to his judgment, the general was doing something that he thought he had better not do." Observing this, many wondered why Grant put up with it. Others believed they knew. "If you hit Rawlins on the head, you'll knock out Grant's brains," they said. But they were wrong. Rawlins was not Grant's brain; he was his conscience, and a rough one, too, especially where whiskey was concerned. "I say to you frankly, and I pledge you my word for it," he had written eighteen months ago to Elihu Washburne, the general's congressional guardian angel, "that should General Grant at any time become an intemperate man or an habitual drunkard, I will notify you immediately, will ask to be removed from duty on his staff (kind as he has been to me) or resign my commission. For while there are times when I would gladly throw the mantle of charity over the faults of my friends, at this time and from a man of his position I would rather tear the mantle off and expose the deformity." Grant had cause to believe that Rawlins meant it. And yet, despite the danger to his career and despite what a fellow staffer called Rawlins' "insubordination twenty times a day," he kept him on, both for his own good and the army's.

Since writing to Washburne, however, the adjutant had either changed his mind about disturbing the mantle or else he had been singularly forgetful. Despite periodic incidents thereafter, in which Grant was involved with whiskey, Rawlins limited his remarks to the general himself, apparently in the belief that he could handle him. And so he could, except for lapses. Anyhow, there was never any problem so long as Mrs Grant was around; "If she is with him all will be well and I can be spared," he later confided to a friend. The trouble seemed in part sexual, as in California nine years ago, and it was intensified by periods of boredom, such as now. Three weeks of slam-bang fighting and rapid maneuver had given way to the tedium of a siege, and Mrs Grant had been six weeks off the scene. On June 5 Rawlins found a box of wine in front of the general's tent and had it removed, ignoring Grant's protest that he was saving it to toast the fall of Vicksburg. He learned, moreover, that the general had recently accepted a glass of wine from a convivial doctor. These were danger signs, and there were others that evening.

"I was not long in perceiving that Grant had been drinking, and that he was still keeping it up. He made several trips to the bar room of the boat in a short time, and became stupid in speech and staggering in gait."

— Sylvanus Cadwallader

Rawlins sat down after midnight and wrote Grant a letter. "The great solicitude I feel for the safety of this army leads me to mention, what I had hoped never again to do, the subject of your drinking. . . . Tonight when you should, because of the condition of your health if nothing else, have been in bed, I find you where the wine bottle has just been emptied, in company with those who drink and urge you to do likewise, and the lack of your usual promptness and decision, and clearness in expressing yourself in writing conduces to confirm my suspicion." Rawlins himself had become rather incoherent by now, whether from anger or from sorrow; but the ending was clear enough. Unless Grant would pledge himself "[not] to touch a single drop of any kind of liquor, no matter by whom asked or under what circumstances," Rawlins wanted to be relieved at once from duty in the department. Grant, however, left early next morning — apparently before the letter reached him — on a tour of inspection up the Yazoo River to Satartia, near which he had posted a division in case Johnston came that way. The two-day trip, beyond the sight and influence of Rawlins, became a two-day bender.

★

Dana went with him, and on the way upriver from Haines Bluff they met the steamboat *Diligent* coming down. Grant hailed the vessel, whose captain was a friend of his, transferred to her, and had her turned back upstream for Satartia. Aboard was Sylvanus Cadwallader, a Chicago *Times* correspondent on the prowl for news. It was he who had ridden into Jackson with Fred Grant in mid-May, when they lost the race for the souvenir flag atop the capitol, and it was he who was to leave the only detailed eyewitness account of Grant on a wartime bender — specifically the two-day one which already was under way up the Yazoo. In some ways, for Cadwallader at least, it was more like a two-day nightmare. "I was not long in perceiving that Grant had been drinking," he wrote long afterwards, "and that he was still keeping it up. He made several trips to the bar room of the boat in a short time, and became stupid in speech and staggering in gait." The reporter of course had heard rumors of Grant's predilection, but this was the first time he had seen him show it to the extent of intoxication. Alarmed by the general's "condition, which was fast becoming worse," he tried to get the captain and a lieutenant aide to intervene. Neither would; so Cadwallader undertook to do it himself. He got Grant into his stateroom, locked the door, "and commenced throwing bottles of whiskey which stood on the table, through the windows, over the guards, into the river." Grant protested, to no avail; the reporter "firmly, but good-naturedly declined to obey," and finally got him quieted. "As it was a very hot day and the stateroom almost suffocating, I insisted on his taking off his coat, vest and boots, and lying down on one of the berths. After much resistance I succeeded, and soon fanned him to sleep."

But that was only the beginning. Shortly before dark, when the *Diligent* neared Satartia, she met two gunboats steaming down, and a naval officer came aboard to warn that it was not safe for the unarmed vessel to proceed. Dana — who later reported tactfully in his *Recollections* that "Grant was ill and went to bed soon after we started" — knocked on the stateroom door to ask whether the boat should turn back. Grant, he said, was "too sick to decide," and told him: "I will leave it to you." Now that he was awake, however, though still not "recovered from his stupor," Cadwallader said, the general took it into his head "to dress and go ashore," despite the naval officer's warning. Once more the reporter prevailed, and got him back to bed. While he slept, the *Diligent* returned downstream in the darkness to Haines Bluff. Next morning, according to Dana, Grant was "fresh as a rose, clean shirt and all, quite himself," when he came out to breakfast. "Well, Mr Dana," he observed, "I suppose we are at Satartia."

Cadwallader relaxed his guard, despite the 25-mile geographical error, presuming that "all necessity for extra vigilance on my part had passed," and was profoundly shocked to discover, an hour later, "that Grant had procured another supply of whiskey from on shore and was quite as much intoxicated as the day before." Again the reporter managed to separate the general from his bottle, only to have him insist on proceeding at once to Chickasaw Bayou. This would have brought them there "about the middle of the afternoon, when the landing would have been alive with officers, men, and trains from all parts of the army." Conferring with the captain as to the best means by which to avoid exposing Grant to "utter disgrace and ruin," Cadwallader managed to delay the departure so that they did not arrive until about sundown, when there was much less activity at the landing. As luck would have it, however, they tied up alongside a sutler boat whose owner "kept open house to all officers and dispensed free liquors and cigars generously." Alarmed at the possibilities of disaster, the reporter slipped hastily over the rail, warned the sutler of what was afoot, and "received his promise that the general should not have a drop of anything intoxicating on his boat." Back aboard the *Diligent*, Cadwallader helped the escort to unload the horses for the five-mile ride to army headquarters northeast of Vicksburg; but when this was done he looked around and could find no sign of Grant. Fearing the worst, he hurried aboard the sutler boat "and soon heard a general hum of conversation and laughter proceeding from a room opening out of the ladies' cabin." There he saw his worst fears realized. The sutler was seated at "a table covered with bottled whiskey and baskets of champagne," and Grant was beside him, "in the act of swallowing a glass of whiskey." Cadwallader once more intervened, insisting that

Former editor Charles A. Dana arrived in Grant's camp as U.S. Secretary of War Edwin M. Stanton's assistant and spy only to become the general's eloquent advocate.

"the escort was waiting, and it would be long after dark before we could reach headquarters." Grant came along, though he plainly resented the interruption. His horse was a borrowed one called Kangaroo "from his habit of rearing on his hind feet and making a plunging start whenever mounted." That was his reaction now; for "Grant gave him the spur the moment he was in the saddle, and the horse darted away at full speed before anyone was ready to follow." The road was crooked, winding among the many slews and bayous, but the general more or less straightened it out, "heading only for the bridges, and literally tore through and over everything in his way. The air was full of dust, ashes, and embers from campfires, and shouts and curses from those he rode down in his race." Cadwallader, whose horse was no match for Kangaroo, thought he had lost his charge for good. But he kept on anyhow, hoping against hope, and "after crossing the last bayou bridge three-fourths of a mile from the landing," caught up with him riding sedately at a walk. Finding that Grant had become "unsteady in the saddle" as a result of the drink or drinks he had had from the sutler, and fearing "discovery of his rank and situation," the reporter seized Kangaroo's rein and led him off into a roadside thicket, where he helped the general to dismount and persuaded him to lie down on the grass and get some sleep. While Grant slept Cadwallader managed to hail a trooper from the escort, whom he instructed to go directly to headquarters "and report at once to Rawlins — and no one else — and say to him that I want an ambulance with a careful driver."

Waking before the ambulance got there, Grant wanted to resume his ride at once, but the reporter "took him by the arm, walked him back and forth, and kept up a lively rather one-sided conversation, till the ambulance arrived." Then there was the problem of getting the general into the curtained vehicle, which he refused to permit until, as Cadwallader said, "we compromised the question by my agreeing to ride in the ambulance also, and having our horses led by the orderly." They reached headquarters about midnight to find the dark-eyed Rawlins and Colonel John Riggin, another staff officer, "waiting for us in the driveway." The reporter got out first, "followed promptly by Grant," who now gave him perhaps the greatest shock of the past two days. "He shrugged his shoulders, pulled down his vest, 'shook himself together,' as one just rising from a nap, and seeing Rawlins and Riggin, bid them good night in a natural tone and manner, and started to his tent as steadily as he ever walked in his life." Cadwallader turned to Rawlins, who was pale with rage — "The whole appearance of the man indicated a fierceness that would have torn me into a thousand pieces had he considered me to blame" — and said he was afraid, from what they had just seen, that the adjutant would think it was he, not Grant, who had been drinking. "No, no," Rawlins said through clenched teeth. "I know him, I know him. I want you to tell me the exact facts, and all of them, without any concealment. I have a right to know them, and I will know them."

He heard them all, from start to finish, but he never reported the incident to Washburne, any more than Dana did to the War Department, not only out of loyalty and friendship, but also perhaps on reflecting that if anything brought about Grant's removal, or even his suspension during an inquiry, command of the army would pass automatically to McClernand, whom they both despised. As for Cadwallader, despite assurances from Rawlins — "He will not send you out of the department while I remain in it," the adjutant told him — he spent an anxious night, "somewhat in doubt as to the view of the matter Gen. Grant would take next day," and "purposely kept out of his way for twenty-four hours to spare him the mortification I supposed he might feel." As it turned out, he need not have worried. "The second day afterward I passed in and out of his presence as though nothing unusual had occurred. To my surprise he never made the most distant allusion to [the matter] then, or ever afterward." From that time on, he said, it was "as if I had been regularly gazetted a member of his staff." Passes from Grant enabled the reporter to go anywhere he wanted; he could requisition transportation and draw subsistence from quartermaster and commissary authorities; his tent was always pitched near Grant's, and his dispatches often were sent in the official mail pouch; in short, he "constantly received flattering personal and professional favors and attentions shown to no one else in my position." All this was in return for his respecting a confidence which he kept for more than thirty years. In 1896, a seventy-year-old sheep raiser out in California, he wrote his memoirs, including an account of Grant's two-day trip up the Yazoo and back. For nearly sixty years they remained in manuscript, and when at last they were published, ninety years after the war was over, they were attacked and the writer vilified by some of the general's long-range admirers, who claimed that what Cadwallader called "this Yazoo-Vicksburg adventure" never happened.

At any rate, no harm had resulted from the army commander's two-day absence from headquarters, drunk or sober. The repulse of Taylor at Milliken's Bend and Young's Point by the gunboats, on the second day, increased Grant's confidence rather than his fretfulness, which in fact seemed to be cured. "All is going on here now just right," he wrote to a friend on June 15, and added: "My position is so strong that I feel myself abundantly able to leave it and go out twenty or thirty miles with force enough to whip two such garrisons." He had small use for Pemberton, characterizing him as "a northern man [who] got into bad company." Nor did he fear Joe Johnston. Though he respected his ability, he said he did not believe the Virginian could save Vicksburg without "a larger army than the Confederates now have at any one place." Next day, moreover, the watchful eye of former congressman Frank Blair enabled Grant to dispose of his third opponent, John McClernand, and thus wind up the private war he had been waging all this time. Scanning the columns of the Memphis

Evening Bulletin, Blair spotted a congratulatory order McClernand had issued to his corps, claiming the lion's share of the credit for the victory he foresaw. Blair sent the clipping to Sherman, who forwarded it to Grant next day, calling it "a catalogue of nonsense" and "an effusion of vain-glory and hypocrisy . . . addressed not to an army, but to a constituency in Illinois." He also cited a War Department order, issued the year before, "which actually forbids the publication of all official letters and reports, and re-quires the name of the writer to be laid before the President of the United States for dismissal."

Grant had waited half a year for this, pass-ing over various lesser offenses in hopes that one would come along which would justify charges that could not fail to stick. But now that he had it he still moved with deftness and precision, completing the

> *"I am prepared to maintain its statements . . . I regret that my adjutant did not send you a copy as he ought, and I thought he had."*
>
> ⸺ John McClernand

adjustment of the noose. That same day, June 17, he forwarded the clipping to McClernand with a note: "Inclosed I send you what purports to be your congrat-ulatory address to the Thirteenth Army Corps. I would respectfully ask if it is a true copy. If it is not a correct copy, furnish me one by bearer, as required both by regulations and existing orders of the Department." Next day McClernand acknowledged the validity of the clipping. "I am prepared to maintain its state-ments," he declared. "I regret that my adjutant did not send you a copy as he ought, and I thought he had." With the noose now snug, Grant sprang the trap: "Major General John A. McClernand is hereby relieved from command of the Thirteenth Army Corps. He will proceed to any point he may select in the state of Illinois and report by letter to Headquarters of the Army for orders." Grant signed the order after working hours, supposing that it would be delivered the following morning, but when James Wilson came in at midnight and heard what was afoot — there was bad blood between him and McClernand; the two had nearly come to blows a couple of weeks ago — he urged Rawlins to let him deliver the order in person, without delay, lest something come up — a rebel sortie at dawn, for example, which might enable McClernand to distinguish himself as he had done at Shiloh — to cause its suspension or cancellation. Rawlins agreed, and Wilson put on his dress uniform, summoned the provost marshal and a squad of soldiers, and set out through the darkness for McClernand's headquarters. Arriving about 2 o'clock in the morning, he demanded that the general be roused. Presently he was admitted to McClernand's tent, where he found the former congressman seated at a table on which two candles burned. Apparently he knew what to expect, for he too was in full uniform and his sword lay before him on the table. Wilson handed him the order, remarking that he had been instructed to see that it was read and understood. McClernand took it, adjusted his glasses, and perused it. "Well, sir, I am relieved," he said. Then, looking up at Wilson, whose expression did not mask his satisfaction, he added: "By God, sir, we are both relieved!"

He did not intend to take this lying down, but he soon found that Grant had played the old army game with such skill that his opponent was left without a leg to stand on. "I have been relieved for an omission of my adjutant. Hear me," McClernand wired Lincoln from Cairo on his way to Springfield, their common home. From there he protested likewise to Halleck, suggesting the possible disclosure of matters that were dark indeed: "How far General Grant is indebted to the forbearance of officers under his command for his retention in the public service, I will not undertake to state unless he should challenge it. None know better than himself how much he is indebted to that forbearance." That might be, but it was no help to the general up in Illinois; Grant challenged nothing, except to state that he had "tolerat[ed] General McClernand long after I thought the good of the service demanded his removal." In time, there came to Springfield a letter signed "Your friend as ever, A. Lincoln," in which the unhappy warrior was told: "I doubt whether your present position is more painful to you than to myself. Grateful for the patriotic stand so early taken by you in this life-and-death struggle of the nation, I have done whatever has appeared practicable to advance you and the public interest together." However: "For me to force you back upon Gen. Grant would be forcing him to resign. I cannot give you a new command, because we have no forces except such as already have commanders." In short, the President had nothing to offer his fellow-townsman in the way of balm, save his conviction that a general was best judged by those "who have been with him in the field. . . . Relying on these," Lincoln said in closing, "he who has the right needs not to fear."

This was perhaps the unkindest cut of all, since McClernand knew only too well what was likely to happen to his reputation if judgment was left to Sherman and McPherson and their various subordinate commanders, including the army's two remaining ex-congressmen Blair and Logan. Among all these, and on Grant's staff, there was general rejoicing at his departure. Major General

Edward O. C. Ord, who had fought under Grant at Iuka, had just arrived to take charge of a sixth corps intended to consist of the divisions under Herron and Lauman; instead, he replaced McClernand. Three days later, on June 22, Sherman was given command of the rearward line, which was strengthened by shifting more troops from in front of Vicksburg. "We want to whip Johnston at least 15 miles off, if possible," Grant explained. Steele succeeded Sherman, temporarily, and the siege went on as before. No less than nine approaches were being run, all with appropriate parallels close up to the enemy trenches, so that the final assault could be launched with the lowest possible loss in lives. Mines were sunk under rebel strongpoints, and on June 25 two of these were exploded on McPherson's front, the largest just north of the Jackson road. It blew off the top of a hill there, leaving a big, dusty crater which

This southern slave survived a mine blast at Vicksburg and became part of the legend of the siege.

the attackers occupied for a day and then abandoned, finding themselves under heavy plunging fire from both flanks and the rear. The mine accomplished little, but contributed greatly to the legend of the siege by somehow lofting a Negro cook, Abraham by name, all the way from the Confederate hilltop and into the Federal lines. He landed more or less unhurt, though terribly frightened. An Iowa outfit claimed him, put him in a tent, and got rich charging five cents a look. Asked how high he had been blown, Abraham always gave the same answer, coached perhaps by some would-be Iowa Barnum. "Donno, massa," he would say, "but tink bout tree mile."

Mostly, though, the weeks passed in boredom and increasing heat, under whose influence the Confederates appeared to succumb to a strange apathy during the final days of June. A Federal engineer remarked that their defense "was far from being vigorous." It seemed to him that the rebel strategy was "to wait for another assault, losing in the meantime as few men as possible," and he complained that this had a bad effect on his own men, since "without the stimulus of danger . . . troops of the line will not work efficiently, especially at night, after the novelty has worn off." Another trouble was that they foresaw the end of the siege, and no man coveted the distinction of being the last to die. Not that all was invariably quiet. Occasionally there were flare-ups, particularly where the trenches approached conjunction, and the snipers continued to take their toll. Though the losses were small, the suffering was great. "It looked hard," a Wisconsin soldier wrote, "to see six or eight poor fellows piled into an ambulance about the size of Jones's meat wagon and hustled over the rough roads as fast as the mules could trot and to see the blood running out of the carts in streams almost." Taunts were flung as handily as grenades, back and forth across the lines, the graybacks asking, "When are you folks going to come on into town?" and the bluecoats replying that they were in no hurry: "We are holding you fellows prisoner while you feed yourselves." There was much fraternization between pickets, who arranged informal truces for the exchange of coffee and tobacco, and the same Federal engineer reported that the enemy's "indifference to our approach became at some points almost ludicrous." Once, for example, when the blue sappers found that as a result of miscalculation a pair of approach trenches would converge just inside the rebel picket line, the two sides called a cease-fire and held a consultation at which it was decided that the Confederates would pull back a short distance in order to avoid an unnecessary fire fight. At one stage of the discussion a Federal suggested that the approaches could be redesigned to keep from disturbing the butternut sentries, but the latter seemed to think that it would be a shame if all that digging went to waste. Besides, one said, "it don't make any difference. You Yanks will soon have the place anyhow."

Grant thought so, too. By now, in fact — though he kept his soldiers burrowing, intending to launch his final assault from close-up positions in early July — he was giving less attention to Pemberton than he was to Johnston, off in the opposite direction, where Sherman described him as "vibrating between Jackson and Canton" in apparent indecision. Blair had reported earlier, on returning from a scout, that "every man I picked up was going to Canton to join him. The negroes told me their masters had joined him there, and those who were too old to go, or who could escape on any other pretext, told me the same story." This had a rather ominous sound, as if hosts were gathering to the east, but Grant was not disturbed. He had access, through the treacherous courier, to many of the messages that passed between his two opponents. He knew what they were thinking, what the men under them were thinking, and what the beleaguered citizens were thinking. He spoke of their expectations in a dispatch he sent Sherman on June 25, the day the slave Abraham came hurtling into the hands of the Iowans: "Strong faith is expressed by some in Johnston's coming to their relief. [They] cannot believe they have been so wicked as for Providence to allow the loss of their stronghold of Vicksburg. Their principal faith seems to be in Providence and Joe Johnston."

y then — the fortieth day of siege — it had been exactly a month since the man in whom Vicksburg's garrison placed its "principal faith" assured Pemberton: "Bragg is sending a division. When it joins I will come to you." The division reached him soon afterwards, under Breckinridge, and was combined with the three already at hand under Loring, French, and Walker; Johnston's present-for-duty strength now totaled 31,226 men, two thirds of whom had joined him since his arrival in mid-May. But he found them quite deficient in equipment, especially wagons, and deferred action until such needs could be supplied. In the interim he got into a dispute with the Richmond authorities, protesting that he had only 23,000 troops, while Seddon insisted that the correct figure was 34,000. Finally the Secretary told him: "You must rely on what you have," and urged him to move at once to Pemberton's relief. But Johnston would not be prodded into action. "The odds against me are much greater than those you express," he wired on June 15, and added flatly: "I consider saving Vicksburg hopeless." Shocked by his fellow Virginian's statement that he considered his assignment an impossible one, Seddon took this to mean that Johnston did not comprehend the gravity of the situation or the consequences of the fall of the Gibraltar of the West, which in Seddon's eyes meant the probable fall of the Confederacy itself. It seemed to him, moreover, that the general — in line with his behavior a year ago, down the York-James peninsula — was moving toward a decision not to fight at all, and to the Secretary this was altogether unthinkable. "Your telegram grieves and alarms me," he replied next day. "Vicksburg must not be lost without a desperate struggle. The interest and honor of the Confederacy forbid it. I rely on you still to avert the loss. If better resources do not offer, you must hazard attack. It may be made in concert with the garrison, if practicable, but otherwise without; by day or night, as you think best." Still Johnston would not budge. "I think you do not appreciate the difficulties in the course you direct," he wired back, "nor the probabilities or consequences of failure. Grant's position, naturally very strong, is intrenched and protected by powerful artillery, and the roads obstructed. . . . The defeat of this little army would at once open Mississippi and Alabama to Grant. I will do all I can, without hope of doing more than aid to extricate the garrison." Fairly frantic and near despair over this prediction that the Father of Waters was about to pass out of Confederate hands, severing all practical connection with the Transmississippi and its supplies of men and food and horses, Seddon urged the general "to follow the most desperate course the occasion may demand. Rely upon it," he told him, "the eyes and hopes of the whole Confederacy are upon you, with the full confidence that you will act, and with the sentiment that it were better to fail nobly daring than, through prudence even, to be inactive. . . . I rely on you for all possible to save Vicksburg."

But no matter what ringing tones the Secretary employed, Johnston would not be provoked into what he considered rashness. "There has been no voluntary inaction," he protested; he simply had "not had the means of moving." By then it was June 22. Two days later he received a message from Pemberton, suggesting that he get in touch with Grant and make "propositions to pass this army out, with all its arms and equipages," in return for abandoning Vicksburg to him. Johnston declined, not only because he did not believe the proposal would be accepted, but also because "negotiations with Grant for the relief of the garrison, should they become necessary, must be made by you," he replied on June 27. "It would be a confession of weakness on my part, which I ought not to make, to propose them. When it becomes necessary to make terms, they may be considered as made under my authority." In other words, any time Pemberton wanted to throw in the sponge, it would be all right with Johnston. However, he prefaced this by saying that the Pennsylvanian's "determined spirit" encouraged him "to hope that something may yet be done to save Vicksburg," and two days later, June 29, "field transportation and other supplies having been obtained," he put his four divisions on the march for the Big Black, preceded by a screen of cavalry.

He had never been one to tilt at windmills, nor was he now. The march — or "expedition," as he preferred to call it — "was not undertaken in

This photograph of a Union trench at a Confederate redoubt near the Jackson road shows a crater made by a massive explosion of 2200 pounds of gunpowder.

★

the wild spirit that dictated the dispatches from the War Department," he later explained, and added scornfully: "I did not indulge in the sentiment that it was better for me to waste the lives and blood of brave soldiers 'than, through prudence even,' to spare them." He never moved until he was ready, and then his movements were nearly always rearward. The one exception up to now had been Seven Pines, which turned out to be the exception that proved the rule, for it had cost him five months on the sidelines, command of the South's first army, and two wounds that were still unhealed a year later. Moreover, it had resulted in his present assignment, which was by no means to his liking, though his resultant brusqueness was reserved for those above him on the ladder of command, never for those below. To subordinates he was invariably genial and considerate, and they repaid him with loyalty, affection, and admiration. "His mind was clear as a bell," a staff officer had written from Jackson to a friend, two weeks ago, while the build-up for the present movement was still in progress. "I never saw a brain act with a quicker or more sustained movement, or one which exhibited a finer sweep or more striking power. . . . I cannot conceive surroundings more intensely depressing. Yet amidst them all, he preserved the elastic step and glowing brow of the genuine hero."

Desperation never rattled him; indeed, it had rather the opposite effect of increasing his native caution. And such was the case now as he approached the Big Black, beyond which Grant had intrenched a rearward-facing line. On the evening of July 1, Johnston called a halt between Brownsville and the river, and spent the next two days reconnoitering. Convinced by this "that attack north of the railroad was impracticable," he "determined, therefore, to make the examinations necessary for the attempt south of the railroad." On July 3, near Birdsong's Ferry, he wrote Pemberton that he intended "to create a diversion, and thus enable you to cut your way out if the time has arrived for you to do this. Of that time I cannot judge; you must, as it depends upon your condition. I hope to attack the enemy in your front [on] the 7th. . . . Our firing will show you where we are engaged. If Vicksburg cannot be saved, the garrison must."

Next morning, however, before he took up the march southward he noticed a strange thing. Today was the Fourth — Independence Day — but the Yankees over toward Vicksburg did not seem to be celebrating it in the usual fashion. On this of all days, the forty-eighth of the siege, the guns were silent for the first time since May 18, when the bluecoats filed into positions from which to launch their first and second assaults before settling down to the digging and bombarding that had gone on ever since; at least till now. Johnston and his men listened attentively, cocking their heads toward the beleaguered city. But there was no rumble of guns at all. Everything was quiet in that direction.

★　★　★

★

Epilogue

★ ★ ★   **O**n the battle front at least, the spring of 1863 seemed auspicious enough for the Confederate states. When a reluctant Admiral Samuel Du Pont — urged on by his superiors in Washington, who had vastly oversold the potential effectiveness of the new "monitor"-class ironclads against reinforced battlements — attacked the forts of Charleston harbor, an ebullient P. G. T. Beauregard, erstwhile Hero of Sumter, handily drove off the Union navy. At Fredericksburg, where Lee's victories had led Abraham Lincoln to sack Burnside and appoint Hooker as commander of the Army of the Potomac, Confederate soldiers accustomed to victory felt confident about facing anything the North might throw at them. There Longstreet, reviewing the area's defenses while Lee was away briefly in Richmond, had already given to military science the one innovation that would shine alongside the storied tactics of Lee and Stonewall Jackson in the military treatises of the future. Shortly before departing beyond the James River for operations in Southside Virginia, he introduced the traverse trench. The art of war was never the same again.

Despite the bad news from Charleston and doubts about the overconfidence of his new commander, "Fighting Joe," Abraham Lincoln was heartened by the high morale and new sense of purpose he discovered during his Easter review of troops down in Virginia. Even the Confederate cavalry learned a new respect for their Yankee counterparts. As Jeb Stuart, Fitzhugh Lee, and John Singleton Mosby dashed around Northern Virginia, they found a Union cavalry that for the first time seemed to give as good as it got. But as Hooker made his move and Lee recalled Longstreet to help in the calamitous fighting around Chancellorsville, Lincoln was to be disappointed once more in his choice. Lee's clear victory cost Hooker his job, but it also cost the South one of its greatest warriors when Stonewall Jackson was shot by his own sentries. Lee had considered Jackson his strong right arm, and more. His loss was a major blow that presaged a change in the fortunes of war for Lee and the South in the course of the coming summer.

Another blow was Grant's investment of Vicksburg. Subordinates, originally pessimistic about Grant's intention to cut free of his supply base, had not only come round to seeing the plan's brilliance, but also executed it perfectly, sacking the Mississippi capital and its rail connections eastward before turning west toward the riverbluff citadel. Meanwhile, Grierson's horsemen had cut a swath through central Mississippi on a two-week raid that brought him to Union-held Baton Rouge, Louisiana, and further exacerbated the confusion of the rebel leadership. Nathaniel Banks, not to be outdone, launched a campaign that secured the west bank of the great river and then besieged Port Hudson. Meanwhile, the Confederates persisted in trying to get behind Grant to cut him off from the supply line his plan eschewed. During one of these attempts at Milliken's Bend, the black Union troops acquitted themselves by driving off their attackers. Instead of stopping Grant's march on Vicksburg, the Southern response only led to Joe Johnston's refusal to come to the city's aid. Admonished by Davis to hold Vicksburg at all cost and by Johnston to abandon it if need be, John Pemberton — mindful of his status as a northern-born Confederate general — hunkered down for a siege. Flush with victory and well fed, the Union army tried twice to take the city by main force, in vain and at great cost. Grant, too, then settled in for a siege. As the daily shellings of Vicksburg and Port Hudson stretched into late June, after ridding himself of John McClernand, a troublesome subordinate, Grant had little to keep him occupied and rumors of renewed drunkenness surfaced.

Back east, Lee boldly invaded the North a second time and even the major Confederate loss at Gettysburg would at first be obscured by his brilliant escape in the face of the new northern commander George Meade's hesitant pursuit. Although Lincoln would have cause to exult when Vicksburg finally fell on July 4, he nevertheless faced a growing discontent with the course of the war, which manifest itself both in political challenges mounted by Northern "Copperheads" and in popular protests such as the New York draft riots. Still, the signs of change were evident in the successful attack on Heth's retreating troops at Falling Waters, in the repulse of an all-out attack on Northern-held Helena, Arkansas, and in the growing criticism of Robert E. Lee by a southern press that had so recently seemed to worship him. Under renewed assault by his political rivals, whose ranks were growing, and mindful of the South's deteriorating economic and social conditions, Jeff Davis would even try secretly, though in vain, to sue for peace. And it would take all his considerable powers of persuasion to keep Lee himself from resigning his post and removing any hope for what some were beginning to recognize as a lost cause.

★ ★ ★

Picture Credits

The sources for the illustrations are listed below. Credits from left to right are separated by semicolons, from top to bottom by dashes.

Dust jacket: Front, Library of Congress; rear, Library of Congress, Neg. No. B8184-10006; flap, photo by Larry Shirley. 8-10: The Museum of the Confederacy, Richmond, Va., photographed by Larry Sherer. 12: National Archives, Neg. No. III-B-1233. 15: By permission of the Houghton Library, Harvard University. 17: From *The Photographic History of the Civil War*, ed. by Francis Trevelyan Miller, © 1911 Patriot Co., Springfield, Mass. 20: Map by Walter W. Roberts. 23: Charles V. Peery, M.D. 26-28: Courtesy Frank and Marie-Thérèse Wood Print Collections, Alexandria, Va. 31: Courtesy Don Troiani Collection, photographed by Larry Sherer, assisted by Andrew Patilla. 33: National Archives, Neg. No. III-B-3320. 34: Drawing by Edwin Forbes, Library of Congress. 37: From *Battles and Leaders of the Civil War*, Vol. 3, published by The Century Co., New York, 1887. 43: Erick Davis Collection. 46: Library of Congress, Neg. No. B8171-7576. 50: Library of Congress. 52-54: The Western Reserve Historical Society, Cleveland, Ohio. 56: Courtesy Lee-Fendall House Museum. 59: From *Detailed Minutiae of Soldier Life in the Army of Northern Virginia, 1861-1865,* by Carlton McCarthy, The Riverside Press, Cambridge, Mass., 1882, copied by Philip Brandt George. 61: Courtesy Commonwealth of Massachusetts, State House Flag Collection, 1987.286, First National, 27th Massachusetts Volunteers. 64: U.S. Army Military History Institute, copied by Robert Walch. 66: Library of Congress. 68-70: Library of Congress. 75: Map by Walter W. Roberts, overlay by Time-Life Books. 79: Library of Congress, Waud No. 97. 84: Fredericksburg and Spotsylvania National Military Park, Fredericksburg, Va.—Library of Congress, Neg. No. B8184-10365. 86: From *War Diary and Letters of Stephen Minot Weld*, privately printed by The Riverside Press, 1912. 93: From *The Photographic History of the Civil War,* published by The Review of Reviews Co., New York, 1912. 96-98: Painting by Julian Scott, © 1983, Sotheby Park Bernet Inc. 103: From *Battles and Leaders of the Civil War,* Vol. 3, published by The Century Co., New York, 1887. 109: Armed Forces Collection, National Museum of American History, Smithsonian Institution. 113: Courtesy collection of William A. Turner. 115: From *Battles and Leaders of the Civil War,* Vol. 3, published by The Century Co., New York, 1887. 120: Virginia Miliary Institute Museum, Virginia Military Institute, Lexington, photographed by Michael Collingwood. 125: Painting by Leo Frankenstein, courtesy Fredericksburg and Spotsylvania National Military Park, Fredericksburg, Va. 130: Massachusetts Commandery Military Order of the Loyal Legion and the U.S. Army Military History Institute, copied by A. Pierce Bounds. 133: The Museum of the Confederacy, Richmond, Va., photographed by Larry Sherer. 136: National Archives Neg. No. 165-JT-317. 142-144: Andrew D. Lytle Collection, Louisiana and Lower Mississippi Valley Collections, LSU Libraries, Louisiana State University, Baton Rouge. 147: Library of Congress. 151: "The Union Fleet Passing Vicksburg" © 1989 Tom Lovell © 1989 The Greenwich Workshop®, Inc., Courtesy of The Greenwich Workshop, Inc., Shelton, Conn. 153: National Portrait Gallery, Smithsonian Institution, Washington, D.C., NPG.81.M219 158: Lloyd Ostendorf Collection. 161: Courtesy Frank and Marie-Thérèse Wood Print Collections, Alexandria, Va. 162: Map by William L. Hezlep. 165: Courtesy Frank and Marie-Thérèse Wood Print Collections, Alexandria, Va. 170-172: Library of Congress. 175: Massachusetts Commandery Military Order of the Loyal Legion and the U.S. Army Military History Institute, copied by Robert Walch. 178: Courtesy Frank and Marie-Thérèse Wood Print Collections, Alexandria, Va. 183: Old Court House Museum, Vicksburg, Miss. 186: Confederate Memorial Hall, New Orleans. 194-195: Courtesy Frank and Marie-Thérèse Wood Print Collections, Alexandria, Va. 198-200: Manuscript Department, William R. Perkins Library, Duke University. 203: Vann Martin Collection, copied by Henry Mintz. 208: Map by R. R. Donnelley & Sons Co., Cartographic Services, overlay by Time-Life Books. 214: Courtesy Frank and Marie-Thérèse Wood Print Collections, Alexandria, Va. 219: Couresy Roger D. Hunt. 222: Map by Walter W. Roberts. 228-230: Massachusetts Commandery Military Order of the Loyal Legion and the U.S. Army Military History Institute, copied by Robert Walch. 233: Drawing by J. E. Taylor, from *Campfire and Battlefield, An Illustrated History of the Campaigns and Conflicts of the Great Civil War,* by Rossiter Johnson et al, ©1894 by Bryan, Taylor & Company, New York. 236: Andrew D. Lytle Collection, Louisiana and Lower Mississippi Valley Collections, LSU Libraries, Louisiana State University, Baton Rouge. 240. Courtesy the Historic New Orleans Collection (Acc. No. 1979.130). 247. MASS-MOL-LUS/USAMHI, copied by A. Pierce Bounds. 250-252: Reproduced by permission of the American Museum in Britain, Bath. 254: Courtesy Frank and Marie-Thérèse Wood Print Collections, Alexandria, Va. 259: Old Court House Museum, Vicksburg, Miss., photographed by Henry Mintz. 260: Chicago Historical Society, Neg. No. ICHi-08019. 262: "The Shell," by Howard Pyle, private collection, courtesy the Brandywine River Museum. 267: Library of Congress. 270: Library of Congress, Neg. No. LC-B811-2430. 273: Library of Congress, Neg. No. LC-B813-6554. 275: Thomas Smith Collection, courtesy L. M. Strayer, Dayton 278: Chicago Historical Society, Neg. No. ICHi-08022.

Index

★

★

SHELBY FOOTE, THE CIVIL WAR,
A NARRATIVE
VOLUME 6 CHARLESTON HARBOR TO
VICKSBURG

Library of Congress Cataloging-in-Publication Data
Foote, Shelby.
    [Civil War, a narrative]
    Shelby Foote, the Civil War, a narrative/by
Shelby Foote and the editors of Time-Life Books.
— 40th Anniversary ed.
        p. cm.
Originally published: The Civil War, a narrative.
New York: Random House, 1958–1974, in 3 v.
        Includes bibliographic references and indexes.
        Contents: v. 6: Charleston Harbor to Vicksburg
        1. United States—History—Civil War, 1861-1865.
I. Time-Life Books. II. Title
E468.F7   1999   99-13486
973.7—dc21   CIP
ISBN 0-7835-0105-6

For information on and a full description of any of
the Time-Life Books series listed at right, please call
1-800-621-7026 or write:
Reader Information
Time-Life Customer Service
P.O. Box C-32068
Richmond, Virginia 23261-2068

TIME® Time-Life Books is a
LIFE division of Time Life Inc.
BOOKS

TIME LIFE INC.
PRESIDENT and CEO: George Artandi

TIME-LIFE BOOKS
PUBLISHER/MANAGING EDITOR: Neil Kagan
SENIOR VICE PRESIDENT, MARKETING:
Joseph A. Kuna
VICE PRESIDENT, NEW PRODUCT
DEVELOPMENT: Amy Golden
DIRECTOR OF MARKETING: Pamela R. Farrell

EDITOR: Philip Brandt George
DIRECTOR, NEW PRODUCT
DEVELOPMENT: Elizabeth D. Ward
Art Director: Ellen L. Pattisall
Marketing Manager: Peter Tardif
Editorial Assistant: Patricia D. Whiteford
Correspondent: Christina Lieberman (New York)

Director of Finance: Christopher Hearing
Directors of Book Production: Marjann Caldwell,
Patricia Pascale
Director of Publishing Technology: Betsi McGrath
Director of Photography and Research:
John Conrad Weiser
Director of Editorial Administration: Barbara Levitt
Manager, Technical Services: Anne Topp
Senior Production Manager: Ken Sabol
Quality Assurance Manager: James King
Chief Librarian: Louise D. Forstall

Volume Six in this series produced for Time-Life
Books by Zenda, Inc.

ZENDA INC.

Editor: Charles Phillips
Managing Editor: Candace Floyd
Administration: Patricia Hogan
Design and Production:
Gore Studio, Inc.: Bruce Gore (cover)
The Graphics People: Susan Ellen Hogan,
Mary Brillman, Roger Neiss, Tasha Nesbitt

OTHER TIME-LIFE HISTORY PUBLICATIONS

What Life Was Like	*Cultural Atlas*
Voices of the Civil War	*Our American*
The American Indians	*Century*
Lost Civilizations	*World War II*
Time Frame	*Echoes of Glory*
The Civil War	*Living Wisdom*